W9-ASO-303

WORLD FAITHS AND THE NEW WORLD ORDER

WORLD FAITHS
and the
NEW WORLD ORDER
A MUSLIM-JEWISH-CHRISTIAN SEARCH BEGINS

Edited
by
Joseph Gremillion
William Ryan

Sponsored by
The Interreligious Peace Colloquium
Lisbon • *7-11 November 1977*

TABLE OF CONTENTS

PART III
Followup and Future

Foreword

Matthew Rosenhaus and Isma'il al-Faruqi

Thirty persons participated in the second conference of the Interreligious Peace Colloquium (IRPC) held at Lisbon, Portugal, 7-11 November 1977. The subject was "The Changing World Order: Challenge to Our Faiths."

Twenty participants were professionals from political, business and academic circles concerned with our theme, adherents of their faith and cultural values as Jews, Muslims and Christians. Eight were religious leaders of these sister communities; two were Buddhist.

We met to address world issues from the dimension of faith, hoping to generate larger vision and moral commitment for human betterment, justice, human rights and peace.

About a third of our number had gathered at Bellagio, Italy, in 1975 for our first Colloquium, on *Food/Energy and the Major Faiths*. A book of this title reports on that first conference. It is prepared by Joseph Gremillion, who is coordinator of our group; the book also tells how IRPC took organizational form after Bellagio. (Orbis Books, 1978 New York)

As president and vice-president of the Colloquium, we are pleased to present now in book form a report on our Lisbon experience. It is co-authored by Gremillion and William Ryan, executive-secretary of IRPC. These two had prime responsibility for the conception and preparation of Lisbon. Their volume gives the ten major papers by distinguished specialists in transnational issues and by well-known religious thinkers. They provide summaries of these papers and the discussion which followed, and their own reflections.

The central piece in this book is the Statement on the Lisbon conference made by the eight officers and directors of IRPC who participated. Besides the four of us already mentioned, these signers are Cynthia Wedel, Theodore Hesburgh, Irwin Blank and Henry Siegman. Other

Colloquium directors are Muhammad Abdul Rauf, Simeon Adebo, Sol Linowitz, Henry Schultz, Philip Klutznick and Maurice Strong. Each played some part in making Lisbon possible.

Cyrus Vance, a founding officer of IRPC and Bellagio participant, must also be named. During 1975-76 he contributed much during the ten meetings our officers held to plan our organization and its programs. Vance resigned as vice-president of the Colloquium in January 1977, when he became Secretary of State in President Carter's cabinet.

More about the short history, purpose and nature of the Interreligious Peace Colloquium is given in this book's appendix. As officers we express appreciation to all who have helped it and our unique gathering at Lisbon.

Gratitude is gladly expressed to the Ford, Rockefeller, DeRance and Rosenhaus foundations for their generous grants. Personal gifts were also made by five friends; for these we are especially thankful because we see that IRPC's future will depend upon relatively small contributions such as they offered, motivated by faith conviction and by love for all God's human family.

May 1978   Matthew Rosenhaus
                                                Isma'il al-Faruqi

1

The Setting

Joseph Gremillion and William Ryan

The Lisbon conference was held in a small hotel on the Atlantic shore twenty miles north of Portugal's capital. We found there the perfect atmosphere for informal interchange and reflection among our thirty participants of diverse religio-cultural and professional backgrounds. This deeply affected our formal sessions and week-long experience.

This volume offers the full text of the papers prepared for our meeting; these provide nine-tenths of its content. Their titles and distinguished authors, and the order in which they were taken up, are listed in the table of contents. A perusal of this table shows how our conference unfolded.

The four papers grouped as Part I, under the heading "Socio-Economic, Political and Cultural Elements," had been circulated to participants several weeks before we met. At Lisbon the authors presented highlights of each paper, then these social and economic, political and cultural factors were discussed as a whole. We the editors give at the close of Part I a synthesis of the four papers and of the discussion they evoked.

The five papers on "The Dimensions of Faith" form Part II, and then follows a synthesis of these and of the general discussion they engendered. A brief summary of each paper, prepared by us editors, is given just prior to the full text, together with a short biography of each author. (In editing the texts, we regret the ambiguity in the occasional use of masculine generic terms.)

Returning to our Lisbon process, at the start of each day an overview of the previous day's discussion was made, by Shlomo Avineri, Nevzad Yalcintas and Ryan. Also, a free flowing discussion was led one evening by Theodore Hesburgh on "Moral Ambiguities Inherent in Decision-making by National Leaders." Three work groups met on the final day. Their recommendations are summarized in this book by Jane Blewett, who is administrative assistant of IRPC.

Part III of this volume entitled "Followup and Future," presents the formal Statement made by officers of the Interreligious Peace Colloquium who participated in the Lisbon conference. We were asked to do this by the participants, who discussed and agreed to the Statement's principal elements in our closing session.

In our final chapter, "Reflections and the Future," we two who conceived and guided our Lisbon process from start to finish, share a few thoughts about this singular experience. We focus on three principal perceptions: 1) The complexities of our interdependent world, groping toward a new human order, can be fruitfully approached by a comprehensive grasp of four categories of transnational actors: economic-political blocs, religio-cultural ethnic regions, faith communities, and ideologies; 2) All of these transnational actors are significantly affected by the dimensions of faith, and in particular the future of the West and Mideast regions are strongly impacted by Muslim-Jewish-Christian belief, values and relations; 3) Relations among these three faith communities, their cultures and social teaching should take on much deeper importance within secular as well as religious bodies, in their regular and specialized programs.

And for these reasons adherents of these three faiths, so long and so often at enmity, can and should come together, as secular and religious leaders in small groups to search, to ponder, to pray.

At Lisbon each day's session opened and closed with five minutes of meditation and prayer, led by a member in ways familiar to his or her own faith. Some forty minutes for formal services by each faith group were scheduled each mid-day. Rooms for this were set aside.

At the opening session participants were asked to introduce themselves by responding to the questions: "Who am I? Why am I here?" This led to an outpouring of self-examination and self-revelation which astonished all. It went on for six hours and began transforming our unusual mixture of individual strangers into a community of human persons, on the way to becoming friends, even brothers and sisters.

PART I

Socio-Economic, Political and Cultural Elements

2

A Comparative Survey of Significant Proposals for a New World Order

Philip Land

Philip Land, a US citizen and Jesuit priest, is presently a staff associate at the Center of Concern in Washington, D. C. Land did his graduate studies at Columbia and St. Louis Universities. As a professional economist and theologian, he has been a member of the Institute of Social Order, St. Louis, Missouri; an associate editor of AMERICA magazine; professor of economics of development and social ethics at the Gregorian University, Rome; and staff researcher in the economics of development and theology of church in the world for the Pontifical Commission Justice and Peace at the Vatican. Land has lectured and written extensively on the church in the contemporary world.

I. INTRODUCTION

II. BACKGROUND
  A) Limits to Growth
  B) The New International Economic Order
  C) Other Studies

III. CONVERGING PERCEPTIONS
  A) Interdependences
    1) Five Crisis Areas
      a) The Energy Crisis
      b) The Food Crisis
      c) Environmental Interdependence
      d) The Use of Resources
      e) Technological Dependence
    2) Two Other Critical Interdependences
      a) Continuing Depression in the Industrial North
      b) Chronic Inflation
  B) Shortcomings of the Old Economic Order
    1) Failures of International Trade
    2) Failures of the Monetary System
  C) A New Development
    1) Basic Needs
    2) The Poverty Gap
    3) Development Is People
    4) Equal Opportunity
  D) A New Development—A New Order
    1) Political Strategizing
    2) Strategies of Structural Reform
    3) Restructuring International Order—RIO's Main
       Recommendations
      a) International Monetary System
      b) Financing Development
      c) Industrialization, Trade and International
         Division of Labor
      d) Energy and Natural Resources
      e) Human Environment
      f) Ocean Management
      g) Arms Reduction
      h) Population
  E) Possible Packages for Comprehensive Negotiations
    1) Bargaining Packages
    2) Packaging and Power
    3) Three RIO Packages
      a) First Package: Removal of Gross Inequities
      b) Second Package: Harmonious Global Growth

I. INTRODUCTION

The Paris Conference on International Economic Cooperation (CIEC) or North/South dialogue ended in June 1977, with little to show for the eighteen months effort. The best the conferees could propose was that the dialogue not end but be carried forward in other forums.

Not to be dismissed, however, are three achievements of a sort. First, the eight industrial representatives did agree in principle to the creation of a billion dollar fund to aid the poorest nations most affected by debt. Second, they reiterated their support of the Common Fund, in terms that sounded, at least at the moment, more affirmative than those used in the United Nations Conference on Trade and Development (UNCTAD) talks held shortly before in Geneva. Third, the North did not make these two points conditional upon agreement on the part of the Organization of Petroleum Exporting Countries (OPEC) to move ahead with discussions on the production and pricing of oil, which had brought the industrial nations to Paris in the first place.

This was surprising because the industrial nations had not come to this bargaining table out of any profound concern for the problems of the poor nations. They were driven there out of national self-interest arising from the uncertainties of the international economic order on which their own prosperity depends. The North—as the richer industrialized nations excluding the Soviet bloc are called—

wants to discuss its own problems. For its part, the South—as the poorer developing countries are called—makes steadily more clear that it is prepared to enter such discussions only if the negotiations open to those more fundamental structural changes that world justice seem to require.

The termination of the Paris North/South dialogue means a shifting of the negotiations to other forums. Far from being a disaster, this may be a return to where they should have remained. Financial questions will now as before be discussed within the International Monetary Fund (IMF) and the World Bank. Trade questions will, as before, be carried out within UNCTAD.

What is the link of the CIEC agenda to the Interreligious Peace Colloquium's (IRPC) Bellagio Conference and its upcoming Lisbon Conference? The food crisis with which Bellagio dealt has ramifications for half the issues on the CIEC agenda. As IRPC now moves ahead to Lisbon to deal with even wider issues of world justice, it finds itself facing all the rest of the CIEC agenda—and that agenda as it will continue being discussed and negotiated in other forums even while IRPC meets in Lisbon.

IRPC might think its resources too modest to contribute in this impasse in CIEC. But this is not so. At Paris, as in a dozen recent similar intergovernmental encounters, there was wide agreement that what is lacking in the world is not so much understanding of the problems as the political will and solidarity to move on them. Here the world's major faiths have potential and bear responsibility to promote that solidarity and affect that political will.

As background for participants' discussions at Lisbon, the present paper attempts an overview of some of the recent thinking on the topic of international cooperation to meet the problems of world poverty. It is not a position paper of the Center of Concern. While the convergence framework here adopted is somewhat arbitrary and limited, it does have the advantage of highlighting a significant hopeful movement found widespread in my survey of the relevant literature.

The changing world order has been analyzed by a variety of top-level professional groups in the past few years, and a series of specific recommendations—with remarkable convergence among them—have emerged from these groups. A look at the analyses and recommendations can show us: (1) the shortcomings of the old international economic order; (2) the shift in thinking toward meeting basic human needs; (3) the proposals for a new economic order; (4) some possible bargaining positions or packages for negotiations; and (5) the significance of the new emphasis on the need for a world authority or authorities. This paper will sketch out these areas, and conclude with some questions for further discussion and action which the Lisbon conference may wish to address.

II. BACKGROUND

To set the Lisbon conference fully within the skein of international discussions preceding and accompanying it would require many pages. Hopefully, the following schematic presentation of both political events and recent studies will suffice for general background information.

A. Limits to Growth

The year 1972 saw the appearance of the Club of Rome's sensational study, *Limits to Growth*. It stated the impending crisis primarily in terms of limits to energy and raw materials. It was severely criticized for its failure to affix to technological advancement the same degree of exponentiality it gave to the ascending curves of population, energy and resource consumption, industrialization and pollution, as well as for its global treatment of all variables. Such treatment concealed both critical areas and potential for resolving crises regionally, if not globally. The Club of Rome took this criticism seriously and while not abandoning the basic thesis of *Limits*, did commission a more disaggregated study entitled *Mankind at the Turning Point, 1974*.

B. The New International Economic Order

This study coincided with an event of much greater significance — the Sixth Special Session of the United Nations, April 1974, with its call for a New International Economic Order (NIEO). That event itself was both preceded by and provoked several conferences of Third World and non-aligned countries' leaders. These in turn both influenced and were influenced by a more private type of consultation, such as the group of experts called together under UN auspices at Cocoyoc, Mexico, in October 1974. The mutual influence of these meetings is largely explained by the fact that often the same experts were present at several of the conferences. For example, one of these competent, ubiquitous experts is Mahbub ul Haq, as is evident in his recent brilliant study, *The Poverty Curtain*, which has been a major resource for this paper. In addition, by 1974, the Club of Rome had already in circulation a first draft of what would be finalized in 1976 as *RIO — Reshaping the International Order*, a comprehensive study coordinated by the Nobel prize-winner, Jan Tinbergen.

In September 1975, the Seventh Special Session of the UN* was held. All commentators have recognized that, however unsatisfactory the results from the view of the Third World, the conference did at least mark a change from the confrontational atmosphere of the Sixth Special Session to one of cooperation, of probing for points of mutual advantage, and of respect on the part of the North for the Third World's economic reasoning.

The substantial demands made by the Third World at the two Sessions, it will be remembered, were these: control of a nation's own resources; greater transfer of real resources; monetary and trade changes; stabilization of prices of raw materials at more remunerative prices; the indexation of the prices of raw materials against industrial prices; and a code of conduct for transnational corporations and for the transfer of technology.

At the Seventh Special Session, the North did seem to seek more accommodation and constructive dialogue and to be better informed on the reasonableness of the South's proposals. But there was still no evidence that the North was prepared to entertain any changes beyond some tinkering here and there with a system which in their view is mainly beneficent and operates according to basically fair rules of the game—a system which supports their own power and privilege and the independence they still treasure over interdependence.

These UN and other conferences of experts have helped nudge thinking in still another direction. The South has begun to acknowledge that a world order offering fairer distribution of opportunity and income also requires reforms within the developing countries themselves. But although governing elites of the South profess concern for this, the situation continues to be one of widening inequality. Indeed, many in the South see that national policies which result in enriching the already rich, weaken Third World demands for changes at the international level, since structural reforms at the world level would only result in benefiting still more the rich elites of the Third World and not their poor.

Signs are emerging from all these world conferences that the nations of both North and South are slowly coming to recognize: (1) the deficiencies of the existing international order; (2) their own national interests can be furthered within the framework of a new international order; and (3) that all can gain from a new creative partnership.

---

*An excellent exposition of the Seventh Special Session—issues, actors, negotiations—can be found in *A New International Economic Order* by Jyoti Shankar Singh (Praeger Special Studies in International Economics and Development, Praeger, New York, 1977).

C. Other Studies

During this time a series of other studies by individuals and institutes, as well as reports of international gatherings, continued to appear. E. F. Schumacher's *Small Is Beautiful* was making remarkable impact with his ideas of "Economics as if People Mattered" or as he entitles one chapter of his book, "Buddhist Economics." Mahbub ul Haq was developing in lectures and articles his own new approaches which would appear in his book *The Poverty Curtain* in 1976.

In 1975-76 four other influential reports appeared. The first was the Dag Hammarskjold Foundation's *What Now — Another Development*. The second was the Aspen Institute's *Planetary Bargain — Proposals for a New International Economic Order to Meet Human Needs*. The third was the International Labor Organization's study on *Employment, Income Distribution and Social Progress and the International Division of Labor*. And the fourth was a study produced by Argentina's Fundacion Bariloche, under the direction of Amilcar Herrera entitled *Catastrophe or a New Society? A Latin American World Model*. Among this growing flood of publications, one other merits special mention. This is the Washington-based Overseas Development Council's *The United States and World Development: Agenda 1977*, a statement of issues on international justice directed to the new administration of President Carter.

President Carter — and several members of his administration — is also associated with another group, the Trilateral Commission, whose studies have been appearing since 1974. This group describes itself as "a private North American-European-Japanese initiative on matters of common concern." Central to trilateralism is the assumption that these industrialized nations must cooperate in reshaping the international structures of finance and trade. While aware of the new demands of Third World countries, the Commission is composed only of First World industrialists, scholars and public officials, and appears to operate on the premise that the industrialized world must first cooperatively solve its own problems before dealing effectively with the Third World. Because of this limiting premise, these trilateral studies do not fit easily within the framework adopted by this paper and so are omitted.*

---

*Two other studies should be mentioned though not included in our convergence group: Allan E. Goodman, *The Politics of the North-South Dialogue: Implications for International Relations,* paper presented at a conference on "New Factors in International Conflict," The Fletcher School of Law and Diplomacy, Tufts, 4-6 May 1977. (The author was in the International Issues Division Office of Regional and Political Analysis, Central Intelligence Agency.) And a second study: Subcommittee on Inter-American Relationships of the Joint Economic Committee, Congress of the United States, *The United States Response to the New International Economic Order: The Economic Im-*

This listing of recent important studies is not complete but will suffice for the purposes of this background paper. Other authors might choose a quite different listing of recent studies for other purposes. •

However schematically and inadequately, all these studies ought to be related. Are they all saying more or less the same thing? What elements are common to them and should one of the studies be the springboard for synthesizing the rest into a background paper for IRPC's Lisbon meeting?

There is, in fact, a remarkable convergence among them. The Club of Rome's *Reshaping the International Order (RIO)* seems particularly suited to demonstrate this convergence. This is so because RIO is a wider statement of problem areas and measures proposed for North/South restructuring and for an international order that will ensure justice among all nations. At the same time, this study tries to meet the industrial nations' needs and to integrate the socialist states and China into a one-world solidarity to serve all peoples. RIO also has the advantage of being the product of a cooperative effort of specialists drawn from a variety of countries, social systems and intellectual disciplines, even though the centrally planned nations were not adequately represented. It also embraces the thinking of the Third World Forum.

But before moving ahead with this, reference must be made to one other study that has gripped the attention of at least the industrial nations. This it the Hudson Institute's *The Next 200 Years*. This "Scenario for America and the World," for which Herman Kahn is mainly responsible, appeared in 1976. It is most noteworthy in its explicit and complete rejection of the pessimism of the Club of Rome's

---

plications for Latin America and the United States, February 23, 1977, US Government Printing Office, Washington, DC.

Goodman's analysis runs, not in terms of needs of the developing countries and justice or equity, but exclusively in terms of how Third World demands impact upon the US and the OECD countries more generally. He weighs Third World ability to bring pressure through cooperation and/or alliances. He concludes with some estimate of the costs of response.

Like the Goodman study, the second one also concentrates on costs to the US of possible concessions within four main fields of NIEO requests: trade in manufactures, in raw materials, in technology and the debt issue. US responses, at that date, are revealed to be very limited on all scores. Emphasis was on reliance on free trade, on the multinational corporation as conveyor of technology to Latin America and on US banking principles as debt criteria.

This present paper should also be complemented by such studies as *International Commodity Agreements,* Hearings before the Subcommittee on Economic Stabilization of the Committee on Banking, Finance and Urban Affairs, House of Representatives Ninety-Fifth Congress, June 8, 1977; and, *International Debt, The Banks and US Foreign Policy,* Staff Report prepared for the use of the Subcommittee on Foreign Economic Policy of the Committee on Foreign Relations, United States Senate, August 1977.

Limits to Growth. It is optimistic about the Third World's prospects. Where the World Bank's officials are still convinced that 750 million people with an average per capita income of less than $100 a year can foresee an annual increase over the next decade of no more than $2 per year, Kahn predicts that by the year 2000, more than two-thirds of the world's people will have passed the level of $1,000. Since only a quarter of the world's population will live in the industrial North by that date, Kahn's expectations must include the masses of the Third World including South Asia.

In a preliminary report for the US chapter of the Club of Rome, Mihajlo Mesarovic and Barry Hughes studied the Hudson Institute's scenario, and following Kahn's own methodology, conclude by totally rejecting his optimism. For them, "the analysis of the assumptions underlying the Hudson Institute scenario for economic transition indicates that impediments. . . . are of such magnitude that none of the measures (in isolation or in combination) could be realistically expected to provide conditions for achieving the stated target."

A key point of the Mesarovic-Hughes attack is that reaching Kahn's target of $1,000 per capita for more than two-thirds of the world's people would require massive transfers of capital from the developed countries on a scale that would, in effect, impose a new — an unrealizable — tax of $1,000 per year on every U. S. family by the year 2000.

Presently Kahn's study stands in isolation among the studies prominently before the world community. Kahn had the opportunity to respond to the charges of Mesarovic in a debate with him sponsored by the Club of Rome in Houston, Texas, October 1977. Unfortunately, this debate added no new light to the discussion but only confirmed how divergent are the worldviews of the two men.

III. CONVERGING PERCEPTIONS

With the preceding background as basis, we are in a position to understand how international perceptions of issues of development are gradually but at a quickened pace converging. In fact, this convergence of perceptions is so striking in the studies indicated — with the exception of Kahn's study — that we will take the liberty in this paper of referring to them as "The Convergence Group."

A) Interdependences

RIO and the Convergence Group (except Kahn) believe that the world is inextricably meshed in interdependences. RIO presents these as crisis areas. They are the following:

1) Five Crisis Areas

a) *The Energy Crisis.* The serious problems caused in the industrial world by the dwindling supplies of cheap oil and gas, together with the price hikes that followed, are a familiar fact of life. Their impact on the poor nations has been far more devastating. Industrial countries manage their oil deficit by sale of commercial aircraft, arms, food, etc. The South, as we shall see, because markets are often blocked to their products and because the prices they get for them run far behind the prices they must pay for industrial equipment, cannot now meet deficits on purchases of energy and food. Yet energy for irrigation, tractors, trucks, and trains is essential to their food production.

b) *The Food Crisis.* This year, the monsoons and increased productivity have brightened the picture for India's half billion people. But monsoons are uncertain. If the U. S. West may currently face another Dust Bowl, so surely may India. Elsewhere in the world, together with some improvement, there are dark spots of malnutrition and hunger. Rapid increases of population still outrun increases in agricultural production in many poor countries. Few experts believe that an early end is in sight for the need of grain reserves, food aid, and aid for increasing agricultural output.

c) *Environmental Interdependence.* The spaceship photograph of the earth compressed our globe into swirls of land masses and water flowing from one hemisphere to another. That is not far from the truth. Air, water, and the upper atmosphere are the world commons we all share. This is true in part even of our soil. For evidence of this commons, we need only think of the swift transfer of pollution from zone to zone. Water carries it. So does air. Heating up the upper atmosphere from industrial activity in one country can bring air disturbances and change of climate to other parts of the world.

d) *The Use of Resources.* There is today great competition for resources. That competition drives prices upward, benefiting those who have a supply of scarce goods. In a world ruled by market prices, the poor inevitably get cut out. Ul Haq, who rejects *Limits* in the sense of physical lack of resources in the immediate future, does agree that future exploration will be at a rising cost which will hit the Third World as it moves into its industrialization. Access to high quality resources will likewise pose serious economic problems for much of the North.

e) *Technological Dependence.* Established trade theory would have it that optimum world output results from an exchange of the North's industrial goods and technology for the South's raw materials. Such a theory binds the Third World once again. These countries must buy the technology for their own development from the North. They have very little to say about whether it is suited to their needs. In fact, it is not suitable. The capitalist nations produce and market to the Third World a technology that meets labor problems by substituting machines and automated processes for labor. The South with their tragically high numbers of unemployed want just the opposite. They need a simpler technology at fairer prices, one that puts more people to work and is more in harmony with their own cultural values.

2) Two Other Critical Interdependences

The critical interdependences of production and pollution are negatively impacted by two others. The second, if not the first, may well become a permanent feature of the world landscape.

a) *Continuing Depression in the Industrial North.* The North's now chronic depression also has a cruel impact on the South. First, it shrinks demand for poor countries' raw materials, since reduced industrial activity cuts back demand for the materials that go into industrial production. Second, because depression brings in its wake heavy unemployment, the industrial world throws up a wall of protection around its jobs by excluding competition from Third World exports. Third, it weakens further the North's already weak political will to meet the UN target of 0.7 percent of Gross National Product in annual governmental (and concessional) aid.

b) *Chronic Inflation.* Because of inflation in food prices, governments of the North, eager though they be to profit through sales of food to the poor, are torn from that objective by the need to retain plentiful supplies for the home market to keep down domestic food prices. The result is that either insufficient supplies are available for the world's needy, or they can have the food only at exorbitant prices.

The North's apparently endless inflation has two other evil results in the South. It makes acquisition of the North's farm machinery enormously costly for poor people. It also eats away at the value of dollars they have already earned.

B) Shortcomings of the Old Economic Order

RIO, if one includes its technical studies in Part Four, together with our convergence group condemns the failure of classical trade theory, trickle-down capitalism, as a force for development—indeed capitalism itself as a model for the Third World. On this last point, RIO, along with most of the convergence group, insists on rejecting "catch-up" with the North as a development model. It points out that going that road means taking on all the economic, social and cultural problems that have grown up around the North's priority accorded to maximum growth.

The Bariloche study in a more Marxian analysis finds the chief cause of present poverty in the domination of the world by rich capitalist nations, supported by Third World elites who imitate the consumption patterns of the North. The real constraints on the South's development are not lack of resources but sociopolitical regimes which support particular patterns of production and consumption in the interests of the rich. While acknowledging the high productivity potential of capitalism, Bariloche, like RIO, believes that the supporting ideology of a new world order will be some form of socialism.

1) Failures of International Trade

On the inequities of international trade, the convergence thinking runs this way. The South believes that the international trade system benefits the North disproportionately. Trade theory as expounded in the North claims that the poor nations gain from the rising prosperity of the rich and that trade is the mechanism of transfer. As the rich grow in industrial prosperity, they require more raw materials. This causes prices of these materials to rise, thus benefiting the developing nations. Also, as labor costs rise in the industrialized world, investors shift their investment to the developing nations where labor costs are lower. This investment launches the poor world into industrialization. Then too, in a system of free exchange, the Third World is at liberty to move its labor as well as its capital into the industrial North.

However, such freedom of labor to migrate is extremely limited in today's world. For example, unskilled labor migrates from South to North in Europe but is returned home when depression hits the Common Market. Meanwhile, the North's capital tends to go where capital already is. The North's foreign investments are found overwhelmingly in other industrialized countries of the North.

If the actual flow of factors of production—labor and capital— bears little resemblance to that foreseen by trade theory, the same, in the view of the Third World, can be said of the flow of raw materials and manufactured goods. The North is able to keep out of its markets competitive products. The North as a whole pours some $20 billion into protecting its farmers from the South's agricultural products. Its industrial workers and investors are also protected.

On one key point of trade, ul Haq has been the strongest spokesperson. This is the need of transferring more of processing to the developing countries. The value added to raw materials in the processing step goes mainly to the rich industrial North. The annual bill paid by consumers in the North for beverages, foods, and manufactured goods originating in the raw materials produced by the South amounts to over $200 billion. Of that, the producers of the raw materials get only $30 billion. Just as within a nation the farmer gets relatively little of the consumer's dollar, with most of it going to processors and distributors, so too in the case of the developing countries. The value added to the product of their fields goes in part to their own middlemen. But largely it goes to those who control most of the processing, finishing and distributing of these raw materials, even within the developing world itself. And these are the processors of the rich world. Think, for example, of the big names in cocoa production.

If the rich industrial world could be persuaded to transfer to the South more of this processing and distribution of the South's raw materials, the developing world would stand, in ul Haq's estimates, to gain as much as $150 billion in annual earnings. If this is contrasted with the meager $8 billion of aid received from the North, it is easy to see where the South's main reliance ought to be placed.

2) Failures of the Monetary System

If trade has failed, so too has the international monetary system which emerged from the post World War II Bretton Woods Conference. Ul Haq himself, a prominent consultant to the president of the World Bank, which with its sister institute, the International Monetary Fund, was the child of Bretton Woods, charges both institutions with many failures. In particular he points to the unequal treatment of rich and poor nation clients by the IMF, as well as by private commercial banking.

Credit, credit creation, and access to credit are the life-blood of a nation and of the whole world. In the developed rich nations the poor get credit, if at all, on terms far less favorable than those accorded the rich and powerful. The same holds true on the world scene. In a recent Manila address, the president of the World

Bank maintains that even though the debt of the poor nations is a great obstacle to their development, it is not as much a problem as is inaccessibility to credit.

What he has in mind is this. A few financial powers like the USA can finance their own deficits by creating their own short-term credit. In addition, they have unlimited access to international credit. The weaker of the industrial nations of the North can get help on deficits from the International Monetary Fund's Special Drawing Rights which are a paper credit created by the Fund. These are also available to the South but on very limited quotas. These quotas will not change easily, given the slight power the South has on IMF decision-making. Established estimates have it that of $130 billion of international reserves only about four percent goes to poor countries.

Credit is one form of purchasing power, and just as the rich within a nation who possess credit can move the market and so production in accordance with their desires, so too at the world level. The rich nations with easy access to credit are in the driver's seat in world production. In the South the poorest nations are considered un-credit worthy. Even the "middle income" countries cannot get credit on the same terms as countries in the North.

This view requires some qualification, for, as we shall see later, the South does receive some credit from Northern governments, the IMF and World Bank, and recently from private banks. But the terms on which they receive much of their credit appear excessively onerous to the South. In any case, it is inadequate to their needs. Here they point out that governments of the North in order to prevent those of their citizens with purchasing power from garnering too much of the nation's goods and services, redistribute income and credit to the poorer. Why, asks the Third World, isn't there some such authority for fairer distribution of credit at the world level?

It pains some leaders from the rich North to be told that the old world economic order has failed. How has it failed? Has it not promoted and maintained a stable and expanding world economy? Have not its specialized agencies provided relief for famine, promoted world health and literacy? Was not aid forthcoming to help the developing nations? Did not the present era witness the practical end of colonialism?

It is not our intention to give explicit answers to these questions at this point. It is sufficient for now to point out that in general the international order of the post-war period was the creation of the USA and Europe and intended to serve the interests of the capitalist world. The socialist states played only a small part in it; the Third World, a weak and vicarious part. Even today their voice is very limited in international institutions. Meanwhile overt colonialism gave way to less overt forms of economic and political domination, in which the transnational corporations play an increasing role, and trickle-down aid both in quantity and quality has been grossly inadequate to keep the North/South gap from widening.

What became increasingly evident was that the capitalist model of development was in grave jeopardy and that "a new development" was emerging.

C) A New Development

This new development—the Dag Hammarskjold Foundation calls it "another development"—has several characteristics. Perhaps most striking is its first priority given to the satisfaction of basic human needs.

For this reason a word must be said about the pioneering work of the International Labor Organization (ILO) in challenging the capitalist development model with its concentration on economic growth and on ever-bigger GNP. The ILO offers a counter proposal centered on a needs-based society. What the ILO is seeking in its study that led to its June 1976 World Conference on "Employment, Income Distribution and Social Progress and the International Division of Labor" is to find a new strategy of development whose goal would be full employment as well as economic growth.

The ILO saw that post-war economic growth had not eradicated poverty, but may even have intensified it. Their report showed how much the North's growth model relied upon employment-destroying automation. Corrective to this, as well as a value in its own right, they outlined a world strategy of production to meet global needs. The "income distribution" element of their conference title is simple recognition that, in money-using economies, production will meet needs only if the needy have income—and employment is usually necessary to acquire money income.

1) Basic Needs

How shall we define basic needs? The ILO has its own definition. Our other convergence studies have their own definitions but here again there is striking similarity. Let us describe a few of these:

For the ILO, basic needs are: (a) essential consumer goods (food, clothes, shelter, home necessities); (b) essential human services (drinking water, sanitation, public transportation, health, education, cultural facilities); and (c) participation through organizations of one's own choosing in decisions affecting one's life. Ul Haq's definition also follows this order.

The Aspen Institute proposes a two-tier list of needs: the first tier is "survival needs," minimum human needs of food, health and education. This parallels numbers one and two of the ILO. The second tier is still basic needs "required for human dignity" but more culturally defined, therefore more relative to a particular people and time.

For the Dag Hammarskjold Foundation, development is geared to the satisfaction of needs, beginning with the eradication of poverty. This definition offers a less systematic division of needs, since needs are as much psychological and political as material. But survival needs obviously precede the others since they are a *sine qua non* of other needs. Survival needs stated in terms of their absence or of poverty include food, water, health, literacy, habitation. Bariloche's study stresses freedom from oppression and from alienation, equality and full participation, as values to be maximized.

The RIO approach builds upon a distinction between basic needs which are mainly individual and material, and collective needs which are "predominantly spiritual." Basic material needs of individuals are survival needs, adequate food, water, health care, and to varying degrees, shelter and clothing. The minimum fulfillment of these needs are basic human rights for the hundreds of millions who at present exist below them. Work is the next basic need both for the human satisfaction it provides as well as for the entree it offers to satisfying other needs through remuneration. Still among basic needs is the need for humane and satisfying environment and for participation in the decisions that affect one's life, livelihood and freedom. Education is another basic but non-material need, as it is also an instrument of physical and economic development.

Only after satisfaction of these needs does RIO turn to needs or "goals" in the field of recreation, leisure and general socio-cultural activities—goals that are at present "largely the prerogative of the industrialized world." These needs are further associated with the individual's rights, not only as a citizen voting and having a voice in planning and decision-making, but also as a producer and consumer. As producer, by the exercise of influence and power through work; as consumer, by a voice in decisions about what should be produced and how.

The Bariloche study runs along the same lines as RIO but is accompanied by a mathematical model to demonstrate the feasibility of a needs-oriented production model. This seeks optimum allocation of capital and labor (interchangeable with maximization of employment through suitable technology) to achieve, not an increase in GNP, but rather an advancement in productive effort to respond to five needs areas. These are nutrition, housing, health, education and final consumer goods and services (presumably other than the four just enumerated).

Can a universally valid index be devised for measuring a country's development in terms of the fulfillment of basic needs? Some groups are trying to construct such an index. For example, the Overseas Development Council is testing a "physical quality of life index" (PQLI) which builds on only three components; life expectancy, infant mortality and literacy.

2) The Poverty Gap

That basic needs of the poorest countries and of the bottom 40% of the population in the middle-income nations of the Third World are not being met constitutes the fact of poverty. World Bank studies, ul Haq's *The Poverty Curtain* and ODC's *Agenda 77* speak of the poverty gap in the following terms.

There exists a wide gap between the North and South with the exception of the wealthiest of the OPEC oil-producers. Up to now, that gap has been looked at in terms of the need to "catch up." Now, more enlightened spokespersons of the South view the gap as a measure of the obstacles to their own self-reliant development, one that does not require "catching up." In this view the gap appears as domination and exploitation on the one side and opportunity denied on the other. Still there is a gap of wealth and income that is terribly burdensome. The World Bank's president, Robert McNamara, in his October 1976 report to the Bank's governors, provided these figures. Income per capita in the North is running at $5,500, with even the richest of the South—a few OPEC nations—running far behind. The "middle income" countries have greater potential to emerge from poverty, though the bottom 40% of their people have seen little of that potential trickle down to them. Later we shall see that even these "middle income" nations encounter obstacles to an indigenous stable development.

Meanwhile, the poorest countries, those averaging an annual income of under $150 per person in 1975 and containing over 1.2 billion people, have to content themselves with annual increases of a bare two dollars per head. At the lower end of the spectrum of poverty, this means further declines from already abysmally low levels of nutrition, housing and health. Over 750 million people, McNamara claims, live at the very margin of existence.

3) Development Is People

Development—to return to our delineation of the traits of a new development—is in the last analysis, people. This is a central theme of the Hammarskjold Foundation study, of ul Haq, of the Aspen Institute, as well as of RIO. The idea is too familiar to require elaboration.

This aspect of development as being people is implicit to two further values which our convergence group defines as integral to development. These are (1) collective self-reliance and (2) participation. On the former, RIO calls for the mobilization of a people's strength, technology, creativity and wisdom in responsible action for its own development. This includes collective self-reliance on the part of a group of developing countries, or indeed of all one hundred and fourteen of them. It also embraces peoples' participation yielding as the end-result, to quote from RIO, "equitable social order" in which "all the world's citizens can achieve a life of dignity and of well-being," of "balance between civil and economic rights"—a point strongly endorsed also by *Agenda 77*.

4) Equal Opportunity

Whatever be the development strategies that these values will suggest, our convergence group is decidedly in agreement on one point—the overall strategy for development, if it be one of equity and redistribution, is not so much a fairer sharing of world income as a fairer sharing of opportunity. Ul Haq puts it this way, "The long-time solution is to change the international system in such a way as to improve the access of the poor to economic opportunity and to increase their long-term productivity, not their temporary income." *Agenda 77*'s equivalent is "equality of opportunity rather than redistribution. . . ." Only the language of the ILO study is different. It talks in concrete terms of what makes that equality of opportunity. This, it claims, is a new international division of labor that looks beyond growth to distribution.

This North/South gap in opportunity, together with massive pervasive poverty among people at the lower income levels of the Third World, calls for the basic needs-strategy delineated below. It also has suggested to several of our convergence group a strategy that, more generically stated, will build upon, to use the expression of *Agenda 77*, the search for "greater equity and growth simultaneously." The Overseas Development Council has, after considerable study, arrived at the conviction that there is much empirical evidence to prove that, where governments of the Third

World (Taiwan, South Korea, etc.) have shifted a fairer share of benefits to the people with lowest incomes, productivity has in fact increased.

D) A New Development—A New Order

If our convergence group is in agreement with RIO on a definition of what development ought to be, they are equally in agreement in recognizing that what the realization of that development will necessitate is a complete overhaul of existing structures. More specifically, if we seek: (1) to break down the existing system of injustice; (2) to meet the basic needs of the human family; (3) to reduce the gap between North and South; (4) to urge upon affluent societies reduction of their consumption; (5) to reduce arms production and sales which consume limited resources; and (6) to control the nuclear threat, then we are called to a radical reshaping of the international order.

1) Political Strategizing

Such considerations lead RIO and other studies to postulate strategies of political feasibility, longer-term political education in view of such political feasibility and finally technical measures to achieve the desired restructuring.

First, the strategies of political feasibility. The questions to be faced here are: How do you induce the powerful to surrender any of their control over world decisions? How do you induce the powerful to take more seriously Third World reasoning? To change their life-style? How to get them to enter into serious political bargaining on the basis of altruism, humanitarianism or the realization of national self-interests, at least in the long-run if not immediately? How do you induce the industrial nations to make the adjustments that fairer trade deals require? In view of the Third World's understandable eagerness to enhance and not diminish their newly won national sovereignty, how do you induce them to surrender that degree of sovereignty required by a new international order? RIO—and others among our convergence group, if not always in the same degree—here makes an explicit and far-ranging call for *world authority* to respond to the questions just raised.

One of RIO's major proposals represents just such an effort at restructuring world power through a new world authority. This we shall see later, but here a word more on the inevitability of some supranational authority. Such an authority is particularly demanded because of the interdependences described earlier as well as because of the reluctance of sovereign states to surrender any of their power.

Such an authority seems inevitable for still other reasons. At some point the world will have to take seriously the question of whether codes of conduct in international relations are to be legally binding. For the interim period, RIO does not insist upon this. Another consideration calling for world authority is the sheet necessity of controlling the capacity of nuclear destruction through phased disarmament for the survival of the planet. Finally, there is little hope of ever asserting a common heritage of the earth's resources and exploitation thereof for the whole human race, and especially its weaker and poorer members, if there is no authority to declare for commonality in the name of the world community.

An extensive look at possible approaches to structures of world authority was taken by the World Order Models Project (WOMP). One such approach can be found in Richard Falk's WOMP study, entitled *A Study of Future Worlds.*

2) Strategies of Structural Reform

RIO is more systematic than the rest of our convergence group in its recommendations for structural reforms. It makes some 80 specific recommendations framed within basic overall strategies of development for the North as well as for the South (and even the Soviet bloc and China, which we omit here).

RIO offers five points for a new development strategy for the Third World. First, they should press for equitable world opportunity and self-reliant growth; they should attack poverty and provide for basic needs, especially of the bottom 40%; second, they should reject imitation of the North, linear "catch-up" development, the creation of luxury and military goods; third, against the vagaries of the North's supply of food, the South should develop its own agriculture through collective self-reliance, land reform, cooperative or collective land tenure; fourth, it should hold as a primary aim the provision of employment and the required redistribution of income that implies, as well as a simpler technology which may even mean some lowering of average productivity. The latter does not preclude development of a modernizing sector in order to compete in world markets. Fifth, taxes or subsidies (with improved tax collections) will be employed to guide policy; and suitable policies for housing, public transportation and equitable income distribution will also be developed.

RIO strongly states the responsibilities that Third World people themselves together with their leaders bear for their own development. The authors are aware that the strong measures they call for of land reform, fairer sharing of taxation, and benefits of public service will be vigorously resisted by the propertied and privileged elites of many Third World countries.

The industrialized countries, though often unaware of it, also need a new strategy for their own development. Today the North is characterized by excessive material growth to meet artificial needs, fostering mass consumerism, and resulting in massive waste of both industrial and food products. Development in the North should, accordingly, mean reduction of consumption and abandonment of an economy of endless growth and accumulation —an economy which in fact is accompanied by high rates of poverty and inequality, dissatisfaction and anxiety. RIO proposes for the North, instead of "economic profit," the value of social profitability. This would include a monitoring of the costs of technology, fairer national and international distribution, reduction of meat consumption, improved durability of consumer goods, public transport and the establishment of maximum limits allowed for a civilized standard of life in a world where millions live in deprivation.

Essential to a basic strategy for development in both North and South is a reinterpretation of national sovereignty. The reasons for this have just been reviewed. What RIO suggests is the substitution of functional sovereignty for territorial sovereignty, at least in some cases. For example, the interests of a nation in its adjacent waters could best be dovetailed with world interests in these waters by allocating to that nation some functional sovereignty beyond a limited territorial sovereignty. That nation would, for instance, see to the protection of the waters from pollution and to their being safeguarded as a reserve for fish. The notion of functional sovereignty would by the same token allot to the world community jurisdiction over the remaining waters as a world "commons."

3) Restructuring International Order—
   RIO's Main Recommendations

Because RIO is concerned with structural reforms, it makes no short-term recommendations. However, it assumes that some structural reforms can be achieved in the next ten years and makes proposals for a medium period, 1976-85. And on the supposition that others will require a longer span, it proposes those as long-term, 1985-2000.

Four relations exist between medium and long-term: (1) most medium-term proposals are initial steps toward the longer-term; (2) they are preparatory and clear the way; (3) attention to the former should not distract from the need now to think about the longer-term; and (4) achievement of the medium does not automatically assure the longer-term. On the contrary, resolution of the energy problem by, for example, the use of nuclear sources, may bring in its wake staggering new long-term consequences.

RIO's study of the development problem was done under ten headings, so it concludes with ten sets of recommendations. These sets include: the arms race, population, food, human settlements, environment, international trade and monetary system, energy and natural resources, science and technology, the oceans and outer space.

For present purposes, we will concentrate on those sets of recommendations closest to the problem areas raised in the Seventh Special Session of the U.N. These will be: (1) the international monetary system; (2) financing development; (3) trade; (4) energy and natural resources; and (5) environment. Food is excluded here only because that was the subject of IRPC's recent Bellagio Conference and forthcoming book. Ocean policy, the arms race, and population will be briefly discussed at the close of this section.

a) *International Monetary System.* RIO finds consensus on the weaknesses in the international monetary system that must be corrected. World reserves serve mainly the interests of the rich world and requirements of the Third World are pretty well ignored, despite token increase of its presence in the IMF. To correct the situation, RIO proposes for the medium range: (1) phasing out national reserve currencies as well as gold; reserve creation should be made progressively more through Special Drawing Rights-type of assets; use of these should be jointly agreed to, keeping in mind especially the development of the Third World; (2) the development of guidelines for official interventions in exchange markets.

In the longer term, a new monetary system ought to be truly global with an agreed international reserve unit as common denominator for exchange rates and contracts, for reserve accumulation and debt settlements. It should aim at sustaining feasible, non-inflationary growth rates of world trade and production. The lending potential of these reserves should serve internationally agreed purposes, due weight being given the financing of Third World development (the so-called "link").

b) *Financing Development.* Here most of the proposals are for the medium-term, so we can first dispose of the longer-run recommendations. These call for a World Treasury which would derive its resources from international taxation and ownership of such productive resources as the oceans. The Treasury's basic purpose would be to promote an equitable world development with eradication of world poverty.

In the medium-term, RIO proposes an aid target of 0.7% of GNP by 1980, for the poorest countries, to be thereafter raised to 1% through international taxation and voluntary transfers.

Because Third World governments know a history of having their development plans thwarted by a cutting off of aid, transfers must become more and more automatic. This could be achieved through linking aid to the creation of international reserves, taxes on undesirable rich world consumption, pollution, arms spending, etc. Such aid transfers should be shifted from middle-income Third World countries to the poorest and have a very strong, ninety per cent grant component. Further, they should be directed to the satisfaction of basic human needs. The figure of $10 to $12 billion in annual transfers is suggested. RIO believes that the debts of the poorest countries should be consolidated and re-financed on highly concessional terms.

For the middle-income Third World countries, *access* is the suggested remedy, access to capital markets on fair terms, to roll-over of short-term foreign debt, to safety nets, and to international liquidity to cushion them against short-term fluctuations in their increasingly vulnerable balance of payments.

c) *Industrialization, Trade and the International Division of Labor.* Unlike most development schemes, RIO treats industrialization and trade together, and links both to the international division of labor. The purpose remains (1) to eradicate poverty, (2) to reduce unemployment, and (3) to satisfy basic human needs.

The underlying economic theory is the optimum use of the world's human and physical resources. It embraces efficiency in production and distribution, equity in distribution, accessibility to consumers—all within a new international order. In addition, optimum use suggests rational management of non-renewable resources and alternative patterns of production and consumption.

The international division of labor as understood today was devised to fill the needs of the developed industrial countries, and made no attempt to embrace all nations or global objectives. RIO recommends that this now be replaced by a truly global and dynamic international division of labor that will look beyond growth to distribution. Today's static theory of division of labor assumes that production will remain within established patterns of distribution or redistribution among nations. A progressive shift in regional patterns must be substituted in order that all nations may benefit from comparative advantage and specialization.

The ingredients of such a dynamic division of labor for global industrialization are to be found in the Second General Conference of the United Nations Industrial Development Organization (UNIDO) held in March 1975. Its main conclusions were included in the agenda of the U.N. 7th Special Session. By the year 2000, the Third World's share of industrial production should increase from today's 7% to 25%. This will require new rules and institutions to regulate and encourage industry, trade and development over against existing bilateral interests which prove incompatible with an equitable international division of labor.

In addition, there is need for a world industrial strategy. This should be approached through interim consultations and agreements between industrial and Third World countries (in which the socialist states should play their role). Such agreements would include commitments, surveillance machinery and obligatory arbitration.

Ingredients of such a world strategy would include: (1) aid to nations in formulating consistent industrial policies; (2) use of the strategy as basis for negotiations especially with transnational corporations; (3) a more rational management of raw materials, minerals and other basic industrial commodities; and (4) codes of conduct for transfer of capital and technology, as well as for trade.

The achievement of Third World goals requires that attention be focused on employment, production of goods that meet basic needs, more local processing of goods, and increase of manufactured goods for export to pay for necessary capital goods and knowledge-intensive technology. For some time to come, the poor countries will have to use a dual technology, one for increasing employment; the other, for increasing capacity to produce goods for export.

Meantime the industrial countries must take seriously their responsibility to make the required adjustments through specialization in knowledge-intensive goods and processes (and environmental protection). They must also reduce tariff and non-tariff barriers to Third World's exports of semi-processed, fully processed and manufactured goods.

An improved international division of labor (including agricultural products) requires the following: (1) identification of products which developing countries could produce with comparative advantage; (2) consequent reallocation in the North to permit this production to take place; (3) more access to industrial markets; (4) the trade measures embraced in UNCTAD's Integrated Commodities Programme (ICP) such as negotiations to improve and stabilize prices of commodities, negotiation of such guarantees as minimum food supplies and the protection of the Third World's purchasing power by indexing and conpensatory financing; and finally, (5) greater Third World participation in such downstream economic activities as local processing, storage, banking, transport and marketing.

d) *Energy and Natural Resources.* It is in this area, as we suggested in the introduction, that Herman Kahn distances himself furthest from RIO and our convergence group. We need mention only one additional point. RIO argues that exaggerated reports on the speed of resource depletion are not warranty for squandering resources, for their availability will depend on factors that ought to be of great concern, for example: the rate of exploitation, especially in attempts to meet the demands of the rich nations; success in proving new reserves; and the discovery of new productive processes and/or substitutes. Technology just may not deliver in time.

With respect to resources, RIO's main concern is that the poorer nations be enabled to earn more from them. Recognizing that many poor nations are not suppliers of most resources and that several industrial countries are heavy exporters of raw materials, RIO calls for selective treatment that will afford the rich world its gains on resources mainly in the form of assurance of access to those supplies in the control of the Third World.

What the poor world needs is assurance of higher prices for some of its commodities and stabilization of prices on as many as possible. RIO here returns to its recommendations on indexing and compensatory financing. It also argues for producers' associations, a topic to be treated below.

Toward the expansion of world resources, RIO calls for such medium-term measures as expanded information via satellites, research into recycling possibilities, into geothermal, solar, tidal, biogas and nuclear-fusion energy, and into measures to save energy and to better use low-grade waste heat.

As to long-range proposals, RIO suggests that energy and minerals be viewed as the common heritage of humankind to serve global needs, including assurance of supplies to the North, eradication of mass poverty in the South and the possible support of domestic policies of redistribution of income within the poor countries from a system of world taxation.

This suggests the need within the U.N. system of a World Agency for Mineral Resources to search out new reserves, investigate and exploit alternative native supplies of energy, oversee work of other U.N. organizations in negotiating remunerative prices, stabilization, indexing, etc. This is another type of functional sovereignty.

This World Authority should tax sales of ores in favor of the poor nations. It is objected that the consuming nations would resist such taxation and as consequence reduce their demand while seeking substitutes or diminished use through, for example, recycling. But RIO believes that the Third World would, nevertheless, gain from the tax and be helped in breaking away from their exclusive reliance on sale of raw materials even while they explore for further reserves of ores, etc. The suggested tax has these advantages over a price hike: (1) the price rise would also benefit the rich nations which do not need it; (2) the tax would not raise the price beyond the market demand, thus leaving the market undisturbed; and (3) it would bring no shift in price between different minerals.

On energy, RIO maintains that savings could be achieved if the rich nations would reduce their consumption through conservation measures and slow the pace of their industrial growth. Inevitably growth of industrialization in the Third World will increase pressure on energy reserves, as well as efforts to process low-grade ores. RIO calls therefore for a search for new sources. It warns here again against the dangers of nuclear fission and recommends a switch to nuclear fusion and solar radiation.

e) *Human Environment.* At this point, RIO shifts its focus from economics of production, consumption and distribution with its concomitants of trade, industrialization, debt, and scarcities of raw materials and minerals, to a much wider perspective—that of the human environment itself viewed as an eco-development system. There is no need to point out the linkages of the eco-system with the system of production and consumption together with its inputs and pollution output.

It is in fact precisely this interface of natural and social processes which leads the authors here to call for "nature accounting" to follow the changes in the stock of natural capital and then to align that with social indicators of quality of life and economic accounting of costs of development strategies.* This will include quantification of the wastefulness in present patterns of development strategies, including technology that permits decentralization of energy sources.

---

*This "nature accounting" is being actively pursued by groups such as Lester Brown's Worldwatch Institute in Washington, D. C.

RIO believes that "we must learn to design techno-industrial structures as true systems and to explore interfaces between life-styles, urban design and production systems." Toward this there must be research on food, health, habitat, education. There must also be "life-size experiments" in changing development styles in various cultures.

All such medium-range strategies must be followed by a more long-term strategy. This is the creation of a global system of planning, management and resolution of conflicts with respect to resources and environment. RIO is pessimistic about the possibilities of nations easily accepting such supranational organization, given their sensitivity to national sovereignty. But it remains "a major challenge to the new international order."

f) *Ocean Management.* Here we mention briefly RIO's set of proposals for medium and long-range progress toward management of the seas, since these are already familiar from other symposia and especially the recent debates in the Law of the Seas Conference.

In the medium range, RIO hopes for more regional cooperation and bilateral treaties eventually leading to an international treaty, the Law of the Seas. Whether under it or outside it, the major objectives must be to protect the living resources of the seas, to research them scientifically and to prepare and transfer an adequate technology for their exploitation. Such objectives will also include peaceful use, freedom of access, and integration of land-locked countries. Finally, the Third World should get a fairer share in world shipping, and shipping rates should be agreed upon in Liners' Conferences.

In the longer range, under a Law of the Sea the world must look to a fully systematic management and development of the living and non-living resources of the waters of the world. This would include international public enterprises for fishing and offshore oil production and for international taxation on ocean usage.

g) *Arms Reduction.* The RIO proposals on the arms race are far-reaching and familiar: nuclear test ban, nuclear disarmament, banning of chemical weapons, regulation of arms' trade and a world disarmament agency. The reduction of military expenditures should permit more generous assistance to the developing world.

h) *Population.* While population is one of the ten problem areas of the RIO report, it is singularly absent in its section on recommendations. Perhaps the authors judged the recommendations included in the U.N. World Plan of Action adopted at Bucharest in 1974 to be adequate. In any case, the only policy hints are contained in the discussion of population as a problem, where the following points are made: (1) it is controversial with some industrial countries attributing all or most world crises to population pressures in the developing world, while some developing countries reject population control even where it could be demonstrated to be needed; (2) some countries suffer from too small a population while others suffer extremely high birth rates; (3) there are limits to the earth's support capacity; (4) the population problem is more acute in poor nations where it puts enormous pressure on resources and appalling strains on people; (5) curbing high birth rates requires a concentrated attack on poverty, unemployment, illiteracy, hunger, and disease together with provision of social services, as well as more direct measures of population control.

E) Possible Packages for Comprehensive Negotiations

How can we manage the mass of recommendations that RIO and the convergence group present in the five areas we have chosen for specific consideration? Can they be integrated further? Can common interests between North and South be discovered in some of them? Are some areas more certain of acceptance and therefore a good point to begin?

1) Bargaining Packages

The Aspen Institute thought there was a good beginning point and titled its report *The Planetary Bargain: Proposals for a New International Economic Order to Meet Human Needs.* Despite conflict of interests, they discern "converging interests." All the world wants to avoid a nuclear holocaust. Positive-sums (all sides gain) can be achieved by pairing *self-reliance* (as opposed to dependence) with *self-restraint* (which requires a global approach to environmental limits). *Fairness* demanded by the Third World can be paired with the industrial world's demand for *predictability* of behavior in international dealings; for example, in the treatment of foreign investments, supplies of raw materials, etc. The Third World wants more *participation* in decision-making in such international bodies as the IMF; this must be combined with *effectiveness* of these agencies in carrying out their tasks. Finally, both North and South are coming closer to agreement on basic human needs. The Aspen Institute believes that these pairings permit bargains to be reached that will stem from common purposes.

Ul Haq, while stressing much more the power of the Third World to push their legitimate demands and reciprocally the obligation of rich nations to rethink their attitudes and give redress, still gives high priority to the search for compatibilities. "Whatever deals are eventually negotiated must balance the interests of the rich and the poor nations," he maintains. Interests on the side of the rich include wanting to avoid the costs of a Third World disruption of the industrial world's operations. The price of avoiding that cost through accommodations will be small. It is equally to be considered small in view of the North's need for an orderly, cooperative world if they want to see continued growth. For their part, the poor nations ought to recognize that "in an interdependent world, they cannot hurt the growth prospects of the rich nations without hurting their own chances of negotiating a better deal," contends ul Haq.

RIO itself offers three reasons for grouping proposals into bargaining packages. First, since the more fundamental proposals for a new order are long-term and therefore to be negotiated "over decades," it will be necessary to order priorities toward that long-term strategy. Packaging can indicate where priorities stand. Secondly, packaging shows linkages among proposals. Thirdly, and most importantly, packaging helps balance divergence of interests between rich and poor nations.

Rich nation gains may be more in the long-run than in the short. Hence, they may resist packaging unless they are given clear understanding of what benefits may eventuate for them. Some examples are: (1) against stable remunerative prices for the Third World's commodities stands the rich nations' long-term benefit of assured supplies; (2) both stand to lose from wasteful use of raw materials; (3) developing countries can make some gains from the operations of transnational corporations and the latter profit by being allowed to stay in host countries; (4) food self-sufficiency is needed in the Third World and this also helps reduce food inflation in the rich world.

2) Packaging and Power

To negotiate a package of proposals, there must be some sort of parity of power. Since power is excessively in the hands of the industrial nations, ways must be pursued of empowering the Third World. Several ways are proposed:

a) Self-reliance built through self-sufficiency in food, more automatic and less dependent transfers from rich to poor, more equitable functioning of international markets and financial mechanisms;

b) Full sovereignty of natural resources, with more control over the processing of them;

c) Collective bargaining using UN forums, regional groupings, collective economic security mechanisms;

d) Producers' associations in selective commodities to face the considerable concentration of power among buyers;

e) Public international enterprises to help the developing countries exploit their resources, codes of conduct for transnational corporations and the transfer of technology;

f) Coalitions with interest groups in the rich nations, for example, a lobby of consumers backing the entry of Third World products; a coalition with equipment producers to help increase financial transfers to poor countries;

g) Common exploitation of the heritage of the seas, to avoid exploitation for the sole benefit of the rich;

h) Democratization of the Bretton Woods financial institutions.

In an important chapter entitled "The Bargaining Power of the Poor Nations," ul Haq argues that present skepticism about the real bargaining power of the Third World is unwarranted in light of the evidence of growth of a "trade union" of poor nations. The North dismisses this development. In their view the economic power of the Third World remains meager. Ul Haq answers that that is not where the power is—it is more political than economic. More importantly, "the Third World *is* the future international order." Here he alludes to the power of sheer numbers of people and to the power of threat in their acquisition of nuclear technology. But he also believes that their economic power is growing, for example, their control over their raw materials and over supply conditions. (It is difficult for the North to turn from natural fibers to synthetics under conditions of the staggering costs of petroleum and the growing need of the Third World as a market.) Just as the capitalist world came around to recognizing the need to sustain purchasing power at home to keep its industry moving, so they will come to respect and sustain the purchasing power of the developing nations.

3) Three RIO Packages

What priority should be established among the bargaining packages? RIO presents three intriguing possibilities. We shall synthesize these here, and then compare them with the set of packages offered by the Overseas Development Council in its *Agenda 77*. The ODC proposal comes from the very different perspective of a challenge for more generosity made to the new U. S. Administration from within basic support of the capitalist system.

a) *First Package: Removal of Gross Inequities.* RIO's first package is one of the highest importance. This is to remove gross inequities in world distribution of income and economic opportunity. Into the package from the Third World side would go: (1) an acceleration of food sufficiency; (2) mobilization of development resources, including human resources; (3) restructuring of investment priorities and of social institutions to favor more the people at the bottom; and (4) population control, for which the preceding measures are incentives.

The North's parallel contribution includes: (1) achievement of the 0.7% target of public development aid; (2) the channeling of aid to help meet the Third World objectives just enumerated; and (3) rescheduling of debt. RIO estimates that the total bill for the rich countries to meet these objectives will be about $10 to 12 billion annually over the next ten years. (This is also ODC's and ul Haq's estimate.) In addition to achieving greater equity and justice, this will help build political stability, population limitation, and the eventual cessation of aid.*

This package requires no technical analysis—only political will. Once the will is aroused, the international community can elaborate strategies to combat poverty.

b) *Second Package: Harmonious Global Growth.* Interruptions in global growth through, for example, the disastrous inflation of the

---

*On October 25-28, 1976, a group of 250 participants from 60 countries met at Algiers to discuss RIO. With slight modifications and shifts in emphasis they gave consensus approval to the general lines of RIO's recommendations and proposed bargaining packages. They emphasized the need to strengthen Third World bargaining power and the need to evolve a World Development Authority. However, they saw lacking in RIO's "poverty" package sufficient analysis and redress of the present net transfer of some $35 billion annually from South to North. They wanted more emphasis on structural change and less on "more help" from the North. They wanted bargaining commitments made binding by giving them international legal status.

The Algiers delegates urged that RIO's proposals be reflected upon world-wide, but they also recognized the need for further study and conceptualization to help translate these proposals into practical measures for the world community. Finally, they agreed with RIO on the urgent need for follow-up on both the political and consciousness-raising level.

last few years, carry heavy costs. Hence there is a large degree of compatibility of interests between North and South in wanting harmonious global growth. Assuming stronger Third World participation, the following four measures can be packaged:

(1) Monetary reforms will avoid unplanned shifts in international liquidity leading to inflation, "stagflation," and depression. Here RIO indicates once again the replacement at the world level of national currencies by an international reserve managed by an international authority in line with genuine needs for growth of the world system and with special regard for the poorest people. Increased Third World food production would decrease inflationary pressure.

(2) The world would have a smoother running economy if information about the operations of transnational corporations and technology transfers were internationalized, and if "appropriate markets were developed to safeguard Third World interests."

(3) This harmonious global growth will require basic changes in consumption habits in both poor and rich nations. The poor should devote their resources initially to the satisfaction of basic needs, the provision of low-cost social services, and the development of consumption more akin to their stage of development as well as to their cultural values. Meanwhile, rich nations should develop less wasteful, less resource-intensive, consumption habits. All this will respect eco-development.

(4) Food and population must be balanced. The vulnerability of poor nations in food should be avoided by creating international food reserves.

c) *Third Package: Global Planning and Management of Resources.* RIO believes that it is only a matter of time before the international community will follow national states in planning and coordinating economic activities within the framework of world objectives. Toward acceleration of this process, it recommends:

(1) World taxation through a World Treasury to meet "the current as well as the development needs of the Third World;"

(2) Creation of an international currency reserve by an International Currency Bank;

(3) The planning of international food supplies, including world grain reserves, emergency relief and the International

Fund for Agricultural Development;

(4) Expanded responsibilities within UNCTAD for overall coordination of trade in primary resources and manufactured goods; participation of UNIDO in planning a more equitable industrial world;

(5) Additional international authorities such as an International Bank, a World Energy Research Authority, an ocean management institute, etc. required to plan and coordinate the global economy;

(6) Fundamental restructuring of the U.N. along the lines already being proposed, to give it broader economic powers and a more decisive mandate for international economic decision-making;

The ultimate objective proposed by RIO for such internationalization of planning and management is "the pooling and sharing of all resources, material and non-material, including means of production, with a view to ensuring effective planning and management of the world economy and of global resource use in a way which would meet the essential objectives of equity and efficiency."

d) *Which Package Has Priority?* The second package deserves priority because its balancing of interests will be most acceptable in the short-run. Yet the first package has top priority on the basis of need. It will take much longer to prepare people for global planning and management, but all three packages can be simultaneously negotiated in different forums with different time spans for achievement. Also, these three packages do not exclude still others. While negotiations will presently be best conducted in such existing forums as UNCTAD, now that CIEC is defunct, the best final forum will be a completely restructured U.N. system.

With respect to these bargaining packages and all the recommendations proposed in the ten problem areas, RIO recognizes that some experts will consider them unrealistic while others will believe them not radical enough. RIO joins neither the pessimists nor the radicals. Rather it sketches the evolution in human institutions which the authors believe could best ensure equality of opportunity.

4) ODC's Bargaining Packages

The study which invites the closest comparison with RIO on bargaining packages is the ODC *Agenda 77*. In this volume, Roger

A Comparative Survey 37

Hansen does a major essay in the form of an open letter to Jimmy Carter, the new president of the United States. We summarize ODC's proposals here because they present concrete examples of a private influential educational group helping the leader of a major power package realistic and significant proposals to advance the North/South dialogue.

Hansen sees the people in the North divided into three broad groups: (1) those who resist the South's revisionist challenge, (2) those who seek the South's cooperation, and (3) those who are genuinely concerned with international equity.

The anti-revisionist's strategy is to resist where possible, co-opt the more powerful of the South where total resistance proves ineffective, for example, Brazil and OPEC, etc., and compromise only if seriously challenged, giving just enough to save essentials. This description fits fairly well the previous U. S. administration.

Then there are those in the North who believe that there are problems which the North cannot solve without the South's cooperation, problems like energy shortage, limitation of resources, exploitation of the seas, open markets, debt repayment, compensation for past and future expropriation of transnationals, etc. Those from the North seeking cooperation of the South on these issues are disposed to more cooperation on issues of trade and aid that concern the developing world.

Finally there are those in the North who are genuinely concerned about development of the South and even more important, with international equity, whether of income and power or of opportunity, and who also translate this to mean within the developing countries, an equity which brings the dispossessed bottom 40% into fairer sharing in the benefits of world cooperation and their own country's development.

ODC's ideal goal, as sketched by Hansen, would meet the realpolitik of the first group, the interdependence demands of the second, and the equity of opportunity and meeting of basic needs of the third.

The ODC proposals work within a presumed broad consensus that the world economic system initiated after World War II, now needs drastic restructuring, but not, however, a scuttling of the basic structures of free trade nor of the Bretton Woods institutions, though both of these need considerable improvements. This consensus reaches out also to recognize that development efforts must focus more on people in the bottom 40% of the poor world. On this basis, Hansen presents to President Carter three possible packages (or options) for consideration. It is ODC's hope that the new administration will embrace all three.

a) *Option One* endorses marginal improvements to make more effective implementation of already agreed programs in aid and trade. Realpolitik will work here to take the heat out of confrontation.

b) *Option Two* accelerates the pace of negotiations. Its basis is an active search for solutions which render positive sums for both North and South. One such solution would be a global fisheries regime, a gain for all and desired by the North, and a global food regime, desired especially by the South.

A second area within Option Two are measures on which the South stands to gain immediately while the North gains nothing at the moment, though it stands to gain in the future. Some of these include: increased self-processing of the South's own products, higher agricultural productivity, entrance to the North's markets, securing of financing on world money markets and orderly rescheduling of debt, commodity agreements, etc.

The measures proposed under Option Two are not very different from those of RIO's second package. Some more far-reaching ODC proposals for institutional reform parallel those of RIO's third package but lack RIO's thorough-going internationalism.

c) *Option Three* favors the poorest within the Third World (the poorest billion found in the lowest 40% of the middle income countries and in the lowest income countries as a whole). Here ODC is in general agreement with the convergence group in identifying basic human needs. However, there is a qualification. Needs are not to be widened to embrace more than an internationally agreed-upon minimum.

Hansen's preferred package combines the three options. Option One, containing pluses for all, will be opposed by no one. Option Two contains only demands from the South issuing in immediate gains for them but none for the North except in the long-run. Obviously, this will be harder to sell to the U. S. Congress.

Here is where Option Three becomes strategic, for it makes demands upon the Third World, its middle-income countries. They must make the above-indicated reforms in land tenure and public welfare in favor of the neglected bottom 40% of their societies. They must also agree to the North's targeting most of its aid to meeting the needs of the poorest. Hansen argues that the U. S. Congress would be more amenable to the demands made in

Option Two if the South were to accept the reforms required by Option Three.

This brings Hansen to the human rights issue. Can the U. S. Administration nudge the South's middle-income countries to such reforms if, at the same time, it is pressuring them on their alleged abuses of human rights? Is that not just too much pressure? Might not the U. S. have to forsake its rights campaign for the sake of securing help for the poor? On the rights issue, the new Administration can also expect opposition from powerful voices in the North—those for whom the number one priority is national security. These stubbornly resist any pressure being brought to bear upon the North's security links in the Third World.

F) Managing a New World Order

This survey of recent attempts to articulate a new international order cannot be concluded without giving serious attention to the implications of such a new order for world government. A few studies such as RIO, the Dag Hammerskjold Foundation and ul Haq's *The Poverty Curtain* are more explicit on these implications. In fact, it is becoming increasingly evident that research into a new international economic order converges with research into world peace in its implications for some kind of world government.

An authority on world government, Theodore Caplow, argues in his 1977 *Feasibility Study for World Government*, done for the Stanley Foundation, that whereas it is feasible within existing mechanisms to imagine a world government for achieving the maintenance of peace, there is at present no feasibility for doing the same for economic activity. Caplow believes that there is still too wide a division among nations for any world authority to reconcile them or even be assigned the task of reconciling them. For Caplow there are irreconcilable differences between reliance on the free market and on the assignment of prices, between centralized decisions and free enterprise, between inheritance and non-inheritance of wealth as well as on such other central issues as labor market goals and world resource management and redistribution. He would assign to his one-world government only such economic responsibilities as control of radioactive material, the ocean deep, and space travel.

As already noted, some of our convergence group are less pessimistic. For example, the Aspen Institute believes that "world opinion is not yet ready for 'supranational' institutions to which they would transfer their sovereignty" but argues for an intermediary 'extranational' solution. This would be an institution like the Common Market "which operates as an executive commission at the political level and draws to itself much of the initiative for action without derogating from the ultimate power of the governments who have, in effect, *loaned* their sovereignty. . . ."

This extranational commission would analyze problems from an international point of view and negotiate with governments at the political level. Its collective leadership would ensure that a wide spectrum of views had been heard in the process. Besides having these functions of conceptualization and negotiation, this commission could implement by means of interpretation, political pressure and incentives and could also adapt or adjust already existing institutions to present needs rather than start from zero in every case.

The Aspen Institute is prepared to make use of any existing international body which demonstrates capacity to exercise extranational leadership, even if it happens to be a single strong leader such as the World Bank. However, if new entities come into existence, such as a regime for the Law of the Seas, they might well incorporate this principle of the extranational commission.

Early in 1975 a group of 25 experts were engaged in a study of the structure of the U.N. system for the purpose of over-hauling it. This group seems to have been strongly influenced by the Dag Hammarskjold Foundation's *What Now*. The core of their proposal is to create within the U.N. a Director-General for Development and International Cooperation. This would raise international economic order to the same level of significance in the U.N. as the maintenance of peace. Under that leadership, the present Economic and Social Council (ECOSOC) would play a larger role in global policy-making and in consultations among groups of nations searching for world solutions. It is clear that such a world organization could not function smoothly, as Aspen warns, if the Third World were to insist—as in UNCTAD—on treating it as their personal forum.

In his call for a single World Development Authority, ul Haq makes explicit what he sees implicit in the proposals of the group of 25. To this Authority he assigns the following tasks: (1) regulation of short-term international credit; (2) provision of long-term development finance; (3) creation of a framework for the expansion of world trade; (4) attempts to balance world population increases with food production; and (5) in general, to act, in an advisory role, as a global economic planning commission. This World Development Authority, itself supported by an International Central Bank, would have four supporting agencies: an International Development Fund, an International Trade Authority, a World Food Authority, and an International Seabed Authority.

Like these other studies of our convergence group, RIO takes the unequivocal position that the problems of international economic order will not be resolved without some world authority. Like the Dag Hammarskjold Foundation and ul Haq, RIO also supports the creation of a development authority within the U.N. "because it (U.N.) is what we have to work with." The essential thread running through RIO's recommendations is that nations are inextricably bound together in a skein of relationships which can only be developed in a world context. Furthermore, a world authority will be needed to plan, coordinate, monitor and enforce compliance.

No single major problem can be attacked in isolation. Such problems themselves are interlinked, as food with energy, the industrialization of the developing nations with pollution and with adjustments in the industrialized world, and population with all the rest. Even apart from these interdependent problems, one nation in resolving what appears to it as a purely national issue can impinge upon other nations. For example, Australia considered the negative impact of atomic experiments in the Pacific an infringement of its national sovereignty.

In addition, countries are as a result of these issues caught up in new and uncertain relationships. Consider, for example, the potential of the Third World possessors of nuclear power to disrupt the security of the North, the rise of the middle-income developing countries into the ranks of the developed, or OPEC's power to disrupt the weaker of the Organization for Economic Cooperation and Development (OECD) group or to establish leadership in creating countervailing Third World power through regional trade, etc. Bilateralism, so prized by the U. S., seems anachronistic in this new world.

RIO, like ul Haq, believes that the Third World has far less confidence than the North in the possibility of resolving the problems of justice among nations through reforms of existing structures. Accordingly, RIO hopes that the nations of the Third World would be prepared to accept some surrender of national sovereignty in favor of the required international authority or authorities. Unfortunately, this runs counter to the present thrust of the Third World to hold on to their sovereignty so recently and so dearly won from colonial powers. Many developing countries are especially jealous of their sovereignty because they now have to contend with insidious neocolonialism in the power of the transnational corporations. Nevertheless, one can hope, argues RIO, that the sheer necessity of relegating some decision-making to authorities at a supranational level will induce the Third World to endorse efforts toward some sort of one-world government.

One of RIO's attempts to cut the Gordian knot of territorial sovereignty is to introduce, as we saw earlier, the concept of functional sovereignty for carrying out specific responsibilities. This is in harmony with its principles of "decentralized planetary sovereignty" which combines as much as possible lower-level or local decision-making with as much as is needed supranational decision-making. These principles provide for the education of all people as world citizens through the exercise of participation in decision-making wherever possible.

IV. SOME QUESTIONS FOR FUTURE WORK

Here our remarks can be confined to broader issues. These are: (1) Does a consensus exist about the bargaining "packages" at least in general outline if not in precise detail (for example, a common fund is accepted in principle—but it could be consequent rather than antecedent to negotiations)? (2) Does a consensus exist that the nature of many of the problems before nations require some form of supranational authority or ad hoc authorities over specific issues? (3) If these do not exist, or too minimally to make further progress immediately possible, what line of action is possible? And (4) even apart from these more global issues, if the rich nations are growing protectionist and unwilling to give more aid, is this due to a failure of political will—and in that case, what line of action is possible? Finally, we list some other general questions—raised but not answered satisfactorily in our survey—that the conference participants should address.

A) Does a Consensus Exist About the Packages?

The burden of these pages is to show that among an influential group of concerned scholars there is considerable convergence. But these are not the people who are responsible for governmental decisions. Hence the question: what impact can the professional have on the leaders and/or politicians of individual countries of the world?

Specific measures requiring such impact have been mentioned throughout this paper, the majority being directed to the North. But experts engaged with development problems often ask why is it so difficult to bring the governments of the South to implement the measures indicated. Take just three examples:

1) Collective Self-Reliance.

Any number of valid proposals which would bring significant pay-offs have general endorsement. Why then is there so little cooperation among developing countries?

2) Appropriate Technology.

The case for it is incontrovertible. Is then the lack of follow-through to be blamed entirely on the industrial nations, or do not some leaders in the South bear a share of blame for having voluntarily succumbed to the allurements of elaborate and showy technology?

3) Land Reform.

There is unanimity among the experts that there can be no development—human, economic, social and political—without land reform, which includes together with the redistribution of land, its reorganization, management and use. Many have made only erratic efforts in this direction. Some confine themselves to laws on the books that remain inactive. Everybody knows the serious obstacles to land reform. But at the same time everyone acknowledges the need for it and recognizes that the problems can be solved. Why then has there been so little progress?

B) Is there Consensus on Supranational Authority?

Here again, among professionals over a wide spectrum of world opinion, one would find considerable conviction, stemming not only from efforts at peace-keeping but also from the more economic problems of a world-in-development. Understandably, division will be wide about what and how much authority is necessary. Here one encounters the need for studies that examine how much can be accomplished by *ad hoc* authorities which take up individual problems, one authority for the seas, another for pollution, still another for food, etc. Has this road the advantage of allowing for learning from experience?

But, conceding that functional authorities are adequate in responding to some of our global problems such as exploitation of the seabeds, can we hope that by accretion of such *ad hoc* authorities we can arrive at the solution of all our global agenda? Does functionalism, in a word, permit us to believe that we can avoid surrenders of sovereignty deeper than functional? If, as indicated in some of our studies, there must be world planning and management of resources, can this too be carried out by another limited functional authority? And by adding still another such limited authority—monetary this time—could we indeed achieve that reform which replaces all national currencies by a single world-bank of reserve deposit and credit emission for all international transactions? could this be achieved remembering that this would be a bank that could authoritatively direct use of reserves more in favor of the poor nations in ways quite beyond all proposed reforms of the IMF?

C) Is It Political Will That Is Lacking – If So, Are We Educable?

Our final two questions can be commented on together. Among the studies considered, it is a main-line conclusion that political will is lacking. On the part of whom? The people? Their political leaders? Some studies indicate in rich countries far more will among people to increase aid than among their politicians. If so, it is the politicians who have to be educated on this issue. Can the same be said of protectionism? Probably considerable sectors of workers in industrialized countries share with certain businesses fear for their industry. Who in this situation needs education? and of what kind? and who dares tells workers to accept "adjustment assistance" when their past experience has usually been derisory.

The question of whether we are educable presupposes of course that we *should* be educated to accept the packages delineated above or specific recommendations for a supranational authority of some sort. Setting that aspect aside, the experience of trying to educate on these issues of world justice has been thus far discouraging. Does not this indicate, therefore, need for the same massive attention to be given to broad general education on these issues as has been previously invested in preparing expert reports?

Some other general questions addressed to the conference participants:

Our preoccupation with convergence has helped to shape our survey of the literature. Has this preoccupation and the omission of more socialist and more conservative studies left our survey somewhat truncated and overweighted with Northern studies?

Does the focus on convergence seem to imply that what converges is already morally good?

Many of these studies used in the survey seem to waffle between a "power-bargaining approach" and a "people-educative-participatory approach." How, in fact, are these two approaches related?

Does the present preference for a basic needs approach provide the rich North with a way to break up the hard-won, fragile unity of the Third World?

Why do the studies surveyed reveal an almost total lack of concern for some kind of explicit value common denominator, both to facilitate and to maintain global interdependence and solidarity?

Even if people are educable and massive efforts are made to educate them and so to change their worldview, will they then spontaneously move to change the world order radically? or will still more severe global crises be necessary to push them to action?

And—a question central to the Lisbon conference—what role can the world's faith communities singly or in cooperation play in this whole process of education and radical change?

V. SELECT BIBLIOGRAPHY

Aspen Institute for Humanistic Studies Program in International Affairs, *The Planetary Bargain: Proposals for a New International Economic Order to Meet Human Needs.* Princeton, New Jersey: Aspen Institute, 1975.

Brown, Lester R., "World Population Trends: Signs of Hope, Signs of Stress" (Worldwatch Paper 8). Washington, D. C.: Worldwatch Institute, 1976.

Caplow, Theodore, "A Feasibility Study of World Government" (Occasional Paper 13). Muscatine, Iowa: The Stanley Foundation, 1977.

Club of Rome and the International Ocean Institute, "Towards a New International Order: An Appraisal of Prospects" (Report on the joint meeting held in Algiers from 25 to 28 October, 1976). Published under the auspices of the governments of Algeria and the Netherlands and in cooperation with the RIO Foundation.

Cocoyoc Declaration (produced by a small conference sponsored jointly by UNCTAD and UNED. It was held in Cocoyoc, Moreles, Mexico, October 1974). U.N. Document A/C.2/292, November 1, 1974.

Dag Hammarskjold Foundation, *What Now: Another Development* (the 1975 Dag Hammerskjold Report on Development and International Cooperation). Sweden, Borgstroms Tryckeri AB, Motala, 1975.

Falk, Richard, *A Study of Future Worlds* (sponsored by the Institute for World Order, Inc.). New York: Free Press, 1975.

Fundacion Bariloche, "Catastrophe or a New Society? A Latin American World Model." Amilcar O. Herrera, Project Director. Ottawa, Canada: International Development Research Centre, 1976.

Goodman, Allan E., *The Politics of the North-South Dialogue; Implications for International Relations,* paper presented at a conference on "New Factors in International Conflict," The Fletcher School of Law and Diplomacy, Tufts, 4-6 May 1977.

Hirsch, Fred, *Social Limits to Growth.* Cambridge, Massachusetts: Harvard University Press, 1976.

International Labor Office (ILO), *Employment, Growth and Basic Needs: A One-World Problem.* Published for the Overseas Development Council in cooperation with the International Labor Office; New York: Praeger Publishers, 1977.

Kahn, Herman, *The Next 200 Years: A Scenario for America and the World.* New York: William Morrow and Co., Inc., 1976.

Leontieff, Wassily et al., *The Future of the World Economy,* A United Nations Study, Oxford University Press, New York, 1977.

McNamara, Robert S., President, World Bank Group, "Address to the Board of Governors" (given in Manila, Philippines on October 4, 1976). Washington, D. C.: International Bank for Reconstruction and Development, 1976.

Meadows, Donella H. and Dennis L.; Randers, Jorgen; and Behrens, William W., III, *The Limits to Growth.* New York: Universe Books, 1972.

Mesarovic, Mihajlo, and Pestel, Eduard, *Mankind at the Turning Point.* New York: E. P. Dutton/Reader's Digest Press, 1974.

Schumacher, E. F., *Small Is Beautiful: A Study of Economics as if People Mattered.* London: Blond and Briggs, Ltd., 1973.

Sewell, John W., Project Director, *The United States and World Development: Agenda 1977.* New York: Praeger Publishers (for the Overseas Development Council), 1977.

Singh, Jyoti Shankar, *A New International Economic Order: Toward a Fair Redistribution of the World's Resources.* New York: Praeger Publishers, 1977.

Third World Forum. Mexico City, Apartado 85-015, Mexico 20, D.F.: Coordinating Secretariat.

Tinbergen, Jan, Coordinator. *Reshaping the International Order: A Report to the Club of Rome.* New York: E. P. Dutton & Co., Inc., 1976.

ul Haq, Mahbub, *The Poverty Curtain: Choices for the Third World.* New York: Columbia University Press, 1976.

ul Haq, Mahbub, *The Third World and the International Economic Order.* Washington, D. C.: Overseas Development Council, 1976.

United States Congress: *International Commodity Agreements,* Hearings before the Subcommittee on Economic Stabilization of the Committee on Banking, Finance and Urban Affairs, House of Representatives Ninety-Fifth Congress, June 8, 1977; *International Debt, The Banks and US Foreign Policy,* Staff Report prepared for the use of the Subcommittee on Foreign Economic Policy of the Committee on Foreign Relations, United States Senate, August, 1977; *The United States Response to the New International Economic Order: The Economic Implications for Latin America and the United States,* Subcommittee on Inter-American Relationships of the Joint Economic Committee, Congress of the United States, February 23, 1977, US Government Printing Office, Washington, D. C.

SUMMARY

Land's paper is not a position paper but rather a background paper which attempts to provide the Lisbon Conference participants with an overview of relevant events, documents, studies and proposals on a new world order. Land sees a widespread convergence emerging among top-level professional groups working in different parts of the world and so adopts a convergence approach to organize his survey. He chooses the Club of Rome's *Reshaping the International Order* (RIO) as the statement that can best stand as paradigm of this convergence, and goes on to trace convergence perspectives in the multitude of analyses and recommendations in the following areas:

1) the shortcomings of the old international economic order;

2) the shift in thinking toward a basic human needs approach;

3) the many proposals made for a new economic order;

4) some possible bargaining positions or packages proposed for negotiations; and

5) the significance of the new emphasis on the need for a world authority or authorities if a new world order is to be more than a cliche.

He leaves his readers with the deeply puzzling question of how such widespread convergence can exist among influential groups of concerned scholars and yet have so little consequent political impact. Clearly the same massive attention that has been invested in preparing these expert reports has to be given to programs of broad general education on world justice issues.

If this is so, what role can the world faith communities play singly or in cooperation in this whole process of education and radical change in world order?

3

World Chaos or a New Order: A Third World View

Isma'il Abdalla

Isma'il Sabri Abdalla, an Egyptian citizen, is presently Chairperson of the Third World Forum, and former Minister of Planning for the Egyptian Government. Until recently, he was Director General of his country's Institute of National Planning. Abdalla did his graduate studies in economics at the University of Paris. Among his many posts and honors, he has been Chief Editor of the State Publishing House, Dar Al-Maarif; head of the Economic Development Organization; member of the Academic Committee, Arab Planning Institute, Kuwait; and member of the Council and Chairperson of the Membership Committee, Society for International Development. He has lectured and published extensively, especially on the international monetary system and the New International Economic Order.

The birthday of a new world is at hand.
Tom Paine, 1775

A new civilization is born.
V. I. Lenin, 1917

I. INTRODUCTION

A New International Economic Order (NIEO)

More than four years ago, the heads of states of the non-aligned nations gathered at their fourth Summit Conference in Algiers, September 1973, considered once more the slow pace of development in the developing nations and the constraints imposed on their efforts by the existing system of international economic relations. This time* their conclusion was that, given the long list of misgivings, nothing short of reshaping the whole system could be meaningful. Accordingly, they proclaimed that what the world needed was a "New International Order."

To its authors this history-making resolution had to be implemented with due care and perseverance. They did not underestimate the hardships of the path they were choosing. Hence their decision to convene a series of specialized conferences of developing nations to elaborate on targets as well as on the ways and means to achieve them. The first of these conferences was to deal with what was considered the most urgent issue: raw materials.**

OPEC and the NIEO

Less than a month later, the October war in the Middle East, the Arab oil embargo and the subsequent rise in oil prices decided by the Organization of Petroleum Exporting Countries (OPEC), made a hot issue of what the international mass-media treated a few weeks

---

*As a matter of fact the issue of development and its links with the relations between "developed" and "developing" countries had always been central to the members of the non-aligned group. Already at its first summit conference, Belgrade 1961, President Gamal Abdel Nasser of Egypt raised it strongly and almost in today's terms. That conference called a meeting of all developing nations to discuss problems of aid and trade. It took place in Cairo, July 1962, and elaborated the first general statement of claims, known as the "Cairo Declaration." Among other things the participant nations asked the United Nations to hold an international gathering to examine the state of affairs and identify possible solutions. Two years later, the UN Conference on Trade and Development (UNCTAD) gathered in Geneva. Faced by the reluctance of the developed countries to comply significantly with any of their demands, the developing nations convened in a separate meeting to state once more their point of view. The "group of 77" was thus born.

** It gathered in fact in Dakar, February 1975.

earlier as mere rhetoric worthy of just limited coverage, if any at all.

The North-South debate gained unprecedented momentum and shifted from one arena to another over the last four years. The sequence of events was briefly the following. First, the US Secretary of State, Henry Kissinger, called for an oil consumers coalition to confront the oil producers. All the developing nations declined his proposals, while many developed nations expressed various degrees of reservation toward a full scale confrontation. Then, President Boumedienne of Algeria, acting in his capacity as chairperson of the non-aligned conference, asked the UN Secretary General to convene in a special session the UN General Assembly to discuss the problems of raw materials and development. President Giscard d'Estaing of France launched the idea of a North-South conference with a limited number of participants representing the different interests. This Conference on International Economic Cooperation (CIEC) would be held in Paris to provide a more adequate forum for negotiation than the UN bodies.

The sixth special session of the UN General Assembly took place in April-May 1974. It raised great hopes when its resolutions 3201 and 3202 gave official recognition to the term "New International Economic Order." Herein the member states solemnly proclaimed their "united determination to work urgently for the establishment of a NIEO based on equity, sovereign equality, interdependence, common interest and cooperation among all states, irrespective of their economic and social systems, which shall correct inequalities and redress existing injustices."

Four Years of Vain Efforts

People of good will and deep insight met in a series of seminars, symposia and conferences to identify the issues at stake, analyze their nature, and point out possible solutions and the necessary adjustments they might entail. The outcome of this world-wide action of dialogue and "thinking together" is an impressive mass of statements, reports and studies ranging from the concise enumeration of a consistent set of measures as in the case of the "Proposals for a New International Economic Order," issued by the Third World Forum, to the far reaching analysis of "mal-development" both in the South and the North found in the Dag Hammarskjold Report *What Now: Another Development.* The elaborate "package of comprises" for the short and medium term found in several studies including the Club of Rome Report *Reshaping the International Order* prepared by Professor Tinbergen and his team took the discussion a step further. This wealth of generous ideas and new analytical concepts enriched our knowledge about development both nationally and internationally. Unfortunately it had little if any impact on inter-governmental negotiations.

The consensus reached at the seventh special session of the UN General Assembly diluted the issues in equivocal general statements of intent. As far as the concrete measures called for by the "Programme of Action" adopted by the sixth special session, developing nations had to seek them in another forum, the Fourth UN Conference on Trade and Development (UNCTAD IV) held in Nairobi.

Again in Nairobi the industrialized nations blocked almost all resolutions, hinting that the Paris CIEC conference would be a more appropriate place for effective bargaining. In that setting, fear of an "automatic majority" and speeches made for the benefit of public opinion at home can be dispensed with and workable solutions based on mutual concessions can be elaborated. Yet one year later, CIEC ended in total confusion.

Thus neither the public fora nor the secret deliberations gave any satisfaction to the developing nations. Four years of vain efforts ended while the state of the globe steadily worsened with more suffering in the South and a prolonged recession in the North.

Shapers of Public Opinion

This situation does not enhance the credibility of decision-makers, those who by democratic vote or otherwise, bear the responsibility of leading their nations and humankind to better living and legitimate hope. Instead of helpless disenchantment, those individuals and groups who influence the shaping of public opinion spiritually, intellectually or morally, should look to the root causes of errors and misunderstandings and never give up. In the name of their respective commitments, they should again and again try to raise public awareness of the fact that many values, attitudes, relations and institutions are bound to change. What counts most is to bring about the change with the least social cost. We have no alternative for our survival.

Thus, it is with this necessary combination of keen desire and cold analysis that I address myself to the urgent need for a new world order. I will skip the details except for illustrative purposes and stick to what in my opinion is the heart of the matter. On the other hand, I am supposed to spell out the point of view of the Third World. Consequently, frankness is here more relevant than any pseudo-objectivity.

II. GENESIS AND CHARACTERISTICS
OF THE PRESENT WORLD ORDER

What Is Wrong With the Existing World Order?

It is quite logical, especially for a good many people in affluent societies, to ask what is wrong with the existing world order that makes it necessary to change it altogether and establish a new one? Has not humankind achieved in two centuries or so under this order much more progress than it had during thousands of years of recorded history? A reply that limits the discussion to the simple enumeration of facts and figures illustrating the tragic conditions in which the majority of the inhabitants of our planet try to survive is not sufficiently convincing. We know in advance the typical reaction of the rich of all times, and we have repeatedly heard their modern version. It goes like this.

The first phases of growth in Western nations were full of sufferings, inequalities, hardships and a slow rise in per capita income. What the people in the Third World are complaining about today is, in fact, the natural course of development. With hard work and enterprise they will some day attain much better conditions, if not full-scale affluence. They have no right to share the fruits of the endeavors and sacrifices of other nations, say many people in the North with full candor.

More generous souls concede in the name of solidarity that some remedy should be found to correct the regrettable side effects of the system and alleviate the pains of the deprived: a bit more aid, some lenient trade conditions, some industrial investment in the manufacturing sector, etc. On the whole, people in the industrialized countries are so accustomed to look at their prosperity exclusively as a national achievement, that it rarely occurs to them that there may be a link between their wealth and the poverty of others.

"Deaf Dialogue" in a Sick World

International negotiations during the last four years have gone more or less along those lines. It is not very astonishing then if they have turned into a kind of "deaf dialogue" with insignificant results. In the sick world of today, dealing with the symptoms and ignoring the disease cannot be of great help. So it is to the disease that I address myself here. It can be identified if we care to have a close look at the genesis and characteristics of the world order. We are so accustomed to live within it that we forget that it is a relatively recent phenomenon in the history of humankind. Unconsciously we admit

its existence and *modus operandi* as the "natural order," in the sense
that 18th century philosophers used this term.

Capitalism

Looking back we can see the genesis of the world order some
two centuries ago. During tens of thousands of years people lived in
separate communities more or less large and sedentary, each community knowing only of the existence of its immediate neighbors.
The empires of ancient times each covered a limited portion of the
globe and never integrated into a single socio-economic system all
the communities they controlled. Travellers who ventured on long
trips were often motivated by curiosity and brought back more tales
than commodities. Until the end of the 15th century, to the people
around the Mediterranean* the world meant, in addition to their immediate surroundings of Europe and the Middle East, China and
India. Needless to recall that "international trade" was still sporadic
and confined to a few luxury items.

Even when Paine was speaking about "the birth of a new world"
in 1775, the globe was far from being known to all its populations.**
It was the nascent socio-economic system of capitalism that spurred
the Europeans in an unprecedented enterprise, the conquest of the
whole planet. The captured riches of conquered nations provided a
good part of the initial capital accumulation that allowed wealthy
Europeans to transform inventions—hitherto considered curiosity
gadgets for the courts of kings and princes—into productive
technology.

Colonialism

Modern industry was born with two characteristics: a voracious
appetite for energy and raw materials and an endless need for ever
expanding markets. Colonialism was the means to insure both. Thus,
capitalism***unified the world for the first time in human history not
only politically, but also economically. It is fashionable today in some
circles in industrialized nations to emphasize the "interdependence"

---

*Literally, the sea in the "middle of the earth," a becoming name for a region con-
sidered—at least by its inhabitants—as the "cradle of civilization."

**Books of history talk about the "age of discoveries." The term is typically ethno-
centric. The Europeans were discovering distant lands and peoples but not the other
way round!

***Here we do not attach any value judgment to this term. It describes simply an
economic system characterized by the search for maximum profit by the owners of
the means of production through the interplay of market mechanisms.

of all nations, including the most powerful* as if it were an entirely new phenomenon. What is really new is only its present magnitude and complexity.

In fact, interdependence started the day the Lancashire textile mills expanded by using cotton from India, Egypt and the United States. In turn the economics of the colonies were shaped by the colonial powers to satisfy primarily the needs of their own industrial growth. Thus, the colonies became economically dependent as well as militarily occupied and politically enslaved.

In the 19th century, "free trade" was the war cry of the most industralized countries, while each power was managing to build its own empire where it enjoyed "imperial preference." By the end of that century the entire globe was under the domination of industrialized nations and most of its population part of one of the colonial empires.** Thus the world economy evolved into an integrated system, parts of which were interdependent. But the central question remains—as it does in the case of the integration of a national economy—who manages the system and thereby draws the major portion of its benefits?

Economists say that the market tends to exclude the sub-marginal producer and favor those who have a "rent position." The classical economists thought that "survival of the fittest" was both natural and beneficial. In fact, the development of the market economy favored growing inequalities regionally and socially. At the national level, only a deliberate state action could bring about a serious reduction of those inequalities. In the absence of a world government, such a corrective action did not exist.

On the contrary, military and political coercion exerted by the colonial powers greatly aggravated the built-in bias of the system. The outcome of this process was formidable industrial growth in a few nations (the center of the system) to the detriment of the rest of the world (the periphery). Underdevelopment is not sheer historical backwardness. It is a distorted, extroverted and dependent development—the by-product of development in the North.

This historical perspective is not meant to revive any bitterness, nor to support any claim for compensation. Problems of the future

---

*See, for instance, Harlan Cleveland *The Third Try at World Order*, American Self-Renewal in an Interdependent World, World Affairs Council of Philadelphia, 1977. It has the great merit of telling the people of the first superpower how their might and prosperity are dependent upon what is going on in other parts of the world, especially developing nations.

**This phenomenon drew the attention of several observers who called it "imperialism" and offered various analyses to explain it. Hence, the word is not a marxist invention. See for example, the works of Hobson and Schumpeter and also H. Kohn, *World Order in Historical Perspective*, Harvard University Press, 1942.

can be solved only by constructive interaction among those responsible for the future without emotional quarreling about the past. I wanted simply to unveil the power structures of the world order that systematically alienate and frustrate Third World people and inhibit their development potentialities through numerous and varied built-in mechanisms. I do this because I believe that unless joint and sincere efforts are undertaken to establish more democratic power structures, words like solidarity, equity, equality of opportunity will long remain in the realm of wishful thinking, if not that of sheer utopia.

Interlinked Power Structures

Now let us try to have a look at the interlinked power structures that form a kind of cobweb in which developing nations find themselves entangled.

a) Military domination

First, military might is in the hands of the most developed nations. It continues to increase at accelerated rates in spite of all the conferences dealing with disarmament. Military expenditure has been increasing during the last ten years at an average rate of 7% and weapons are becoming more and more devastating. The impact of this armament race on Third World countries is many faceted. It is a permanent threat to their independence. Many of our nations gained their sovereignty after bitter, long and destructive wars. Others have been victims of aggression. The Namibians, the Palestinians, the Zimbabwe people and the Blacks of South Africa are still under military coercion.

In some parts of the world, a prolonged war-like state forces some national governments to divert an appreciable proportion of their GNP from development in order to buy weapons, increasingly sophisticated and costly. In other areas, the complacency of some governments of the North, and/or the desire to increase their share in a particularly lucrative trade allows some Third World regimes to buy equipment necessary to strengthen military dictatorships, to wage local wars over conflicts that could be otherwise peacefully settled, or even simply to satisfy the megalomania of some heads of states.

In addition, the "balance of terror" having made military adventures among Northern powers almost suicidal, the Third World, in its own process of transition, offers an easy market for weapons considered technically obsolete. These weapons can be used in local wars often provoked by the struggle for influence among the big powers. The Third World becomes a ballpark where risks of global confrontations seem easier to control.

Finally, developing nations have to depend on arms producers in the North for their supplies and know how in order to provide for their national defense requirements in a world that lives in a state of "armed peace," and in which aggressions and subversions occur only in the Third World. World peace and generalized disarmament are thus the best of gifts the big powers can offer us.

b) Economic domination

Second, the key factors of economic power such as industry, technology and finance are concentrated in the hands of a small number of industrialized nations. Some salient features of this kind of domination should be mentioned. The total share of all Third World nations in the world industrial output amounts to only 7%, less than that of the United States alone. Noteworthy is the fact that this industrial explosion in the North is heavily dependent on the Third World for energy and raw materials. The case of oil dependency is all too well known. But the dependence of the United States, Japan and the European Economic Community (EEC), for their supplies of 13 strategic raw materials is also striking.* Excluding phosphates, US dependence ranges from 20% in iron ore to 98% manganese and 100% natural rubber. The EEC relies on imports for 100% of its needs in five of the thirteen commodities, and Japan in seven.

Yet, economic power belongs to those who process and manufacture these raw materials because they have a precious accumulation of capital and technology. In the field of technology, beside the accumulated know how, there is the ever growing concentration of research capacity. Over 90% of all scientists and technologists are at work in the industrialized countries, even though many of them are people from the developing nations. Furthermore, over 90% of their activities are concentrated on research for the rich world and on converting their findings into protected technical processes.

The international monetary system is based on the paper-dollar and managed in fact by the five major industrialized powers: United States, West Germany, Japan, Great Britain and France. As a result, the developing nations own only 4% of world reserves, and inflation imported from the industrialized countries

---

*These are bauxite, chromium, cobalt, copper, iron ore, lead, manganese, natural rubber, nickel, phosphates, tin, tungsten and zinc. Cf. *International Economic Report of the President to the Congress,* US Government Printing Office, Washington, DC. March 1976.

reinforces local inflationary pressures.* The external debt service added to returns on foreign investments often reverses the financial flows. In addition, the South pays more than it receives if we take into consideration the terms of trade for raw materials. The high concentration in the "international capital market" easily explains this damaging fact.

Again, the world food market is dominated by three countries, United States, Canada and Australia, who provide 69.7% of the total world exports of grain. And the list of instances of economic domination goes on—but we already have sufficient for the purposes of this paper.

c) Cultural domination

Last but not least, there is the cultural domination of Western civilization** exerted through education, information and communication systems. Modern education is widespread at all levels in industrialized nations, while the majority of Third World people are still illiterate. This in itself is a decisive factor of supremacy.

But more relevant to domination is the fact that our intellectuals are trained in Western or Western-like universities. The whole education system in our countries has been tailored after Western patterns irrespective of the differences of national cultures and the local socio-economic and physical environment. As a rule, national languages have been discarded as being inadequate vehicles for modern scientific knowledge. The inefficiencies of our systems of education are generally recognized even at home, but very little attention has been given thus far to their inappropriateness and the possible link between the two phenomena. Yet, those systems contributed greatly to the formation and shaping of Third World elites with all the incalculable consequences of their being ever fascinated by the West.

One chief thing I would like to emphasize is the lack of knowledge of our own national history and culture among our people and the lack of knowledge about other Third World nations. A dichotomy persists in many cases between an out-dated traditional education and a modern one which reinforces a "dual economy" with a "dual culture." Needless to say, I am not denouncing access to the fruits of the formidable scientific progress achieved by Western countries. It goes without saying that the universal

---

*While a rate of inflation of 20% is exceptional and considered very alarming in the industrialized countries, rates around 80 to 100% have become a way of life in many developing countries. See the International Monetary Fund, "Financial Statistics," issues of the last four years.

**Understood as Euro-American including East European countries.

laws of physical and mathematical sciences should be studied and propagated. But the ways and means of conveying scientific knowledge should be related to local conditions.

On the other hand, social sciences are too greatly influenced by the societies in which scholars carry out their research so that their findings cannot *a priori* be accepted as valid all over the world and at all times. Our societies remain virgin land, so to say, for national research work, in need of new tools of inquiry and analysis. New findings that may be thus discovered will enrich the social sciences and broaden their overly narrow Western focus.

The situation in the field of information is even more dramatic. Four Western news agencies have, practically speaking, monopoly of news dissemination all over the non-socialist world. Without going as far as accusing them of systematic and international distortion of facts—even though this happens sometimes—misinformation is the logical result of an inevitably value-laden process of selection that raises some events to the rank of "news" and dismisses others as insignificant or of no interest. Consequently, information within the Third World and about the Third World is inadequate and often biased or misinterpreted.

Mass media transmits its message around the clock, a one-sided flow of news ideas and images from the North to the South. Our broadcasting stations are not powerful enough to reach the public in rich countries, and in any case, nobody would care to listen to them. Our newspapers are read only by some specialized scholars. Movie-goers in a few Western cities occasionally watch films from developing countries, when these films win a prize at a Western festival and are introduced in Western distribution circuits, that is to say when they satisfy Western tastes and are more or less in conformity with preconceived images. Third World populations, on the contrary, are literally flooded with information about the astronauts and the "mafia," the bright scientific discoveries and the "merits" of gadgets, as well as the whims of fashion makers and product designers.

The technical revolution in communications aggravates the situation both by the new instruments it provides, such as TV satellites which poor countries cannot afford to buy, and by the capacity it confers on those who handle them to reach illiterate people in the remotest villages of developing nations. Thus, political propaganda, business advertisement, social and cultural values are constantly hammering the citizens of the Third World, reshaping their tastes, changing their behavior for better or worse and altering their culture.

Once more, I am not advocating cultural chauvinism or defending parochial values and concepts. On the contrary, I believe that cross-cultural fertilization has played a decisive role historically in human advancement. It could now play a far more important one, if cultural diversity were recognized, national cultures given equal opportunities to flourish, and cultural exchanges were genuinely multilateral and less unequal. Free circulation of information reminds me of free trade in commodities, insofar as both can be benficial to all partners only when power relations do not allow some partners to keep most, if not all, of the benefits for themselves.

To conclude this section, I would say that we in the Third World believe that we cannot achieve overall, self reliant, self centered and self sustained development without changing the present world order. True enough many individuals and groups in the developed nations have their own good reasons to welcome the change. But the purpose of this paper is first of all to spell out the directions of change that developing nations seek earnestly to introduce.

III. WHAT IS THE THIRD WORLD AND WHAT DOES IT WANT?

What Is the Third World?

The term "Third World" was first coined by French authors.* For them "Tiers Monde" was in analogy with "Tiers-Etat" (Third Estate), a term that designated before the French Revolution those who did not belong to either of the two privileged "estates," namely, the nobility and the higher clergy. A revolutionary priest, l'abbe Sceyes, wrote at that time, "What is the Third Estate? Everything. What has it been hitherto in the political order? Nothing. What does it desire? To be something." Except for the "everything," his statements sum up remarkably well the status and desires of the Third World.

a) Great discrepancies in wealth

Some governments of industrialized nations and a good number of authors reject the concept of "Third World," on the grounds of the great discrepancies in wealth and economic growth found among developing nations. They divide these nations into four groups: OPEC, middle income, less developed and least devel-

---

*The most famous among them was Alfred Sauvy.

oped nations. Arguing in terms of per capita GNP, it is rather easy to dispel this kind of categorization.

Let us look first at the rich among the developing nations, those with per capita income over $2,000. They are 8 countries totaling only 13 million people. The "fabulously rich" Saudi Arabia has a per capita income of only $2,630, less than Italy ($2,820) and slightly more than Spain ($2,490). On the other extreme, the poorest among the poor are 7 countries with per capita income of less than $100, and a total population of 31.5 million. The rest of the "group of 77," the more than 100 countries with a population exceeding two billion people, have a per capita income between $100 and $2,000, the better off having 20 times the per capita income of the poorest. In contrast, the richest among the OECD group of nations,* are only 10 times richer than the least rich. Nevertheless, what is more telling is the fact that the middle income countries and the majority of OPEC countries** have a per capita income in the $1,000 to $2,000 bracket, which is the lowest bracket in the OECD.***

The conclusion is obvious. By industrialized nations' standards all developing nations are more or less poor, and not more or less rich, with the insignificant exception of those 8 countries with their 13 million people, mentioned above. We have no grounds to predict that a fairly large number of developing nations, representing an appreciable percentage of total Third World population, will in the forseeable future join the "club of the rich" and enjoy therein comfortable and permanent seats.

b) Historical and structural ties

However, what is common to all developing nations is not simply this unequal sharing of poverty, but the historical and structural ties that maintain them in a position of inferiority. Three basic facts have to be brought into the discussion in this respect.

Political domination. First, almost all developing nations have been the victim of Western conquest, military occupation and political domination. They have been for decades or centuries colonies of this or that European power. The trauma of foreign domination explains the ambivalent love-hate relationship between most of the newly independent nations and the former colonial powers.

---

*North Atlantic Community, plus Japan, Australia and New Zealand.

**They are 12 countries with total population of 150.4 million.

***Two countries whose total population amounts to only 30 million, are in this bracket.

Economic exploitation. Second, all of them have been subjected to economic exploitation. I have hinted in the first section at the impact of this process on the economies of the colonies and how it produced "under-development" as a state of affairs that has nothing to do with the concept of historical backwardness. Let me repeat that what counts is not the time lag, but what happened during it, since the dynamics of world capitalist expansion left no place for a "stationary state."

Political decolonization has now been achieved with few exceptions. Unfortunately, since it did not bring with it economic decolonization, exploitation continues. It has become more subtle, hiding behind the opaque curtain of market forces. The combination of the expansion of transnational corporations and inappropriate development strategies adopted by Third World governments has given this exploitation new dimensions in both depth and magnitude.

I will not elaborate on this phenomenon in this paper, since it is well covered in the available literature. However, I will dwell briefly on one example because of the confusion it has created, namely, the oil exporting countries whose billions in income are one of the favorite topics of the mass media. From the outset, let us agree that national interest should push an oil producing nation to export only to the limit of its need for foreign currency, since oil is obviously an exhaustible resource. When it exports more, it complies with the needs of other nations, especially the industrialized ones. By so doing, it exchanges a real asset, whose value is bound to increase, for a financial asset whose purchasing power will continue to decline, given the chronic situation of world inflation.*

The monetary wealth it can get in excess of its needs for rational development stimulates conspicuous consumption and investment in inordinate prestige projects, as well as the acquisition of weaponry to the detriment of real overall independent development.

Moreover, surpluses of petrodollars are deposited or invested mainly in industrialized nations. Thus most petrodollars are in fact recycled, leaving the exporters too often with consumer goods and gadgets, as well as some uneconomic infrastructures, industrial plants and nuclear power stations.

---

*In a speech delivered at the Society for International Development (SID) conference on "Equality of Opportunity Within and Among Nations" (Amsterdam, November 29-December 5, 1976), Minister Pronk of the Netherlands said that oil prices had already lost more than 30% of their overall purchasing power, while prices of equipment imported by OPEC nations had doubled.

Cultural aggression. Third, most developing nations suffered from cultural aggression. Western people were, and to a great extent remain, convinced that their civilization is radically superior to all others. For centuries they used to equate it with human civilization tracing it back to the ancient Greeks, in complete ignorance of and disdain for the remarkable achievements of the Chinese, the Indians and the Arabs, etc. They had a good conscience during the colonial era because they were bringing the benefits of civilization to the barbarians. In addition, they did not bring only new scientific and technical knowledge, but mainly a way of life, social values, and languages that were alien to the people they conquered.

In their typically ethnocentric drive, they denigrated national cultures *en bloc* and taught the happy few of their subjects who were given access to modern education that in order to be civilized and cultured, they had to mimic Europeans and drop their native cultural and social values. Languages which carried sophisticated scientific knowledge for centuries were abandoned in favor of foreign ones. Our societies became the subject matter of a new science, "ethnology," because traditional comparative studies presuppose a minimal degree of equality. Such equality remained until recently a strange and shocking idea.*

The effects of cultural colonialism are the more lasting. They explain the fascination the West exerts on our upper and middle classes, the cultural schizophrenia of many of our intellectuals and their lack of confidence in the capabilities of our people, the recurrence of "fanatic" politico-religious movements rejecting all that comes from the West and seeking salvation in a return to the "purity" of ancient times. They explain chiefly why we in the Third World were unable for decades to identify paths to development other than the historical Western model.

These historical and structural ties having been laid out, it still is important not to underestimate differences, conflicts of interest and contradictions among and within developing nations. It is our duty to identify them and to deal with them in a manner less costly in human lives and wealth than used by the Western nations until World War II. On the other hand, we should do everything possible to strengthen our collective bargaining power with the industrialized countries. We are often told by

*The new *Encyclopedie Francaise* published in the thirties by a group of authoritative scholars under the auspices of the Minister of Education, offers a striking example of ethnocentrism. The authors contrast "pensee orientale" to "pensee occidentale" and characterize the first as "prelogique" and the second as "logique." They simply forgot that they were using Arab figures to explain algebra and chemistry, among other "oriental" products. See vol. 1 pp. 10-13, Paris, 1937.

Western people: put your own house in order before blaming us for your sufferings. And they point out the privileged minorities in the Third World who absorb most of the foreign aid and govern their countries in more or less undemocratic styles.

Let me say one thing here. If the rich minority are able to keep their privileges and dictatorships in the Third World continue to spring up and remain in power, it is partly because of Western backing. For decades, Western countries used to label any national or social liberation movement as "communist," and hence under Soviet obedience and thus suspect in the game of the Superpowers. Accordingly, rich minorities, accommodating leaders, and dictators proclaiming their faith in the values of Western civilization, were supported against Soviet "totalitarianism" in the name of defending the "free world." In all objectivity, one must concede that these policies often paid off well in profits, military bases and zones of influence. The question now is how long are these practices to last? What will be the cost of the inevitable change? And who will pay for it?

What Does the Third World Want?

The answer to the question in a nutshell is that the Third World wants structural changes, not mere marginal concessions in the world order.

a) Structural changes

Transfers, both financial and technological, have proved to be disappointing and sometimes deceiving. There is abundant literature about aid, how its importance is declining and its concessionary element shrinking.* Moreover, aid is tied for all practical purposes to buying in the donor countries. Export credits and other short term facilities promote the exports of the creditor's products and services. The external debt of the Third World has reached the astronomical figure of about $300 billion. The burden of servicing this debt is exorbitant, and it absorbs a large portion of foreign currency earnings. Returns on direct investment often offset the direction of financial flow to the benefit of industrialized countries. More dramatic still is the fact that availability of foreign financing often determines development priorities. No wonder then if growth is often unbalanced and economies distorted.

---

*For OECD countries, Official Development Assistance (ODA) as percentage of GNP declined from 0.52% in 1960 to 0.35% in 1976. For the United States in the same period, the decline was from 0.53% to 0.26%.

What we ask for is international taxation on the use of non-renewable raw materials, on polluting activities in the use of the world commons, etc., to be received and redistributed by a multi-lateral international agency run democratically—one nation, one vote.

In the area of trade, we should recognize the fact that the world markets of primary commodities are oligopolistic. This calls for either inter-governmental regulation, like national antitrust laws and stabilization funds, or the organization of producers associations to enhance the bargaining power of the exporters. Competition cannot continue to operate only among sellers.

In the field of technology we want the Third World nations to develop their own technological capacities and to use technologies appropriate to their specific conditions, instead of acquiring inappropriate technologies at high prices. Technical assistance is of a dubious character. A computation carried out by the UNCTAD secretariat estimates the value of technology transfers from the United States, Canada and Great Britain to developing nations (1960-1972) at $46.3 billion, compared to an estimated imputed value of $150.9 billion for the skills of technicians from developing nations who immigrated to these three industrialized countries.

We want the monetary system to become truly internationally controlled by an International Central Bank, itself managed in a democratic way.

Last but not least, we want real world peace, effective disarmament and a renovated UN system reflecting equitably the legitimate interests and aspirations of all nations in their diversity. It is inadmissible that one big power can block any UN resolution while the so-called "automatic majority" can only vote "recommendations."

b) The process underway

How can such changes in power structures be introduced? First of all let us agree that today's world is facing a set of inter-linked crises. History shows that crises of the magnitude of our times forecast periods of disruption. We cannot look for solutions to our crises in the past, which in any case was not all that successful if judged in terms of social and human cost-benefit analyses. History also shows that significant transformations usually take place under the pressure or by the action of the destitute. When those who retain wealth and power do not understand the pressing need for change, this action of the destitute can become devastating. Harlan Cleveland explains how vulnerable the big industrialized powers are precisely because of the complexity of their technological urban societies and sophisticated weaponry.*

Without dismissing the possibility—even likelihood—of such action by the destitute, one can easily think of other kinds of concerted Third World action—raising the prices of raw materials and regulating their supply, boycotting international arrangements that require universal consent (from nuclear safeguards to narcotics smuggling) or reducing dramatically their imports from industrialized countries by barring unnecessary consumption, etc.

In a more constructive approach, a good number of Third World nations will try to become self-reliant nationally and regionally. The advocated new development strategies will gradually materialize in one way or another. Awareness of environmental issues will push some nations to be more prudent in exploiting their non-renewable resources and more selective to avoid importing technologies that pollute.

The process of change has already started and nobody can stop it. Today the people of the Third World have the same awareness and emotional involvement toward issues of equity, equal opportunity and justice that they used to have toward political independence. The anti-colonial struggle had its ups and downs, its successes and failures, its heroes and its compromisers. Yet the end of political colonialism came because it was inevitable. The same applies to the present struggle for a new world order, because it involves the economic and cultural decolonization of developing nations.

IV. A POSITIVE SUM GAME

The new world order for which we are struggling will be beneficial to the people in industrialized nations as well. It is not a zero sum game, taking from one exactly what will be given to the other. At the present historical juncture, and as a result of the irreversible interdependence of all nations, problems facing any group of nations are linked in one way or another to those confronting other groups of nations. Only a global approach to global interrelated issues can facilitate the tackling of even national problems. Some issues illustrate convincingly what we are stating here.

The irresponsible arms race imposes growing burdens on the industrialized nations, while total aid to developing nations amounts to only 3-4% of the world military expenditure. A significant cut in

*op. cit. p. 95. The recent power failure in New York City can be repeated by a band of "desperados." See also: Paul-Marc Henry, *La Force des Faibles*, Paris, Editions Entente, 1975.

this expenditure can at the same time alleviate the burden to industrialized nations, allow for a meaningful transfer of real resources to developing nations and lessen the danger of war. On the contrary, if this race is allowed to continue, more resources will be diverted to useless production and nobody can guarantee an absolute control over the stocks of deadly weapons.

The nuclear powers can find themselves involved in Third World wars originally meant to be limited or local armed conflicts. Of more concern is the access of some racist regime to nuclear weapons. Or even worse, a group of individuals can easily and cheaply fabricate an atomic bomb that might be a kind of detonator of a thermo-nuclear apocalypse. A climate of exasperation, despair and successive confrontations between the rich and the poor of the world dramatically increases the risks of this kind.

Another example is provided by what has been called the problem of the "outer limits." Without speculating about the finite nature of our resources, one can safely predict that the traditional wasteful patterns of growth and consumption of the industrialized nations, added to the unavoidable industrialization of the developing nations, will certainly increase the demand for energy and raw materials. This will push their price upward and shorten the life-span of exhaustible resources. New life styles on the contrary that give more attention to the satisfaction of immaterial needs and new patterns of industrialization and technology can secure more rational use of energy and raw materials.

A third example can be found in the growing concern for the quality of life. Reducing pollution, due respect for the natural environment and improvement of urban life in manageable agglomerations go hand in hand with irradication of poverty, slum clearing and rural development. It is now an established fact that pollution spreads across national borders and extreme poverty is as damageable to the environment as over-industrialization, over-urbanization and over-consumption. Once more we face a one-world problem.

Finally, unless the international community becomes capable of handling adequately and democratically the introduction of necessary changes, confrontations conducive to disruptions cannot be avoided. It is high time that our global community measure up to what the word "community" means. In the 19th century, the world community was reduced to the big European powers that constituted the "concert des nations," because we in the Third World were still colonies and not nations. After World War II, the United States became the unquestioned leader of the "free world," that is, of all nations except the Socialist countries. Since the sixties, detente has replaced the cold war and the role of the Socialist nations in world affairs has become a fact of life. Now the emergence of Third World nations should radically change the international scene. Most of these nations belong to the non-aligned group which rejects any allegiance to big powers and insists on the recognition of all nations as full-fledged members of the international community.

Only this recognition can make of this community a reality and empower its democratic structures to tackle global issues and manage universal interdependence equitably. Thus both the rich and the poor can find their share in the new set-up.

Wealth and power are by nature factors of conservatism. Therefore, it has been the destiny of the poor to promote the radical advancement of civilizations—those same poor who followed Jesus and Muhammad, to speak of two religions familiar to me, and whose action changed the world to the benefit of all. The poor of the Third World should do the same. The outcome of their struggle should be the "birth of a new world" or "a new civilization" in a more global sense than that imagined by the authors of the two quotations with which I have prefaced this paper.

FOOTNOTES

1. Third World Forum, *Proposals for a New International Order*, Mexico City, August 1975; Jan Tinbergen et al, *Reshaping the International Order* (RIO Project), a Club of Rome Report, Amsterdam 1976. Also the Report on the Algiers Conference, October 1976, where the RIO was presented and discussed.

Dag Hammarskjold Foundation Report, *What Now: Another Development*, on Development and International Cooperation, Uppsala, 1975.

2. See illustrations of today's inequalities and frustrations in Mahbub ul Haq, *The Poverty Curtain: Choices for the Third World*, Columbia University Press, New York, 1976.

Robert S. McNamara, *One Hundred Countries, Two Billion People*, Praeger Publishers, New York, 1973.

John W. Sewell and Staff of the Overseas Development Council, *The United States and the Developing World: Agenda 1977*, ODC, Washington, DC, 1977.

3. Cf. *RIO Report*, p. 39 and also p. 270 on "brain drain."

4. Ibid., pp. 199-205

5. See Sewell

6. See UNESCO, *Draft Medium-Term Plan*, submitted to the 19th General Conference, Nairobi 1976, and the proceedings of the Conference itself. Many of the topics outlined in this section are discussed extensively therein.

7. As translated in the *Encyclopedia Britannica*.

8. All figures are quoted from the "World Bank Atlas" 1976 edition.

9. See for instance, Raul Prebisch, "Peripheral Capitalism," *CEPAL Review* 1976; and Celso Furtado, *Developpement et sous-developpement*, Presse Universitaire de France, Paris, 1966.

10. See L. J. Calvet *Linguistique et colonialisme* Payot, Paris, 1974.

SUMMARY

Abdalla first outlines the events that lead up to the Sixth Special Session of the UN General Assembly, April-May 1974, an event that greatly raised Third World nations' hopes by giving official recognition to the term "New International Economic Order." For him, the ensuing years have been marked by vain efforts and fruitless discussion. Witness the failure of the Fourth UN Conference on Trade and Development (UNCTAD IV) and the unresolved confusion of the Conference of International Economic Cooperation (CIEC).

Abdalla goes on to analyze, from a Third World viewpoint, the genesis and chief characteristics of the present world order. He dismisses the thesis that the wealth of rich nations is the rightful fruit of their own labors. He concludes that present underdevelopment in the Third World is not mere historical backwardness. Rather it is "distorted, extroverted and dependent development"— the by-product of development in the rich North and of military, economic and cultural domination for centuries.

He argues that in spite of significant differences and conflicts of interest, Third World countries still form a homogeneous group in their common exclusion from the "club of the rich."

Today the Third World no longer wants marginal concessions but rather major structural changes in the present world order. To replace dwindling and sporadic aid, they want an international tax on non-renewable raw materials, on polluting activities in the use of the world commons, etc., administered by a fully democratic multi-lateral international agency. Regarding trade issues they want significant inter-governmental regulations or producers' associations to enhance their bargaining power. In technology, they want assistance to develop their own appropriate technological capacities. Finally, they want a truly internationally controlled Central World Bank, effective disarmament, and a renovated United Nations system that removes the veto power of big nations.

For Abdalla the present struggle for a new world order is as inevitable in its outcome as was that to end colonialism. Both Jesus and Muhammad taught us that it was the destiny of the poor to promote the radical advancement of civilization. Nevertheless, rich and poor alike will profit from a genuine world community of equal nations.

4

Basic Human Needs and the New International Economic Order: A Northern View

James Grant and John Sewell

James P. Grant, a US citizen born in China, has been President of the Overseas Development Council since its establishment in 1969. He was formerly Assistant Administrator of the US Agency for International Development (AID), and a Deputy Assistant Secretary of State for the Near East and South Asian Affairs. In his AID work, he has lived many years in India, Sri Lanka and Turkey. Grant is currently the Vice President of the Society for International Development (SID). His recent analyses have centered on the world food situation, major structural changes taking place in the international order, and the effectiveness of various development strategies.

John W. Sewell, a US citizen, is Executive Vice President of the Overseas Development Council, Washington, D. C., and directs the Council's program of research and public education. He joined the Council's staff in 1971 after serving as Assistant to the President of the Brookings Institute and as a foreign service officer in the Department of State. Sewell has written and lectured on US public opinion concerning developing countries, on ethics of development assistance, and on the African Sahel.

I. INTRODUCTION

Pessimistic Perspectives

The past few years have been marked by a spate of books and articles from various writers and commentators in the industrialized North questioning the ability of the individuals and their leaders to resolve the problems now facing both rich and poor countries. They predict the end of "civilization" as defined by the industrialized countries, either because we are pushing towards the earth's physical capacity to sustain or accommodate continued acceleration of economic activities, or because humankind lacks the political will and intelligence to deal with current pressing problems. The title of these works—*The Limits of Growth* is the best example—bears witness to this growing pessimism. It is perhaps deepest in the writings of an American economist, Robert Heilbroner, who asks if there is any hope that humankind will be able to meet the current challenges now facing the world without paying a fearful price, he responds ". . . no, there is no such hope." [1]

This pessimism is directly attributable to the growing, but still not widespread, understanding in the industrial countries that the world is in the midst of the transition from one era to another . . . from the period in which the international political and economic system was dominated by the power arrangements established as a result of World War II and by the institutions created in the years immediately following that event, to an era whose shape is yet uncertain and whose institutions are yet to be defined.

Optimistic Perspectives

Yet other observers in both developed and developing countries see the transition period as a marvelous opportunity. The optimist realizes the current period also is an era in which humankind and the leaders of the world's nations have the physical resources to eliminate the worst aspects of absolute poverty by the end of the century, as well as the political possibility to create a more just and equitable series of relationships between rich and poor countries. It was in this vein that President Carter spoke in an inaugural message to people outside the United States of "the basic right of every human being to be free of poverty and hunger and disease and political repression"; he also called for ". . . a joint effort to move the reality of the world closer to the ideals of human freedom and dignity."

To Sketch an Optimistic Northern Perspective

The purpose of this paper is to sketch out a Northern (and perhaps even more specifically, a United States) perspective on the background to the current situation, the possible shape of the "joint effort" to which President Carter referred, and the problems and dilemmas posed for both the developed and developing countries by any effort to link the "new international economic order" and the address of basic human needs.

The attempt to deal with the "Northern perspective" on these issues should fill any author with trepidation. There is as much diversity of opinion in the North as in the South concerning the overall shape and specific details of a new international economic order. Statements and proposals from individuals and groups in the developed countries range from those favoring virtually no change in existing international economic and political relationships, to those who would support wholesale reform and restructuring of the current nation-state system. This essay is merely one perspective on the current discussion and debate, albeit one written from those perspectives of the United States which are sympathetic to the proposals of the developing countries.

II. NEW NORTHERN PERCEPTIONS OF THE DEVELOPING COUNTRIES

Not an Undifferentiated Bloc

For years analysts and policy makers in the developed countries tended to consider the developing countries as an undifferentiated bloc, making no real distinctions between Mexico and Mali in terms of economic and social structures and potential. This aggregation is perhaps not surprising given the nomenclature of a "third world" and the unified position of the developing countries on many international issues. Indeed the *overall* development record of the past three decades reinforces that viewpoint and belies the pessimism of some observers. As a recent World Bank study by David Morawetz points out, the economies of the developing countries as a group grew faster than either the developed or the developing nations had grown in any comparable period prior to 1950, and at a rate which exceeded both official goals and private expectations. In addition, average life expectancy in the developing countries is now 50 years, comparable to the level reached by Western Europe at the beginning of the twentieth century and infant mortality has dropped sharply.[2]

The sudden massive price increases of 1974 in oil, food, and fertilizers combined with the still ongoing global economic slowdown have tended to obscure the longer term record. Most developing countries dealt with these economic shocks better than expected. They did so, however, mainly by borrowing; as a result, their outstanding debt has grown 80 per cent since 1972. This debt will pose a growing burden unless special measures are taken to change the various international economic systems and unless the industrial countries resume the economic growth rates of the past.

Two Distinct Groups

In reality, both the price rises and other economic "shocks" of recent years greatly widened differences among the developing countries in terms of the state of their economies and their development prospects. Among the market-economy developing countries, two distinct groups of countries have emerged, groups with quite different needs in terms of their external economic relationships: the "middle-income" developing countries and the poorest countries. The middle-income nations consist mostly of the countries of Latin America, North Africa, the Middle East, parts of the rest of Africa (notably Nigeria), and the countries of East Asia; they have a total population of approximately 900 million. The poorest countries, concentrated primarily in South Asia, Sahelian Africa, and much of sub-Saharan Africa, have a total population of approximately 1.2 billion.

a) Middle-Income Developing Countries

The middle-income developing countries as a group (i.e., countries with a per capita income of $300 or above in 1974 dollars) are among the fastest-growing in the world. Over the past decade, they have achieved an overall growth rate of 6.8 per cent—about 4 per cent in per capita terms. Some of these countries are demonstrably better off than others because of their rich endowment of natural resources. Most conspicuous within this group are the countries which export petroleum, but others, such as Malaysia, which is virtually self-sufficient in oil as well as a major exporter of tin and rubber, also fall into this category. Another group of middle-income developing countries consists of those nations which have been able to increase their exports of processed and manufactured goods. Countries as diverse as Taiwan, the Ivory Coast, Brazil, and Mexico fall into this category.

In many of these countries there is still a great deal of poverty. However, with sufficient national political will, economic recovery in the industrialized world, and supportive reforms in the international economic systems (none of which can be assumed as certainties), these countries should prove to have resources adequate for addressing their poverty problems. Per capita income differences between these middle-income countries and the developed countries appear to be narrowing (at least in relative terms); more important is the likelihood that these countries may be able to narrow greatly the "gap" in terms of many of the most basic indicators of economic and social well-being (such as life expectancy, infant mortality, and literacy) during the remaining years of this century.

b) Low-Income Group

On the other hand, the more than forty nations that constitute the poorest or "low-income" group have the slowest growth in output of any group of countries in the world. Average per capita incomes in the poorest nations grew at an annual rate of only 1.5 per cent, or $2 per year, during the past decade, in contrast to annual per capita increases of $30 in the middle-income countries and $130 in the high-income countries. The future prospects of these poorest countries are not bright. The World Bank estimates that, over the ten-year period 1975-1985, the per capita income of the 1.2 billion people living in these poorest nations will increase by only 20 percent (from $150 to $180), even under the most optimistic circumstances. And even if the per capita income in these countries were to grow at the rate of 3 per cent annually until the end of this century—which is unlikely—it would only then begin to approximate that of England and the United States in 1776. (See table below.) Therefore it seems clear that there is likely to be little improvement even in the physical well-being of people living in these countries unless special and extraordinary measures are taken by both developed and developing countries.

c) Gaps Continue to Widen

Not only is the gap between the developed countries and the developing countries still very great; income disparities between rich and poor people *within* most developing countries actually appear to be growing. The ratio of income received by the top 20 per cent of the income recipients to that received by the bottom 20 per cent is about 6:1 in the United States and the United Kingdom, and 4:1 in Poland; but it is 29:1 in Ecuador, 20:1 in Brazil, and 15:1 in Mexico. In most developing countries, moreover, this ratio is worsening.

The result of all of these trends is that, despite the trebling of world output since the 1940s, nearly one billion people today subsist in chronic poverty in the developing world. Most live in the poorest countries; but significant numbers reside in the middle-income countries and in rich countries. Stark as these numbers are in themselves, they cannot begin to convey that in human terms they mean a vicious cycle of widespread illiteracy, unemployment or underemployment, malnutrition, hunger, ill health, and short life expectancy.

Disparities Between Groups of Countries, 1975
(millions and $)

Population
(millions)

	Total	Absolute Poor	Under-nourished
Poorest Countries (under $200 per capita GNP)	1,200	750[e]	600
Middle-Income Developing Countries (over $200 per capita GNP)	900	170[e]	140
Developed Countries	700	<20[f]	<20[f]

Per Capita Income[a]
(in constant 1975 U. S. $)

1965	1975	1985[bc]	2000[bd]
130	150	160-180	180-230
630	950	1,130-1,350	1,510-2,400
4,200	5,500	6,700-8,100	9,000-14,600

[a] Based on official exchange rates rather than purchasing power comparisons and therefore represents only broad orders of magnitude.

[b] Long-term projections of economic growth are, of course, highly speculative; they are presented here not as predictions, but only to call attention to problems that may develop if present trends continue.

[c] The higher figures are World Bank projections based on 1975-1985 annual per capita growth rates of 1.6% for the poorest countries, 3.9% for the middle-income countries, and 4% for the developed countries. The lower figures are ODC projections based on annual per capita growth rates only half that good.

[d] ODC derived the higher figures by projecting a continuation of the 1975-1985 growth rates assumed by the World Bank and the lower figures by projecting a continuation of growth rates half that high.

[e] In the developing countries, defined as those with annual per capita incomes of less than $100 in 1975 U. S. dollars. They are considered to have only a slight chance of being able to increase their incomes by more than $2 annually over the next decade. In addition, there are hundreds of millions more with incomes that are somewhat above this minimum level of poverty but still less than one third the national average.

[f] Even in the rich countries, there are millions who suffer from poverty and undernourishment.

NOTE: Data for centrally planned economies are not included in this table.

SOURCES: Adapted, with revision, from Robert S. McNamara, "Address to the Board of Governors," Manila, Philippines, October 4, 1976 (Washington, D. C.; World Bank, 1976), pp. 3, 5, and 15.

III. A CHANGING POLITICAL ENVIRONMENT

The increased urgency of the problems facing the developing countries comes at a time of far-reaching changes in the international political environment within which a new set of relationships between rich and poor countries must be created.

Growing Global Economic and Political Interdependence

The last decade has been marked by the emergence of global political and economic interdependence on a scale hardly imaginable only twenty-five years ago. This interdependence has been manifested in such seemingly unrelated phenomena as continued "stagflation" in the industrialized economies, the depletion of the world's fisheries, the continuing threat of a world food shortage, and the impact of a fourfold increase in the price of oil. This interdependence, however, is not a new phenomena for leaders in developing countries. They have long realized—and chafed against—their dependence on the policies and actions of the industrial countries. But the understanding that the needs and desires of the developing countries must be taken into account in formulating global policies is a new phenomenon for policy makers in the industrial countries. In many ways it is a healthy development to the extent that the industrial countries enter into negotiations with the developing countries based on a perception not of the need for charity, but rather on their own long-run self-interest.

This perception of pyramiding interdependencies has for some given rise to the pessimism described earlier; but for many observers in the rich countries (and indeed in the poor countries) it has led to the conclusion that global problems will not be resolved unless they are addressed by most, if not all, nations working together. Such attempts are already in progress in a number of areas: reform of the world monetary system, discussion of new and as yet undefined commodity arrangements, negotiation of a new regime for the oceans, organization of a network of both altered and new institutions for increasing the world food supply and stabilizing grain prices, and growing awareness that a cooperative international approach is needed in the energy field.

Clearly, the world in which these changes must be negotiated is very different from that which emerged at the end of World War II. The present period is one in which no one nation is dominant. Even while many observers in the North are experiencing increasing global interdependence, recognizing inadequacies in the operation of existing international economic systems, and witnessing dramatic shifts in the development prospects of specific groups of developing countries, the international political environment in which changes must be negotiated is being transformed.

Continuous Restructuring in the International System

The current political situation is in fact only a stage in the process of continuous restructuring in the international system that has been going on for most of this century. The disappearance of colonial empires and the emergence of new nations are all part of a process of accommodating to the emergence of new states as participants in the international system and adjusting relationships among already participating states.

One major aspect of this new environment is that the developing countries are currently pressing for major changes in the economic and political structures that have governed international relations since 1945. Their demands for greater participation and decision-making power have many precedents, both international and domestic, in the actions of countries and groups that considered themselves disadvantaged in the past. It is analogous, for instance, to Japan's drive prior to World War I, and then in the interwar period, to equal standing in the international system. It also bears some similarity to the emergence of organized labor in the United States in the late 1920s and 1930s, and the drive of Black Americans for legal equal rights in the 1960s. In each of these cases, it became apparent, after much resistance by those in power and after prolonged struggle and strife, that accommodating the reasonable demands of those on the outside for effective participation within a changed system paid both political and economic benefits to all concerned.

Current Upsweep in Nationalism and in Collective Self-Reliance

Inherent in the present drive of the developing countries for increased power, status, and access to resources is another major characteristic of the current environment: the continuing post-colonial upsurge of nationalism and the consequent emphasis on national sovereignty. At a time when many in the North are beginning to realize that the nations of the world are becoming increasingly interdependent, this strong insistence on national sovereignty is a complicating factor in developing new cooperative mechanisms to deal with the world's pressing economic and social problems.

This emphasis on nationalism and sovereignty both reinforces and is reinforced by growing developing-country interest in the principles of *national*—as well as *collective* "self-reliance"—that is, the measures that developing countries themselves, individually and collectively, can take in support of their national or collective development. The interest in self-reliance stems from the desire to fashion economic policies according to what the developing countries see as their own needs, problems, and historical experience. It is also partly an expression of long historical experience and frustration with the lack of development results derived from two decades of applying conventional development strategies patterned after those conceived and followed in the industrialized world.

Neither "self-reliance" nor "collective self-reliance" are new concepts; indeed, collective self-reliance was implicit in the shaping of the European Communities and the Atlantic Community. There also have been many attempts at economic cooperation among *developing* countries, usually with relatively little success, partly because one vestige of the colonial era is the continuing close economic linkage of many of these countries with specific developed countries, and partly because a considerable number of developing countries perceive their best prospects for development to lie in greater integration into the world's trading and monetary systems.

Both developing and developed countries might benefit from some varieties of developing-country "self-reliance" — for example, for expanding trade among developing countries and, equally important, from the lessening of the "psychology of dependence" through increased interdependence among developing countries. Collective "self-reliance" approaches pose choices for *both* developed and developing countries. The latter will have to decide the degree and the manner of their integration into the world's various economic systems, and the former must decide whether or not to encourage increasing autonomy on the part of the developing world.

Only the Demands for a NIEO Are New

The demands of the developing countries for a "new international economic order" that seemed to emerge full-blown in 1974 in various international forums took most Americans by surprise. Encouraged by the successful boycott and price increases of the oil-producing states in late 1973, the developing countries used a number of both official and unofficial international gatherings to press their proposals for reforms in the operation of international institutions and systems created in the post-World War II period. The major explicit components of the "new order" — the "NIEO" — called for by the poor countries of the Southern hemisphere are by now quite familiar.

They include: market access for their manufactured goods, stable and higher prices for their agricultural and other commodities, renegotiation of their growing external debt obligations, restraints of the activities of multinational corporations, greater access to existing technology, an expanded share in the production of the world's industrial goods, an aid relationship that relies less on short-term legislative appropriations and more on various forms of more automatic resource transfers, and, above all, a major adjustment of existing international decision-making procedures to give the Third World a greater voice in the governance of the world's trade and financial systems.

Often overlooked in the initial furor, particularly in the United States, was the fact that the demands of the poor countries did not emerge *de novo* in 1974, but, rather, were the predictable outcome of more than a decade of largely fruitless efforts of the "Group of 77" developing countries to evoke in various international forums a positive response from the developed countries on issues of crucial importance to the Third World. The proposals that attracted the limelight in 1974 under the "NIEO" label had evolved over the past fifteen years at a series of international meetings and discussions, mainly within the Group of Non-Aligned Countries and, since 1964, within the United Nations Conference on Trade and Development (UNCTAD). Underlying them all is a strong feeling on the part of developing countries that they are subject to rules of international economic institutions and systems that discriminate against them, but in whose creation they did not participate and in whose decision making they still have relatively little voice. The events of the mid-1970s merely provided—in the role of the oil-exporting countries—the lever with which developing-country demands could be presented in a variety of international forums with greater effectiveness than in the past.

OPEC Supports the NIEO

Many Americans looked upon these proposals as a fundamental challenge to the dominant position that the United States has enjoyed in the world since the end of World War II. Indeed, some people in the United States initially feared that the demands signaled a "new cold war," and there was much talk of the need to meet the new "threat" to the United States and its industrial allies head-on. This initial reaction was muted—at least in governmental circles—when it became apparent in mid-1975 that the United States would not get agreement from the OPEC nations to discuss the price and supply of oil, which the U. S. saw to be the most pressing problem, until it also was willing to discuss the concerns of the developing countries set forth under the rubric of the New International Economic Order. The result of this impasse was a change in U. S. policies marked by Secretary of State Kissinger's speech to the Seventh Special Session of the United Nations and the subsequent establishment of the Conference on International Economic Cooperation.[3]

US Wants No Fundamental Structural Change

Yet despite intensifying discussions between North and South in a variety of forums both sides seem far apart on their diagnosis both of what is wrong with the present international economic system, as well as their prescription on what can or should be done to change it. Policy makers in Washington now recognize that there can be benefits to both rich and poor countries from some changes in existing policies and institutions, but there is little desire to alter the basic structure of the system created after 1945. Therefore, the emphasis is still put on increased aid and lowering of tariff barriers, combined with a willingness to talk about some new types of commodity arrangements (including a common fund although not necessarily as proposed by UNCTAD). This attitude is perhaps best caught in the recent report to Congress by Under Secretary of State for Economic Affairs, Richard N. Cooper, who himself is a distinguished international economist. Cooper said:

"We believe the North-South dialogue in CIEC and other forums, should emphasize improving, rather than restructuring, the existing international economic system, thus enabling the developing countries to participate fully in this system. Appropriate and efficient transfer of resources to developing countries through direct mechanisms, such as foreign assistance, as well as the importance of trade and investment, are the essential elements in an improved economic system. We believe—and seek to convince LDC's [less developed countries]—that indirect mechanisms of resource transfer, such as generalized debt relief and indexation of primary product prices, would be inefficient, largely ineffective, and actually contrary to LDC interests."

The U. S. response to the NIEO proposals has been strongly affected by a number of factors. Some concern a perceived dilution of power; others reflect ideological differences between policy makers who emphasize heavy reliance on the corrective powers of the market mechanism itself and those who perceive a need to introduce varying degrees of market intervention. Moreover, the discussions that have taken place to date suggest that there is still inadequate information available to policy makers, in the United States and other developed countries, on the economic and political costs and benefits

—for *both* the developed and the developing countries—implicit in specific proposals to change present practices.

Several questions in particular have received very little attention. What can the United States itself expect to gain from reform of international economic arrangements? Do the NIEO proposals put forward by the developing countries imply nothing but economic losses for the rich countries and gains for the poor countries? Or are there potential solutions that would result in gains for *both* sides? Alternatively, if the "losers" and "winners" vary depending on the issue, is it possible to assemble packages of bargains so that the gains and losses at least roughly balance out? If the United States and other developed countries determine that certain short-term economic costs are necessary in order to achieve national and international long-term economic and political gains, who would bear these costs *within* the United States?

The present world political situation is further complicated by the fact that pressures in the developed countries for governmental action to ensure full employment and to address the social welfare needs of all their citizens have grown steadily since the late 1940s. These pressures, described by sociologist David Bell as the "revolution of rising entitlements," have led to a variety of domestic social welfare programs that in many cases were overdue; at the same time, however, they have limited the negotiating freedom of governments on foreign policy issues which touch the welfare of their own citizens. Thus trade negotiations, for example, have become increasingly difficult as organized labor, fearing the loss of U. S. jobs, has opposed tariff-cutting measures that would permit the increased import of low-cost consumer goods—including imports from developing countries.

Impact of LDC's Greatly Increased

However, few observers realize that the aggregate economic impact of the developing countries on the United States and on the industrial world as a whole has greatly increased in recent years. What happens in the developing countries can affect inflation, growth, and jobs in the United States and other industrial countries. U. S. exports, for example, currently account for about 5 per cent of our gross national product. By 1975, some 27 per cent of total U. S. exports went to non-oil-exporting developing countries—more than were purchased by the European Communities, Eastern Europe, the Soviet Union, and China combined.

One recent study concluded that the continued high imports by the developing countries in 1974 and 1975 (financed mainly by the foreign borrowing from a variety of sources) had enabled the industrialized countries of North America, Europe, and Japan, to maintain economic growth at relatively high levels in spite of the negative effects associated with the oil price increases.[4] In addition, American consumers benefited during this time from a wide variety of low-cost imports—particularly textiles, electronic equipment, and shoes—from developing countries. Indeed, some observers have begun to raise the question of whether or not the United States (and the other developed countries) will be able to regain the high growth and the relatively low inflation of the 1960s *without* accommodating to the needs of the developing countries.

Who Pays Cost of Change?

There is, of course, another side to the impact of increasing North-South economic interdependence. The developing countries can only increase their purchases of industrial-country goods if they can earn money through exporting their own products to the United States and other developed countries. Yet those exports, in turn, have a direct impact on certain segments of American industry. In the United States this is at the moment most apparent in the shoe and textile industries, which are facing severe competition from imports. The same situation is likely to arise in other industries in the near future. How can costs of having access to lower-cost consumer goods be distributed so that they are not concentrated on the workers in a few industries? And how can it be assured that all of the potential anti-inflationary gains to be realized from a global grain reserve system will not fall hardest upon individual American farmers in the form of lower prices? Can both the costs and the benefits of change be equitably shared by a broad spectrum of American society?

Arms Race and Sales Waste Resources

U. S. policy on North-South relations clearly will have to reconcile the traditional American goals of minimizing international conflict and maintaining international stability with the demands of the developing countries for sometimes far-reaching changes in existing economic and political systems. In recent years, many of the areas of potential "superpower" confrontation have been in the Third World. The points of tension have not been Berlin or Eastern Europe, but areas of turmoil in Southeast Asia, the Middle East, and Southern Africa. Considerable political and social turbulence can be expected in many developing countries in the years ahead. Contrary to the conventional wisdom of the 1950s and early 1960s, it now is generally accepted that development progress in and of itself will not bring peace and stability. Indeed, it may even have the opposite effect in the short run as the process of development itself creates stresses and strains within heretofore largely traditional societies. Yet in the *long run* the *lack* of development progress is likely to give rise to even greater conflicts within these societies which may also intensify tensions between the superpowers.

The prospects for conflict within the Third World — and perhaps between the First and Third Worlds — are further complicated by the likelihood that many developing countries will be turning to nuclear power as a source of energy (with all the attendant risks of proliferation of nuclear weapons) and by spiraling military expenditures in both rich and poor countries. World military expenditures have grown from $198 billion in 1963 to $350 billion in 1976. Much of this growth has taken place in the developed world (including the Soviet Union) but expenditures by developing countries also are growing. In fact, the developing country *share* of total world military expenditures has grown from 4 per cent in 1957 to 14 per cent in 1976; while world military expenditures are growing about 3 per cent per year, expenditures by the developing countries are increasing at 10 per cent each year.

Some of this growth undoubtedly has been stimulated by arms sales by the major powers. U. S. arms transfers to developing countries alone have grown from under $1 billion in 1970 to nearly $6.2 billion in 1975. Other suppliers have shown an equal growth. Yet it also is clear that weapons salesmen find a ready market among those developing country governments who for a variety of reasons are spending scarce resources on these largely unproductive military programs.

Grappling with these issues in the future will pose difficult questions for both sides. The developing countries guard their sovereignty and in some cases have legitimate internal or external needs for military equipment and training. Developed countries find arms sales useful as sources of foreign exchange and fear that renunciation of sales by one supplier will simply allow another to fill the gap. Yet the resources dissipated by both developed and developing countries demand address of this issue, especially at a time when other global problems and needs are competing for the financial, technical, and material resources which military spending absorbs.

IV. THE EMERGENCE OF A BASIC NEEDS STRATEGY

In the mid-1970s nearly one billion people are believed to live in absolute poverty around the world. They exist in two overlapping groups. Absolute poverty in a global context characterizes the condition of more than a billion people living in the poorest countries—some 40-odd countries with average per capita incomes of $150. Absolute poverty also refers to the condition of a partially overlapping group of people who are poor, regardless of where they live. This latter group includes some 700 to 800 million in the poorest countries, some 150 to 200 million in the middle-income countries, and some 35 to 70 million in the high-income countries.

The Concept

The continued existence of this large group, despite the fact that world output has trebled since the late 1940s, has led to an intensive rethinking of development theories and strategies among economists and development practitioners in both developed and developing countries. A new understanding is now emerging concerning development strategies that could be effective in alleviating poverty in the developing countries in a relatively short time. Recent academic studies and the experiences of several countries indicate that it is possible to achieve greater equity and growth simultaneously.

For instance, in such widely different societies as Sri Lanka, South Korea, Taiwan, China, and the Indian state of Kerala it has been possible to achieve a wide dispersion of improvements in the basic quality of life—such as low death and infant mortality rates and high life expectancy and literacy rates—at relatively low levels of per capita income. A direct improvement in the condition of the very poorest groups constitutes an investment in human capital which, along with labor-intensive development policies, can itself contribute to the growth process. The application of strategies focused along these lines would, however, require most poor countries to allocate their resources differently in the future and in ways much more appropriate to countries which lack capital but not labor.

ILO Basic Needs Strategy

These concepts were much debated at the World Employment Conference held in Geneva in June 1976 under the auspices of the International Labor Organization (ILO). The policy conclusions of the World Employment Conference included a call for an international "basic needs strategy" that would assign first priority to meeting certain minimum human requirements for jobs, food, shelter, and clothing, as well as to providing access to basic health, education, and other services to all people. The program of action adopted by the Conference—which won the endorsement of both developing and developed-country participants—is an important first step in the acceptance of these new development strategies.

Possible Applications

a) In Rich Countries

Recent OECD studies indicate that relative poverty in the industrial countries results mainly from inadequate political will to address the problem seriously. Those countries which have introduced policies to eliminate internal poverty problems (e.g., Germany and the Scandanavian countries) have only some 3 per cent of their populations living in relative poverty and a much smaller proportion living in absolute poverty. The proportion living below the relative poverty line in the United States decreased substantially after sustained attention was devoted to anti-poverty programs in the 1960s, with the number living below the relative poverty line having been more than halved since the mid-1960s.

b) In Middle-Income Countries

Changes in the various international economic systems along the lines suggested below could provide the governments of many of the middle-income developing countries with the additional income needed to eliminate the worst aspects of absolute poverty in their countries within the next twenty-five years—provided that these countries themselves adopt policies for securing the more effective participation of the majority of their citizens in development programs and for delivering services and benefits to the poor majority. As in the developed countries, the question of meeting the needs of the poorest people within these countries therefore becomes one of the political will of those in power and of the internal distribution of political power among groups. Mahbub ul Haq points out that the developing countries must:

"... pass on whatever gains are achieved internationally to the masses rather than to a handful of privileged groups. It also is vital in order to gain credibility for the demand for a new international economic order. We cannot very well ask for equality of opportunity internationally if we in the Third World deny the same equality of opportunity to our own people." [5]

c) In the Poorest Countries

However, eliminating the absolute poverty of one billion people who live mainly within the more than forty *low-income* countries raises a quite different set of questions. Because of their lower gross national product levels, these countries face not only more difficult political problems in redistributing both income and productive assets but also far more intractable *economic* problems than the middle-income countries in attempting to finance health, education, and other services for the "poor majority" of their populations. In many cases it will be virtually impossible for these countries to overcome their problems in the years immediately ahead without substantial outside concessional assistance. The poorest countries are not just last in the world's economic growth race. Their per capita incomes—averaging $150 in 1973—are approximately half those of the United States in 1776, or of Great Britain at the beginning of the Industrial Revolution. They are pervasively poor in a way that was not true of today's rich countries in the early stages of their own development—when Europeans by the millions were free to settle in the vast, lightly populated lands of the Americas, Australia, and Siberia. The ability of these countries to meet the minimum human needs of most of their people may depend very much on the willingness of others to share the financial burden.

RIO Targets

As noted earlier, there is a growing consensus among development specialists in both rich and poor countries concerning the set of development strategies that could be most effective in eliminating the worst aspects of absolute poverty in the developing countries by the end of this century. In this connection, the Club of Rome report entitled *Reshaping the International Order (RIO)*—suggests that such a common goal for *all* countries might consist of the achievement of the following targets by the year 2000: life expectancy of 65 years or more (compared with 48 years at present in the low-income countries), a literacy rate of at least 75 per cent (compared with the present 33 per cent), an infant mortality rate of 50 or less per thousand births (or less than two fifths of the current average), and a birth rate of 25 or less per thousand (compared with the current 40 per thousand in the low-income countries).

V. A NEW WAY TO MEASURE PROGRESS

The increasing interest in meeting basic human needs also has led to an increasing dissatisfaction with the concept of gross national product (GNP) as a way of measuring development progress. GNP — whether recorded as a national total or on a per capita basis — does not say much about the quality of life results achieved. It cannot measure the extent to which the human needs of individuals are being met simply because there is no automatic relationship between any particular level of GNP and improvement in infant mortality, life expectancy, death rates, or literacy. Also, growth of average per capita GNP may not improve the well-being of large portions of a country's population since income may be distributed among groups in very unequal proportions.

ODC's "PQLI"

In order to supplement the GNP measurement the Overseas Development Council has developed a "Physical Quality of Life Index" to measure how basic human needs are being met. Three indicators were selected — infant mortality, life expectancy, and literacy — because they appeared to represent adequately the wider range of conditions that a minimum human needs program seeks to improve. The PQLI consolidates these three indicators into a simple, composite index.*

The data for these three indicators, while still rather uneven in quality, are readily available and express relatively unethnocentric objectives. Improvements in these categories are fairly universally sought, and the indicators do not make any assumptions about special patterns of development. Moreover, they measure *results* rather than inputs. And because these results reflect more or less universal objectives, they are appropriate standards for performance comparison among countries.

Life expectancy and infant mortality seem to be very good indicators of important aspects of social progress. In essence, they sum up the effects of nutrition, public health, income, and general environ-

---

*Life expectancy, infant mortality, and literacy figures are each rated on a scale of 1 to 100, within which individual countries are ranked according to their performance. For the life expectancy index, for example, the most favorable figure achieved by any country in 1973 (75 years in Sweden) was valued at 100 and the most unfavorable performance in 1950 (28 years in Guinea Bissau) was valued at 1. A composite index was calculated by averaging the three components of the index, giving equal weight to each of them. 1950 was chosen as the year for poorest performance because it was the year in which the lowest performance by any country was registered for each indicator. 1973 was chosen as the year for best performance because it marked the highest postwar performance in the world by any country for each indicator.

ment. At the same time, they reflect quite different aspects of social interaction. ODC's preliminary work suggests that infant mortality rather sensitively characterizes the position of women (not only in the household but in the society at large), while life expectancy is a reflection of much more general environmental characteristics. Literacy is a measure of both well-being and of a skill that is important in the development process. The extent to which poor groups are literate helps determine the extent to which they do share or will be able to share in the benefits of economic growth. While it is an indicator that goes beyond a narrow definition of physical well-being, it is an important element in a society's ability to satisfy elemental human needs; and this, ultimately, is what we seek to measure.

What PQLI Measures and Does Not Measure

It is important to be clear about what the PQLI does and what it does *not* measure. First, it measures only certain basic physical requirements of life; it says nothing about other important aspects of the "quality of life" such as justice, freedom, and a sense of participation and happiness. Second, it does not measure "economic" development, which still is best expressed by GNP. Third, it measures *results*, not inputs, and thus leaves each society free to determine how it wishes to achieve these results.

As can be seen from the accompanying tables, some countries have been able to achieve a high PQLI at a low per capita income. Sri Lanka and the Indian state of Kerala stand out in this regard. Other countries—such as Iran and Algeria—have a low PQLI despite much higher incomes.

The PQLI is a way of measuring not only the starting level of a country's achievement, but also the rate at which it is able to move toward some attainable level that is more or less fixed. In this sense, PQLI trends suggest something different from the discouraging evidence provided by GNP comparisons over time, which indicate that rich countries are steadily widening the gap between themselves and poor countries. When physical quality of life attainments are measured, the gap between the industrialized countries and most developing countries appears likely to be narrowed over time. For example, India's PQLI rose from 28 to 41 between the 1950s and the early 1970s; during the same period, the PQLI in the United States rose from 91 to 96. Nor is the PQLI a falsely optimistic instrument designed to mislead. Rather, it reminds us of some important matters— that rapidly rising GNP may go for fancy gee-gaws, nuclear explosives, or great armies; but the PQLI measures success in attaining certain basic conditions that contribute to a satisfactory quality of human existence.

Low-Income Not Synonymous With Abject Poverty

The evidence that some low-income countries have been able to attain fairly high PQLI rankings suggests that there is hope that substantial improvements in at least these minimum human requirements can be provided much more quickly than increases in per capita GNP. The PQLI has the advantage of underscoring that truth that low national income need not be synonymous with abject poverty and its consequences.

THE PHYSICAL QUALITY OF LIFE INDEX

PQLI and GNP for Selected Countries

	Per Capita GNP ($)	PQLI
Low-Income Countries:		
(under $300 per capita GNP)	152	39
Afghanistan	110	19
Egypt	280	46
Ethiopia	100	16
India	140	41
Kerala State	110	69
Indonesia	170	50
Mali	80	15
Nigeria	290	25
Sri Lanka	130	83
Lower Middle-Income Countries:		
($300-$699 per capita GNP)	338	59
Albania	530	76
Cuba	640	86
Ghana	430	31
Guyana	500	84
Honduras	340	50
Korea, Republic of	480	80
Morocco	430	40
Thailand	310	70
Tunisia	650	44
Upper Middle-Income Countries:		
($700-$1,999 per capita GNP)	1,091	67
Algeria	710	42
Argentina	1,520	84
Brazil	920	68

Gabon	1,960	21
Iran	1,250	38
Iraq	1,160	46
Mexico	1,090	63
South Africa	1,210	48
Taiwan (ROC)	810	88
Yugoslavia	1,310	85

High-Income Countries:		
($2,000 or more per capita GNP)	4,361	95
Kuwait	11,770	76
Libya	4,640	42
Sweden	7,240	100
United Kingdom	3,590	97
United States	6,670	96

NOTE: The PQLI ratings (as well as life expectancy, infant mortality, and literacy figures) of all countries are provided in *The United States and World Development: Agenda 1977*, by John W. Sewell and the staff of the Overseas Development Council, pp. 160-71.

PQLI Rankings for Selected Countries, 1950-1970

	1950s	1960s	1970s
Algeria	35	38	42
India	28	36	41
Egypt	32	41	45
Brazil	53	—	66
Sri Lanka	62	77	83
Poland	72	86	93
France	87	94	97

PQLI Rating for the United States (1900-1973)

	1900	1939	1950	1973
All U. S. Population	63	85	91	96
White Population	65	87	92	97
Other Races	30	71	81	89
Selected States				
Mississippi		81	87	92
New Mexico		69	85	94
Texas		81	87	95
Wisconsin		89	93	97
Minnesota		91	95	98

VI. CHOICES FOR THE NORTH

It is against this background of increasing interrelationships between developed and developing countries and a growing understanding of the problems of the world's poorest countries that the proposals for a "new international economic order" must be considered. Policy makers in the Northern industrial countries currently are faced with two separate sets of issues concerning the developing countries. The first encompasses those issues involved in creating a new set of economic and political relationships between sovereign countries. These issues involve relations between states and fall under the heading of the "new international economic order." At the same time, however, policy makers must decide what approach to take to the issue of meeting the most basic human needs of the world's poorest billion people.

Given the fact that both sets of issues are terribly complex and difficult, and because there is not any *necessary* connection between equity among nation states and the condition of human beings within those states, it may seem better public policy to keep the two issues separated. Indeed this has been the argument of some in the industrial North who see the need to restructure the world's economic and political systems to be of overriding importance, and who fear that too heavy an emphasis on meeting minimum human needs will complicate and perhaps even thwart these badly-needed international reforms.

NIEO Linked to Basic Human Needs

However, in practice it will probably be impossible to keep separate the issue of a new international economic order and of meeting basic human needs for a variety of reasons. First, the demands of the South are based, at least in part, on claims to equity and justice. Northerners can ask with at least some justification why they should be concerned about equity *between* states if such equity will not materially enhance the condition of people *within* these states. At the same time, many in the industrial countries (and particularly in the United States) are compelled by their own political philosophy to be concerned about human rights. Yet Southerners ask—also with some justification—why be concerned only with human *political* rights when human economic and social rights are just as important, and indeed are recognized as such on the United Nations Declaration on Human Rights? In practice, therefore, it seems inevitable that the two concepts will be linked.

Having said that, however, it is important to emphasize that the linkage cannot be made in a facile or naive manner. Rather the emphasis should be on forging a coherent series of development strategies that simultaneously meet the needs of the poorest countries, the middle-income countries, and, indeed, the industrial countries. Obviously, the two sets of issues cannot be linked at every stage and in every negotiation in some sort of formalized "global compact." The political and bureaucratic obstacles, were such a herculean task attempted, would be a nightmare.

Yet it is important for those engaged in deciding on and negotiating these issues, and equally important for those who will be directly affected by them, to link a new international economic order and basic human needs both in conceptual terms and particularly in terms of outcomes. The challenge for all parties is to work toward a world order in the year 2000 which meets the needs of all people on a self-sustaining basis.

By now it is generally accepted that some type of response will have to be made to the demands of the developing countries for changes in the existing economic and political systems. The major question then becomes what kind of changes and how far-reaching they should be. Currently these broad policy choices are being debated in the developed countries. Some advocate a continuation of present policies with only marginal improvements; others are looking for accelerated reforms of the existing international political and economic systems; or they can undertake a concerted attempt to meet basic human needs, either alone or in conjunction with either of the first two policy choices.

Policy 1: Marginal Improvements

The first policy choice is premised on the belief that the existing international system has worked well for the developed world and that only minor changes are needed in existing policies and structures. It is based on a judgment that a combination of policy changes within the developing countries combined with a return to the growth rates in the OECD countries that characterized the 1960s will solve the problems of both developed and developing countries. The specifics of such a policy would resemble proposals made by the United States in 1975 at the Seventh Special Session of the United Nations. The ultimate aim would be to preserve the essential elements of the present international system, to blunt the confrontation with the developing countries, and ultimately to dissolve what seem to many in the North to be the unnatural alliance between the OPEC members and the non-oil-producing developing countries. Proponents of this policy choice usually favor concentrating attention on a relatively few of the more powerful and prosperous countries of the Third World — the so-called "local leviathans"—and paying much less attention to the low-income smaller countries.

Policy 2: Accelerating Reform of World Order

The second policy choice involves a series of accelerated reforms and is based on the judgment that the present world order is not serving the needs of either the developed or the developing countries. Therefore, an active search must begin for more far-reaching solutions that will be necessary if the progress and well-being of both North and South is to be assured. Advocates of this policy would agree with the justice of developing-country demands for a more equitable international economic order and would recognize that to an increasing degree the industrial countries must cooperate with the countries of the Third World if they are to regain the economic progress of the recent past. This policy choice would emphasize the gains that can be made for both sides, particularly in the area of trade, and would look to the creation of a series of new global systems to deal with such issues as the oceans and the world food problem. Proponents of this approach would not, however, automatically accept all the current proposals of the developing countries, but would carefully analyze each, searching for arrangements that could directly benefit economically or politically both developed and developing countries.

Policy 3: Concentrated Effort to Meet Basic Needs

The third broad policy choice centers on a global effort to eliminate the worst aspects of absolute poverty and calls for the meeting of minimum human needs in some manageable time frame, say by the end of the century. Advocates of such a policy recognize that changes in existing international systems and policies may not necessarily benefit poor people, and that even if they did the changes would benefit middle-income countries to a much greater degree than the poorest countries. Special measures will be needed, therefore, to deal directly with the circumstances of the people within the poorest countries, as well as with the poorest people within the middle-income and rich countries. In this case, a variety of policy instruments would be pursued, but in each case the aim would be to enhance the ability of poor people and poor countries to support their own development.

Two comments are in order. First is that these choices are not mutually exclusive. The "basic human needs" choice can be combined with a series of "accelerated reforms" of existing international systems. There is no inherent conflict between the two and indeed, there may even be a certain synergism in choosing to deal simultaneously with both sets of policies.

Policy of "Creative Incrementalism"

The other caveat is more serious and of potentially greater difficulty. Even with the best will in the world, it will be politically and administratively very difficult and perhaps impossible for the industrial countries to institute overnight many of the changes called for in the proposals for a new international economic order. It becomes crucial, therefore, to judge what can be seen as incremental changes in light of ultimate goals. For instance, it clearly will not be possible to eliminate at one stroke all of the barriers to the exports of the developing countries that now exist in the industrialized countries despite the fact that were such steps taken the developing countries according to World Bank estimates could earn an additional $30 billion a year by 1985. A policy of "creative incrementalism" therefore could identify policy changes in both international trade policy and in domestic industrial and employment adjustment that would enable the rich countries to absorb an increasing share of the manufactured exports of the developing countries. The difficulty of course comes in identifying which changes are indeed creative—that is changes which would lead to more equitable international economic systems—and those that merely are palliatives.*

VII. A NORTHERN PROPOSAL: A "TRIPLE TARGET" APPROACH TO MEETING BASIC NEEDS

General Goals

The proposal set forth in this paper seeks to encompass both the "accelerated reform" and "basic human needs" policy choices and to set as its target the meeting of minimum human needs within the framework of a restructured international economic and political system that will meet the needs of all countries, both rich and poor. Its objective is for participating developing countries to become self-reliant in meeting the most basic human needs of their people within a generation or less.

---

*We are indebted to our colleague Denis Goulet for this concept.

Reaching this goal will require:

Requirements:

1. Progress in meeting basic human needs of the poor majority within developing countries to enhance their capacity to participate in their own development, which in many cases entails a redistribution of power and wealth.

2. Increasing agricultural production and rural employment through labor-intensive means (because 80 per cent of the population in the poorest countries live in the rural areas).

3. Increasing growth in GNP, both to provide employment in the urban as well as the rural sector and to enable the low-income countries to gradually reduce—and eventually eliminate—their dependence on large-scale foreign assistance.

4. Restructuring the relationships between rich and poor countries in order to permit the latter equal access to the benefits of the system and an equitable return for their own efforts.

In effect, the international community would mount an expanded and redirected effort to help countries meet the most basic needs of their people through national efforts that significantly advance growth of output while giving primacy to the address of basic needs. Such an effort would have the following "triple target" objectives by the year 2000:

Triple Target for Low-Income Countries

1. Overcoming the worst aspects of absolute poverty (including the poverty suffered by the 20 per cent of the world's poorest billion living in the middle- and high-income countries); this would be accomplished by halving the present disparities between the birth rates, life expectancy, infant mortality, and literacy between present levels in developing countries and in the advanced countries, and by a substantial reduction in underemployment;

2. Doubling food production in developing countries by effectively utilizing existing human as well as physical resources in those countries; and

3. Doubling the per capita income in each developing country.

Attaining these goals would bring most low-income countries to levels close to the goals proposed by the RIO group mentioned earlier.

Specific Results in Low-Income Countries

An effectively mounted "triple-target" program by the year 2000 should have the following specific results in the low-income countries: a) increasing their grain production by approximately 250 million tons (equivalent to current U. S. production) to a total of 500 million tons; b) raising their PQLI from approximately 40 to 70 (the U. S. level in the early 1900s), e.g., raising their life expectancy and literacy from approximately 50 years and 35 per cent to some 63 years and 70 per cent respectively, and reducing infant mortality and birth rates from 134 and 40 per 1000 to 71 and 25 respectively; and c) doubling per capita GNP, to $330 in 1974 dollars. This would "graduate" most low-income countries into the lower middle-income category in terms of per capita GNP and into the upper middle-income category in terms of meeting basic needs; it should also greatly reduce and possibly eliminate the need for continued large-scale assistance on highly concessional terms to continue their basic needs programs.

Required Commitments for Industrial Countries

But while a consensus may be emerging on the need to focus development efforts on both growth and meeting the minimum human needs of the world's poorest people, the implications of this consensus for the industrial countries—and particularly for the United States—are only beginning to be explored. If the developing countries are to accept a series of targets—whether to increase GNP and agricultural production, or to make measurable progress in improving certain social indicators—the industrial countries also must be prepared to accept a parallel set of commitments not only for levels of development assistance, but also on *some* of the issues raised by the developing countries under the rubric of a "new international economic order." In other words, the industrial countries must not only be willing to provide additional concessional assistance, but also to continue to reduce trade barriers to developing-country manufactured goods, to give developing countries greater access to international financial markets, and to establish buffer stock programs for grain and other commodities on a basis that is of mutual net benefit to both categories of countries.

The political attractiveness of this program to the countries of both the North and South would be enhanced if it were made an implicit part of a much broader North-South "bargain" emerging from the NIEO negotiations. It would add to those negotiations the missing ingredients of 1) a direct effort to meet the urgent material needs of the poorest countries, and 2) the broader dimension of moral and human concern which such a bargain will require if it is to provide an enduring framework for North-South cooperation.

VIII. IMPLEMENTING THE PROPOSAL

The broad outlines of such an approach have been laid out elsewhere in both general and specific terms.[6] This section deals specifically with questions of increasing trade, which will benefit mainly the middle-income countries (as well as the developed countries), and development assistance, which is needed by and large only by the poorest countries.

Trade

The bulk of the resources needed by the middle-income countries to address the problems of absolute poverty within their own boundaries should come from increased trade, investment, and access to commercial credit. It is in the area of trade that some of the greatest gains can be made by the middle-income countries *if* they are willing to make the necessary policy changes internally and *if* the industrial countries are willing to permit expanded access of the developing countries to their natural markets in the developed world.

The table below indicates some of the gains that can be made by the developing countries in the area of trade. The exports of the developing countries grew from $10 billion in 1965 to $33 billion in 1975 (1975 prices). Under a continuation of the policies that existed in the past, the exports of the developing countries might be expected to rise to $94 billion by 1985. But higher gains are possible. Indeed, if all barriers existing in the OECD countries to developing-country manufactured goods were dismantled, these countries could earn an additional $24 billion per year by 1985. And if the developing countries themselves were to remove all their own supply constraints, they could gain yet an additional $21 billion per year by 1985.

More Realistic Estimates

The table presents more realistic estimates of the gains from trade that could be realized by the developing countries on the assumption that a decade is a short time to eliminate all trade barriers and redirect internal policies.

LDC Earnings from Export of Manufactures
($ billion, 1975 prices)

	Poorest Countries	Middle-Income Countries	Total
1965	$ 2.4	$ 7.6	$ 10
1975	3.4	29.6	33
1985—Present Policies	7.3	86.7	94
Possible Additions from:			
• Tokyo Round	.3	3.7	4
• Partial Relaxation of Non-Tariff Barriers	1.0	5.0	6
• Improved LDC Policies	2.5	7.5	10
1985—New Policies	11.1	102.9	114

Source: World Bank

Through a combination of tariff reductions negotiated at the current "Tokyo Round" of trade negotiations, of a partial relaxation of non-tariff barriers, and of improved internal policies, the developing countries could earn an additional $20 billion by 1985. These gains, however, will occur largely to the middle-income countries. With these changes the trade earnings of the middle-income countries could rise from $7.6 billion in 1965 to nearly $103 billion two decades later, a gain of over $95 billion. The exports of the poorest countries, however, would increase over the same period by just under $9 billion, from $2.4 billion in 1965 to $11.1 billion in 1985. In trade, as in most other areas, the poorest developing countries stand to realize much lower gains than the better-off developing countries.

Costly Changes for Both Rich and Poor

It also is worth noting that the developing countries can gain as much by internal policy changes as by lowered trade barriers in the developed countries. The implications for both sides therefore are far-reaching for costs will be incurred by both rich and poor countries if these gains are to be realized. For the poor countries, it will be a matter of redirecting internal resources and stimulating increased efficiencies. For the rich countries it will mean shifting workers from low efficiency employment in industries in direct competition with those in the developing countries—for instance, textiles and shoes—to other sectors where the industrial countries maintain a comparative advantage. Obviously, such a transition cannot be done in a short period without causing disruptions in the lives of communities and individuals that would be ethically disturbing and politically impossible. It may be possible, however, during the current round of negotiations to lower tariffs on the manufactured goods of the developing countries to the maximum extent possible (a cut as high as 60 per cent for example) and also negotiate some reductions in nontariff barriers.

Much more must be done, however, if the industrial countries are to gain the anti-inflationary benefits of lower cost goods as well as to ensure that developing countries can earn the resources necessary to support their own development.

The policies that must be followed if all states are to gain the potential benefits of expanded world trade will entail substantial shifts within the economies of the developing countries away from labor intensive industries. Such shifts will pose difficult questions of planning and of equity for workers in affected industries. But they will be necessary if the developing countries are to increase their self-reliance as well as to continue to grow as markets for industrial country exports and suppliers of low cost consumer goods. The industrial countries should be undertaking now the studies and planning necessary to effect this transition within their own economies.

Concessional Transfer

As we pointed out earlier, the gains that can be realized from many of the measures proposed by the developing countries for reform and restructuring of the existing economic and political systems will be much greater for the middle income countries than for the poorer countries. This observation holds true for commodity agreements, debt rescheduling, technology transfer, as well as for many other issues. The strong implication, therefore, is that for the poorest countries, concessional resource transfers—development assistance —will continue to be of increasing importance for meeting basic human needs even though the instruments through which it is provided and the amounts of aid will have to change drastically.

Additional Transfers Necessary

How much would a cooperative effort to eliminate the worst aspects of absolute poverty in the terms defined in this paper cost? Several different estimates using different methodologies suggest that it would take some $12-$15 billion annually (in 1973 dollars) for the next ten to twenty years. This sum is the equivalent of 0.35 of the 1976 GNP of both the "old" rich and the "new" OPEC rich and is nearly equal to total flows of official development assistance at present. The $12-$15 billion would require a trebling of concessional development assistance to the poorest billion people, 80 per cent of whom live in the 40 poorest countries. (Most of the remainder live in pockets of poverty within the middle income countries in areas such as Northeast Brazil). Some of this increase could be realized by redirecting existing concessional flows either from middle income countries to poorer countries or within countries to the poorest people. But even if this were done, (and it would not be easy in the very poor countries) additional concessional resource transfers totalling $8-$10 billion still would be necessary.

The importance of assistance from the industrialized countries becomes clear when it is recognized that the sum of $10 billion represents about 6-7 per cent of the GNP of the low-income countries; this percentage of GNP, in turn, roughly equals their total current revenues from taxation. This "fact of life" makes it quite apparent that undertaking the political and economic costs of such programs would call for great political courage—and strength—on the part of political leaders in developing countries. It also makes it amply clear that the action to implement such programs may, in many developing countries, depend *very significantly* on the degree to which the industrial countries are willing to ease the political burdens by sharing the costs during the initial years, with the poor countries themselves providing, over a longer period, a progressively larger share of the total out of their own growth.

With the difficult reality firmly in mind, it certainly should be recognized that the sum of $10-$15 billion appears much more manageable if assessed in comparison to the $13 billion official development assistance provided by the industrial countries in 1975. Of course most of this $13 billion was not targeted to reach the poorest groups within the poorest countries. In fact, most did not even go to the poorest countries. (A major portion of U. S. development assistance was provided to a number of relatively higher-income countries—including, among others, Egypt, Syria, Israel, and Jordan—for a variety of political, economic, and military reasons.)

Conditions for Effective Aid

A $10 billion increase in aid for the purpose of meeting basic human needs would in fact be feasible a) if the developed countries were to reach or exceed an aid level of at least 0.5 per cent of GNP by 1981; b) if some portion of the aid now going to middle-income countries were redirected to low-income countries; and c) if these increases were to be earmarked solely for a more effective address of basic human needs for jobs, health, nutrition, education, and other essential services.

The incentive in human terms to undertake a joint effort to meet the human needs of those suffering from absolute poverty is great indeed. As indicated earlier, a few low income countries have achieved levels of life expectancy, infant mortality, and death and birth rates that are usually achieved only in societies with much higher income. Sri Lanka and the Indian state of Kerala—while their per capita incomes were less than $150—and South Korea, Taiwan, and probably China—while their per capita incomes were still less than $300—are five such cases. The benefits of rapid GNP growth may trickle down only slowly—and sometimes barely at all—to poorer sections of many societies in the absence of major and conscious efforts to involve the poor majority in development and to address directly their basic needs. To pick one example, Iran in 1970, (when it already was a middle-income country with a per capita income well above $300) had more than 200,000 deaths and 500,000 births than it would have had if it had achieved the norms reached in the countries mentioned above at per capita incomes that were far lower.

No Alternative To Productive Employment

Over the longer term, there is no alternative to providing the poor majority with more productive employment, particularly in the rural areas, and with access to low cost health and elementary education services if their basic human needs are to be met on a minimally satisfactory basis. This objective should be pursued with all possible vigor by developing countries and by the multilateral and bilateral programs providing development assistance. However, dramatic progress toward this goal over the next ten to twelve years in the poorest countries is not likely—many would say not politically feasible—given the limited income of these societies and the current restricted scale and form of the external resources available to them. The elites in the upper ten to twenty per cent of these countries—still quite poor compared to their counterparts elsewhere—probably are not prepared to implement voluntarily a shift in their income and economic and political power scale that would effect a rapid and significant improvement in the lot of the poor majority in their countries over the next decade.

The question is, therefore, whether leaders in both the developed and developing countries have the political will to undertake the efforts that will be needed to meet the most essential needs of the poor majority in the low income countries on what ultimately can be a self-sustaining basis. If so, the countries participating in such an effort could before the year 2000 attain a per capita income of perhaps

$300 or more (in 1970 dollars) and bring about a dramatic improvement in the lives of a majority of their citizens. With a basic human needs approach to development, the low-income countries could expect by the end of the century to experience some 8 million fewer deaths and a far greater reduction in births annually, life expectancy 6 or 7 years longer, literacy 30 to 35 per cent higher, than will be achieved under the present strategies now being followed by most developing countries.

IX. CHOICES AND UNRESOLVED QUESTIONS FOR BOTH NORTH AND SOUTH

The foregoing proposal is suggestive of the kinds of proposals that could provide a basis for further discussions between developed and developing countries concerning both the reform and restructuring of the existing economic and political order and of a concerted address of basic human needs. It is, however, a proposal from a *Northern* perspective and thus warrants much further examination and reflection by leaders and specialists from both North and South. Further, it raises perhaps more questions and poses more choices than it resolves. Some of these questions and choices are discussed in the final section of the paper.

What Overall Strategy Should Be Followed?

A more comprehensive and effective mix of developed country policies is required if a steady worsening of North-South relations is to be avoided and if the international economic and political orders are to be reshaped to better meet the urgent needs of both developed and developing countries. Should the North essentially continue present policies, making only incremental changes? Should it take only the minimum steps necessary to meet the most compelling demands of the world's "South" on the grounds that domestic economic and political forces will not allow more?

Or should the developed countries seek a new policy of accelerated and far-reaching reform which carefully considers each of the issues under discussion between the countries of the North and those of the South and, where possible, seeks those solutions, compromises, and alternatives that can benefit both sides either directly or indirectly—by providing substantial gains for *world* development?

And to what extent should the North, together with both the other developed countries and the developing countries seek to devise *jointly* and carry out policies that would make it possible for the world's poorest people (the majority of whom live in the world's poorest countries) to acquire within the foreseeable future at least the minimum physical requirements for basic human life and dignity?

What Kind of "New International Economic Order"?

What is the desired end for negotiations over a new international economic order? Is it merely an ameliorated nation state system with more national actors welcome into the First World? Or is the aim of the present struggle the creation of some as yet unspecified equitable and just global society in which the needs of all human beings are met, no matter what sovereign entity they inhabit? If the latter, what is a "strategy for the transition"? Clearly a new international economic order will not be created overnight. Yet are there measures that can be taken in the context of an overall strategy to achieve such an order?

How is such a world order to be created at a moment when nationalism (and indeed even sub-nationalism) seems to be on the rise? This paradox puzzles thoughtful observers in the industrial countries precisely at the time when many in the developed world are questioning the ability of the nation-state to deal with the pressing internal problems of their societies. The American sociologist Daniel Bell has written: ". . . in a world marked by greater economic interdependence, yet also by a growing desire of people to participate at a local level in the decisions that affect their lives, the nation state has become too small for the big problems of life, and too big for the small problems."

How Far-Reaching Should Specific Policy Choices Be?

The choices to be made on specific issues obviously will depend in considerable part on the strategy chosen for overall American policy on world development and North-South relations.

In each of the areas being discussed in the various international forums — trade, commodities, monetary reform, debt, technology transfer, food, energy, and a regime for the oceans — choices between incremental approaches and more far-reaching solutions will have to be made. The temptation in the Northern countries will be to choose those policies which respond to a problem at the lowest possible immediate economic and political costs. Yet following this path may mean missing the opportunity to resolve many problems in a manner more congruent with the needs of the future than of the past. In the field of trade, for instance, the tendency will be to reduce tariff barriers only for those products that do not affect many U. S. jobs — particularly at a time when large numbers of Americans already are unemployed. Yet the potential *gains* from trade liberalization—including *overall* increases in employment, higher wages, and easing of inflationary pressures for both the United States and the developing countries—are so great that the short-run costs make a renewed commitment to lowering tariff barriers to the maximum degree possible both far-sighted and realistic.

What "Packages" of Bargains Can Be Assembled?

In the next few years, the developed and the developing countries will be involved in both negotiating changes in a variety of global systems and hopefully also in a concerted address of absolute poverty within the world's poorest countries. But the short- and long-run gains, both tangible and intangible, from specific policy changes will vary greatly depending on the particular issue and on the countries most involved.

The development of "packages" of agreements cutting across issues may make compromise on individual issues more attractive for both rich and poor countries. For example, the developing countries need greater access to the markets of the industrialized world; the developed countries need greater assurance of access to adequate amounts of raw materials. The linkage of these two concerns might make a potential package of agreements more politically acceptable for a considerably greater number of countries than if each of these issues were considered separately.

What Form of Cooperation for Addressing the Basic Human Needs Problem?

Even while a consensus is beginning to take shape on the need to focus development policies on meeting the minimum basic human needs of the world's poorest billion people, a host of new questions is emerging on how such an approach should be implemented. What specific development strategies would best enable the developing countries to meet the needs of the majority of their population? To what extent should external aid be concentrated on meeting basic needs and shifted away from the prevailing pattern of supporting economic development in general? How much can or should basic human needs strategies be supported by outsiders—whether other countries or international organizations? Are leaders within the developing countries willing to commit themselves and their governments to specific targets concerning the results of development—for instance in literacy, infant mortality, etc.—in return for commitments by the industrial countries on levels of resource transfers? Conversely, to what extent does the whole approach of a concerted address of minimum human needs involve "intervention" from the outside?

If a minimum human needs approach to development cooperation were accepted, a host of operational questions still would need to be resolved. How much aid would be necessary either to achieve certain economic goals (such as a specific growth rate in gross national product) or social goals (such as targeted reductions in illiteracy, infant mortality, birth rates or malnutrition)? What should be the "fair shares" of the donor countries? Should the industrial countries adhere to some existing standard (such as the objective of the International Strategy for the U.N. Second Development Decade that each "donor" nation should provide 0.7 per cent of GNP in the form of development assistance), or should a new formula for participation, based on an assessment of the needs of the developing countries for resource transfers be developed?

Through what channels and to what countries should aid be provided? The argument between the proponents of bilateral aid and multilateral aid has a long history, and no conclusion as to a desirable balance between the two forms has been reached. What should be the relative roles of private and governmental channels of development assistance? And should concessional aid concentrate primarily on the poorest countries while reforms of international economic systems are relied upon to provide the middle income countries with the resources necessary to address their poverty problems? Or should aid be provided to any country and program which is seriously committed to ensuring that the benefits of its development effort reach the poorest people? To what extent should such a strategy include special measures to assist women, whose contributions and needs often have been neglected by past strategies? Finally, how can a basic human needs approach contribute to an earlier stabilization of the world population? These are not easy questions to resolve, but they must be addressed if the effectiveness of development assistance is to be improved in the years ahead.

What Kinds of Equity?

Among the most crucial of all the questions to be resolved is the relationship between the issues of a) equity *between* states, and b) equity among people *within* states. The question of equity between states is at the base of the demands of the developing countries for changes in existing international and political systems. But the question of equity *within* states will grow increasingly important as it becomes apparent that certain states—or important groups within states—may have to pay costs, at least in the short run, to increase equity between states. Even short-run political costs to the developed countries of changes in political and economic systems may become impossibly high if it is not apparent to the public in these countries that major efforts are being made by the developing countries to ensure that the benefits of development reach their poor majorities.

This view is reflected by Richard N. Cooper who recently wrote:

> "The view that natural rights pertain to individuals rather than to nations has strong implications for a number of the proposals put forward by developing countries toward implementation of a new international economic order. It rules out justifying on *ethical* grounds any proposal that transfers resources unconditionally to developing countries, without serious inquiry into whether the resources thus transferred are in fact serving the ethical purposes—support of the basic needs of life and self-improvement—that provide their rationale."

The evidence is increasingly clear that changes in the external economic order as well as in the internal structure of the developing countries themselves will be necessary if the problems of the world's poorest people are to be alleviated in the foreseeable future. But what commitments will the developed and the developing countries be prepared to assume to achieve this end? Are the developing countries willing to undertake difficult domestic reforms? And can the developed countries be relied upon to offer enough help from the outside to permit developing-country leaders to make the far-reaching, politically difficult changes required to provide a greater degree of equity within their own societies? Some will conclude that the past record indicates that no major changes are likely; others will argue that the growing costs of inaction may be so great as to impel changes, and that the present circumstances provide an opportunity for both rich and poor countries alike.

How Best Advance Human Rights?

The present United States government is giving greatly increased and more comprehensive attention to the human rights issue. This issue area poses many difficult questions. To what extent should the United States attempt to protect human rights in other countries? What are the most appropriate ways to do so? What is the relationship between *human political rights* and *human economic rights*? The industrial democracies tend to give higher priority to the former, and the developing countries tend to give higher priority to the latter. Can a common ground be found?

What Should Be Done About Global Military Expenditures?

The issue of global military expenditures, especially in its North-South context, is certainly one of the most complex and perplexing of all international problems. Developed and developing countries share a grave interest in and responsibility for controlling the world's arms race and military expenditures, particularly in light of international negotiations concerning the form of the "New International Economic Order," as well as discussions about the framework for and levels of development assistance—which today are far overshadowed by the value of arms imports to the developing countries. Military expenditures and arms transfers have direct and indirect implications for virtually all aspects of North-South relations. Should, then, a reduction in military expenditures be part of the general set of negotiations now going on between the developed and the developing countries? If so, will the developing countries be willing to discuss seriously a reduction in their military budgets with some portion of the savings being used for economic and social development, and will the superpowers cut back their own military programs?

How Best Organize for Global Cooperation?

At the international level, there will be a need to determine which existing forums—whose membership must include both the developed and developing countries—can best undertake the multiplicity of negotiations and discussions under way. Also to be considered is the creation of new forums for handling current negotiations and discussions as well as future needs to effect changes in the existing international economic and political systems. Many observers had hoped that the Conference on International Economic Cooperation would provide a central forum for these purposes. Yet for a variety of reasons, there was widespread disillusionment with the CIEC and both developed and developing countries apparently were eager to see it end. There is likewise considerable dissatisfaction with the various organizations of the United Nations system on the grounds that most of these bodies, as now constituted, are too large and unwieldy for negotiating purposes.

Another major question is the extent to which the Soviet Union and China need to be brought into these discussions. The Soviet Union, the Eastern European countries, and China have remained on the sidelines throughout most of the international economic discussions that have taken place over the past several years. Soviet and East European aid to the developing countries also has diminished during the same period. Is the involvement of these countries in

North-South negotiations essential only on global problems which their actions affect greatly (e.g., the world food problem and nuclear proliferation, in the case of the Soviet Union), or on all issues?

A Concluding Note

At an ecumenical meeting at the beginning of the Second Development Decade, Dom Helder Camara remarked that "the present situation of mankind may be described briefly as follows: a sad reality, marvelous prospects, the possibility (even the probability) of a tragic conclusion." Dom Helder was prescient in foreshadowing the series of shocks that the world has undergone since that time, but his basic judgement remains true. Therefore, it may be worth concluding with the thought that to turn the prospect for the world—and most importantly for the people who inhabit it—from "tragic" to "marvelous" by the end of the century will depend on decisions taken within and among developed and developing countries in the next few years for the end of the century is not all that far away. Likewise, what the leaders of the developed and developing world do in the next few years concerning the basic human needs of the world's people will be crucial in determining what the shape of the world will be for future generations.

FOOTNOTES

1. Robert L. Heilbroner, *An Inquiry Into the Human Prospect*, New York: W. W. Norton & Company, Inc., 1974, p. 136.

2. David Morawetz, "Twenty-five Years of Economic Development," *Finance and Development*, Vol. 14, No. 3 (September 1977), pp. 10-13.

3. For background see Jahangir Amuzegar, "A Requiem for the North-South Conference," *Foreign Affairs*, Vol. 56, No. 1 (October 1977), pp. 136-159.

4. John A. Holsen and Jean L. Waelbroeck, "The Less Developed Countries and the International Monetary Mechanism," *American Economic Association*, Vol. 66, No. 2 (May 1976), pp. 171-176.

5. Mahbub ul Haq, *The Third World and the International Economic Order*, ODC Development Paper 22, p. 49.

6. See John W. Sewell and the Staff of the Overseas Development Council, *The United States and the Developing World: Agenda 1977*, Overseas Development Council, Washington, DC, Chapters II and III. Also James P. Grant, *Basic Human Needs, Food, and the World's Poorest Billion—What Future Prospects?*," ODC Development Paper (Forthcoming Spring 1978).

SUMMARY

Policy makers in Northern industrial countries are currently faced with two separate sets of issues concerning the developing countries. In the changed political environment, growing global interdependencies and the use of oil power by the OPEC nations have put the demands of the developing nations for a New International Economic Order (NIEO) at center stage. But at the same time the stubborn problem of nearly one billion people living in absolute poverty—at levels of average income of $150, half that of the US in 1776—has prompted the rejection of many traditional development theories and the emergence of human needs strategies, with a target of meeting the basic needs of all by the year 2000.

The US is still unwilling to accept fundamental changes in the basic structure of the economic system created after World War II, and it is not clear who will bear the burden of these costly changes. However, the cost of meeting minimum needs may be somewhat reduced if the approach of ODC's new "Physical Quality of Life Index" (PQLI) meets with wide acceptance, for it does demonstrate that low-income is not synonymous with abject poverty in terms of infant mortality, life expectancy and literacy. This is evident in areas such as Sri Lanka, Kerala, etc.

There is no *necessary* connection between the NIEO and meeting basic needs. However, the ODC team, while clearly more concerned with their basic human needs strategy targetted at the year 2000, still argue that in practice such a strategy must be linked to the NIEO in any acceptable policy in the future.

The authors then set forth a Northern proposal. It seeks to encompass both the "accelerated reform" and "basic human needs" policy choices and to set as its target the meeting of minimum human needs within a framework of a gradually restructured international economic and political system. These needs pertain to all countries, both rich and poor. The proposal's main objective is for participating developing countries to become self-reliant in meeting the most basic human needs of their people within a generation or less.

They conclude with a series of choices and unresolved questions for both North and South.

5

Satisfying Human Needs in a World of Sovereign States: Rhetoric, Reality and Vision

Richard Falk

Richard Falk, a US citizen, is currently Acting Director of the Center of International Studies at Princeton University. He did his graduate studies in law at Yale and Harvard. Among his many past posts and honors, Falk has been Professor of International Law at Princeton; Fellow at the Center for Advanced Study in the Behavioral Sciences, Stanford University; a Senior Fellow at the Institute of World Order, New York; Vice President of the American Society of International Law; and Chairman of the Consultative Council, Lawyers' Committee on American Policy Toward Vietnam. Falk has lectured and published widely on international law, the Vietnam war and international law, and world order models.

I. INTRODUCTION

No Quick Solution to World Poverty

The enigma of world poverty continues to baffle people of good will. Why are there so many poor people despite a long period during which the gross planetary product has steadily increased? Some blame capitalism or imperialism; others stress selfish leaders and ruling groups; some talk of the ignorance, corruption, and inefficiency of governments or the backwardness of societies; still others point to nefarious money managers and to obscure machinations by multinational corporations; some suggest that the *real* problem is a result of unchecked population growth; and some contend that poverty remains engrained because the planet is running out of cheap resources.

Of course, there are elements of truth in each line of explanation, and yet we lack the knowledge to assert with any real confidence that a single line of explanation is definitive. We are faced with a reality: grinding poverty for the mass of humanity. And we posit a goal: a world economic and political order that produces enough goods and services and distributes them in such a way as to satisfy the basic material needs of everyone. The gap between reality and goal is what defines the scope of our inquiry.

At the outset, it seems important to assert that there is no technical way to close this gap rapidly. It exists, not out of necessity, but because of the way in which states and the system of states are organized. To change organizational patterns on this scale is a complex, difficult, perhaps impossible undertaking that depends on shifting patterns of perceived interests and on changing value formations. It is a formidable challenge to our institutions and traditions, and calls for a wide range of responses. It calls, especially, on our religious heritages to provide us with clues as to what is wrong and what to do about it, as well as with inspiration to strengthen our resolve.

New Stress on Needs Is Ambiguous

The stress on "needs" is, at once, obvious and problematic. It is obvious because the poorest people in the world are numerous and miserable, as well as because the overall arrangement of wealth that allows such disparities to persist is an assault upon our most primitive ethical sensibilities. It is problematic because it encourages a kind of patronizing, philanthropic concern about doing something for "others," conceived as helpless objects, and, therefore, resists the understanding of poverty as a "structural" consequence of the way in which power and wealth are and have been deployed. Nevertheless, we shall focus on needs because that is the way people are thinking about meeting the challenge of world poverty. This stress on needs proceeds from a non-philanthropic outlook that asks how we must transform domestic and international structures to enable *all* people to enjoy a satisfying life; it does not isolate "the poor" as a distinct category.

The diagnostic question is why it seems so difficult to achieve distributive patterns that satisfy the basic material needs of all people. How should we understand and explain this difficulty? This paper argues that the principal difficulty arises at the interface between politics and economics on both national and international levels. It also argues that mass denial of human needs is not inevitable, but results from the contingent structures of inequality existing between and within states. This can be rectified, although only after an intense and prolonged struggle.

The therapeutic question is what to do to achieve distributional patterns that are designed to satisfy basic material needs. The argument sketched here is that political structures will have to be fundamentally transformed by struggle, facilitated by cultural innovation, and pursued by a variety of non-violent strategies ranging from education to mass civil disobedience, general strikes, and the like. Values constitute the core of what the struggle is about, in reality translating the great religious vision of what has been ethically presupposed for humanity into the actualities of political, economic, and social arrangements. Such an imperative is reinforced by the apocalyptic dangers of persisting with behavioral and organizational patterns premised on the acceptability of *exploitation* (giving rise to personal and collective inequality, including deep poverty for large numbers), of *fragmentation* (associating well-being with a part—whether territory, class, race, religion—rather than the whole of the human species). The possibility of a positive human destiny then, depends upon suffusing activities with a vivid and intensifying sense of human solidarity on all levels of societal interaction.[1]

Obviously, such a vision of the future can only begin to be approximated after a long process. The process can be initiated immediately in appropriate forms within every setting of choice and action. We can begin now, and, given the urgency of the undertaking, there is no time to lose. Yet we cannot expect to achieve rapid results except within domains under our direct control. The length of time needed for a cumulative shift of structures may be as short as several decades or as long as several centuries. We have no way of knowing, or even of assessing the probabilities. The correctness of the stand, and not its rewards, provide us with the basis for action. At the same time, the present rewards are tangible because we are allowed the experience of transformation to the limit of our capacities. We can realize now the emergent future order to some extent by putting into practice the principles and values of humane governance in as many activities as our strength and our circumstances allow.

Overview of the Paper

a. Structural and Ideological Impasse. In this paper, I shall pursue these themes by considering the current impasse over methods to reduce world poverty and cut the disparities between rich and poor countries. The main conclusion of this first section is that there is no way to circumvent this impasse, given prevailing secular structures and their supportive ideological outlooks. Furthermore, frustration occasioned by this impasse is likely to grow even more acute, resulting in a violent cycle of repression and resistance. In effect, therefore, violence on both sides, repressive violence by those who would manage the status quo, versus revolutionary violence by those who would change it, will increase.

Such a cycle leads to a political dynamic that is mutually futile, as one side fails to achieve "order," and the other side fails to achieve "justice." Without a greater consciousness for what is necessary, the conception of what is possible will remain excessively modest, dooming the revolutionary attempt, even if successful, to shifts in policy and personnel, but failing to break through the cycle of violent and inhumane governance. The effects of the Soviet Revolution are illustrative.

Of course, structural constraints are not everything. The particular orientation of individuals and elites toward global policy issues may be more or less generous, imaginative, and effective. These variations of outlook could make the difference between a relatively steady voyage into the future and disastrous shipwreck. At the same time, the constraints on official leadership arising from the demands of domestic social forces, from the influence of perceived interests, and from traditions of behavior associated with national security and sovereignty, are so great as to make it highly unrealistic to expect much aid and comfort for transformative demands emanating from the centers of established power and authority.[2]

b. Evolution of a Consensus. After considering this challenge to the legitimacy and capability of the existing system of world order, I will examine the more encouraging evidence of the evolution of a consensus that is beginning to grasp and depict what is needed to evolve patterns of humane governance for the planet. This consensus is gradually forming despite the practices and tendencies of constituted power. In effect, we cannot, at this stage, expect most official institutions and governing groups, given their sense of priorities, to support a social movement for planetary renewal, although individuals serving in these structures will be influenced by the movement to varying degrees, and may keep the processes of governance from veering to extremes.

c. Uneven Process of Renewal. This transnational movement of renewal will proceed unevenly. In the advanced industrial countries, the crux of the problem lies in the interplay between runaway technology and the apparatus of state power. The state is too large for humane governance, and yet too small to cope functionally with the planetary agenda. To overcome the predominance of the state presupposes a dialectical unfolding toward values that are simultaneously more communitarian and personally felt, producing decentralization and more universalistic and functionally successful, and as such, requiring greater centralization of organizing structures.[3] Decentralizing potentials are more significant than centralizing ones because it seems so essential to reduce, to the furthest extent possible, the intrusion of bureaucratic ways and means on the life experience of people.

In less industrialized countries the emergence of strong state structures is part of the phenomenon of "catching up," and provides some assurance that political independence can be safeguarded and that global issues will be dealt with in a fairer way. Statism as a short-run response to imperialism enables Third World societies to make effective their quest for national self-assertion, including achieving greater participation in international arenas and more regulation of foreign penetration in their own societies. Such nationalist strategies interfere with interim, stopgap globalist adjustment processes (e.g. inhibits formation of an enlightened law of the oceans), and may have some unfortunate domestic effects, such as a tendency to smother the domestic self-determination dynamic beneath the weight of an effective machinery of repression.

Overall, however, and given sufficient time, it remains a matter of letting history run its course. The dynamic of self-determination at the national level, and of globalization at the international and individual levels, are both reinforced by the weight of social pressures to such an extent that efforts of resistance are led to choose more and more desperate tactics. These pressures may make the interval and process of transition a dangerous and confusing one, as well as making its outcome uncertain. These pressures also establish the specific context in which religious and cultural perspectives possess their greatest relevance: to facilitate transition by reorienting consciousness toward the satisfaction of human needs and the fulfillment of human potential for individual and group development.

II. COMMENTS ON THE MAINSTREAM DEBATE ON THE WORLD ECONOMIC SITUATION

Some widely accepted generalizations can be set forth to provide a normative sense of direction:

— a large and growing number of people live near or below subsistence;

— the overwhelming concentration of these poor people is among non-white populations located in Asia, Africa, and Latin America;

— a much more rapid and relative rate of population increase exists among the non-white poor of the world;

— a widening gap exists between the per capita GNP of rich and poor countries currently estimated as 11:1 or 12:1;

— an even more rapidly widening income gap exists within poor countries, resulting in the relative, and in some instances, the absolute decline in the purchasing power of the poorest 40% or so of the population despite overall societal growth;*

— a corresponding absence of influence and power on the part of poor countries in international economic and political arenas;

— a disproportionate use of scarce resources by the rich countries of the North relative to their population, perhaps at a ratio of 15:1 on a per capita basis, affecting price and availability of resources required to meet basic needs;

— a strong correlation since 1945 between the poorest sectors of world society and the location of most instances of large-scale collective violence, including warfare;

— an equally strong correlation between the rich sectors of world society and outlays for defense spending;

— an intensification of arms race behavior, including nuclear weapons innovations by superpowers, the spread of nuclear capabilities to many additional countries, and the rise of arms spending

---

*"The costs to the poorest 40 percent of the population in many countries that followed this *'trickle-down'* strategy have now become clear. Not only have their relative incomes and standards of living decreased, sometimes markedly, but there is considerable evidence to suggest that the *absolute incomes of the bottom 10-20 percent may also have fallen.*" (emphasis in original). James Grant and Mahbub ul Haq, "Income Redistribution and the International Financing of Development," Annex 2, in Jan Tinbergen, coordinator, *Reshaping the International Order (RIO)*, New York, E. P. Dutton, 1976.

for sophisticated conventional weaponry; this dynamic increases the likelihood of the outbreak of various forms of warfare, including nuclear war;

—an intensification of authoritarian tendencies, especially throughout the Third World, signifying the decline of moderate politics;

—a mood of growing despair in the rich countries about their economic and political prospects as a consequence of energy costs and options, sustained unemployment and inflation, environmental pressures, terrorist activities, increasing protectionism, and spreading mass disaffection among all societal classes.

These elements of the international situation are not meant to be exhaustive. The purpose of this enumeration is to clarify the grounds of concern about the workings and prospects of the international system. In addition to these various factors, two kinds of linkages, the first between political and economic strategies, and the second, between the domestic political order and the international order, are of fundamental importance.

Idealistic Rhetoric

My analysis proceeds from the conviction that political factors severely constrain available economic policy choices within unacceptably narrow limits and vice versa. These narrow limits reflect a certain stress upon selfish, short-term, domestic concerns that dominate governmental policy-making procedures and make it unrealistic to anticipate any major voluntary adjustments in the international system that could result in substantially greater satisfaction of basic human needs. Put differently, despite idealistic rhetoric, as well as a sense of what needs to be done, altruistic motivation is an exceedingly weak premise for any meaningful program of global reform and perceived selfish motivations are not likely to work for the benefit of the poor.[4]

The only way to avoid this assessment is to envision a reorientation of domestic élites around a more planetary interpretation of national interests coupled with the success of populist politics that successfully revises the domestic allocation of income and wealth. Neither shift is remotely plausible without prior drastic changes in prevailing political consciousness. This will include the emergence of new belief/value orientations that reflect a simultaneous emphasis on the worth of the individual person, on the solidarity of humanity, and on the value of human persistence and evolution.

Such shifts are already underway to some extent, but it will take several decades, at least, until they become dominant; in the interim, stiffening resistance from more traditional and conservative assessments of human nature and political optimality will be encountered. Only by careful examination of prevailing configurations of political power, including their economic dimensions, can we begin to appreciate the magnitude of creating an overall social order of planetary scale that endows all classes and peoples with the opportunity to satisfy basic human needs, a goal more dynamic and ambitious than the elimination of poverty.[5] Poverty could, in theory, be virtually eliminated by welfare payments on an international level without creating a social environment where people have their basic needs, including their sense of dignity, satisfied. Our concern rests with the greater organic attainment of a development process that encompasses everyone, providing work as well as sustenance, dignity as well as material wherewithal, participation as well as benefits.

This insistence on grounding inquiry within the realm of power is especially important where normative concerns are as prominent as they are here. There is often a tendency in international relations to substitute high-minded intentions and words for policy and behavior, or to assume that benevolent adjustments in economic relationships can somehow be achieved by the right technical "fix." The issue of world poverty and the related "development gap" are especially prone to simplistic rhetoric and mechanistic proposals.

Leaders of both rich and poor countries, for a variety of pragmatic reasons, endorse the goals of eliminating poverty as rapidly as possible from the face of the earth. President Jimmy Carter of the United States exhibited a characteristic understanding of this view in a major foreign policy address delivered at Notre Dame University on May 22, 1977: "More than 100 years ago, Abraham Lincoln said that our nation could not exist half slave and half free. We know that a peaceful world cannot long exist one-third rich and two-thirds hungry."[6] To similar effect is a statment by Julius Nyerere, President of Tanzania: "If the rich countries go on getting richer and richer at the expense of the poor, the poor of the world must demand a change, in the same way as the proletariat in the rich countries demanded change in the past. And we do demand change. As far as we are concerned the only question at issue is whether the change comes by dialogue or confrontation."[7]

The formal consensus seems virtually unanimous at such levels of abstraction. Rich and poor leaders alike accept the normative and pragmatic case for a world campaign against both poverty and global disparities. The extent of formal support is also disclosed by the virtually unanimous approval given to the postulates of the new international economic order in key votes at the United Nations; disagreement emerges as soon as action proposals are put forward (e.g. debt cancellation; indexation of commodity prices; national control of foreign investment).

Southern Perspectives

However, even the apparent consensus on goals is deceptive as sharp disagreement becomes quickly evident on the level of explanation and remedy. Third World representatives, regardless of political orientation, tend to put the blame for Third World poverty on the rich countries and naturally expect these countries to bear the moral and material burdens of rectification. As Adam Nsekela, an African World Bank official, puts it: ". . . why are the poor states poor? The answer is that they are poor because they have been colonized, dominated, drained of their surpluses, locked into bondage in which they are poor and are becoming ever poorer because the rich are rich and are becoming relatively richer." [8] Such a perspective leads, at the very least, to an insistence that a feature of any new international economic order that emerges is that states in the poor sector are helped to become economically more secure. In Mr. Nsekela's words, "The New International Economic Order is about distribution: the distribution of world production, the distribution of the surpluses derived in any country and the distribution of economic power." [9] The standard proposals to achieve these results are outside the scope of this paper, but do include such measures as debt relief, stabilization of commodity prices, increased direct assistance, indexation of prices for primary and finished goods, increased Third World voting power in international economic institutions, and improved terms of trade.*

Whether or not such a Southern perspective also includes a transformation of distributive patterns within the state is, of course, a more sensitive issue. To look outward at other governments or global institutions for capital, technical assistance, or social reform may be to invite intervention that endangers political autonomy. In many instances upholding autonomy is a national goal that is as important, and on occasion, more important, than even economic development. To look inward at inequity is to challenge the legitimacy of the state as currently constituted in a political setting where opposition and dissent are increasingly regarded as criminal activities by the leadership of the society. The more radical positions on social change have certainly concentrated upon the need for drastic restructuring on the

---

*The terminology for generalization about rich and poor countries is woefully inadequate. In this paper as generalizations, in some respects deceptive, I refer to poor countries as Third World and Southern, realizing full well that very diverse countries are caught within the net, including rich countries, especially the OPEC members. And for rich countries, with similar caveats, I use the notion Northern, and refer to the market economies of the North as OECD countries.

domestic level and have regarded international restructuring as desirable, but definitely subsidiary. Whether this domestic restructuring is, in effect and unavoidably a call for some variety of socialism, is an important issue. Can governments that rely on private domestic and foreign capital for development purposes, in other words, achieve distributive justice if they are, indeed, operating from an initial circumstance of mass poverty? How? [10]

Northern Perspectives

The governments of rich countries respond to Third World claims in several ways. The most sophisticated and euphemistic line of resistance is to emphasize the automaticity of mutual benefit created by the positive linkage between "growth" for the North and the South, contending that only adjustments based on the imagery of "mutual gain" are politically feasible, economically effective, and morally persuasive. Such an outlook argues against placing additional burdens on the North that will retard its engine of growth to any extent, on the morally self-serving ground that such an effect would be especially harmful to the South. As a consequence, large-scale transfer or redistribution proposals are rejected as "counter-productive" and "irrational." The most authoritative statement, perhaps, of this convenient outlook is contained in the Communiqué of the Economic Summit Meeting held in London during May 1977, and issued on behalf of the seven leading "industrial democracies":

> The well-being of the developed and developing countries are bound up together. The developing countries' growing prosperity benefits industrial countries, as the latter's growth benefits developing nations. Both developed and developing nations have a mutual interest in maintaining a climate conducive to stable growth worldwide. [11]

Even if one grants this dubious premise, what remains to be accounted for is the assessment of whether or not the character of such growth projected for the South is likely to benefit the poorer countries and the poorer segments of these countries. Growth of what? for whom? and over what time period? These critical normative questions are rarely addressed by liberal internationalist advocacy.

The more moderate versions of this mutual gain position argue that the prosperity of the North is the key to market outlets for the products of the South, and that the poor countries are poor for reasons disconnected with their colonial heritage. The essential point in the argument is that these countries would be no less poor had they not been colonized, and that the rich countries would be as rich (or richer) even if there had been no colonial system (e.g. Sweden and Switzerland had no colonies and are rich; Portugal had colonies and is relatively poor). [12]

Some Northerners go further and provide an even more self-vindicating account of economic disparities. For example, the British economists Peter Bauer and John O'Sullivan write that: "Surely the principal reason [for global disparities] is that nations, peoples, tribes, communities are not equally endowed with those qualities which mainly determine economic achievement." [13] That is, the inequality of result in the world of the late 1970s is an inevitable reflection of the inequality of endowment and to allege exploitation and injustice is to offer a rationalization for poverty ungrounded in fact or evidence. Bauer and O'Sullivan go on to attack Northern statesmen for their fatuous acquiescence to the Southern indictment. They argue that indigenous failures of leadership in poor countries are generally responsible for the mass economic plight of their peoples.

This debate as to causation and tactics remains intense and inconclusive. A focus on the level of argumentation tends to overlook more critical issues of political will and capability. The North lacks both the *will* and the *capability* to depart significantly from what it has been doing. Domestic demands for jobs, profits, and inflationary control are predominant, and equalizing concessions to the South are perceived as needless exercises in self-sacrifice for which there is no domestic political constituency of any consequence.

III. SOME PERSPECTIVES ON REFORM.

There are a variety of approaches to global economic reform. The strengths and weaknesses of the principal approaches will be examined in this section.

Capital Transfers and Reallocations

a) A Painless Economic Fix? Many Northerners continue to believe it is possible to help the South with massive capital transfers, coupled with domestic reallocations of investment priorities. Barbara Ward, for instance, proposes "a planetary bargain" between the North and South comparable to the Marshall Plan. As of 1947, the United States made large resource transfers (up to 2% of U. S. GNP per year) for a period of years to stimulate European economic expansion. The result, point out its enthusiasts, has been 25 years of mutually beneficial growth. Arguing that a comparable growth potential exists for North-South trade, Barbara Ward calls for a similar resource transfer, but at the level of .7% of GNP (compared with the current .3%) for a sustained period, perhaps for several decades. Her economic case rests on the view that legitimate demand for goods among the Trilateral countries is largely saturated, leading to increasingly destructive competitive interactions, whereas the demand potential in the Third World remains mostly undeveloped ("there is no doubt where marginal productivity is highest—among still undeveloped people, areas, and resources.").[14]

The incentive for Northern [in conjunction with the Organization of Petroleum Exporting Countries (OPEC)] bounty is the lure of mutual benefit associated with the prospect of major increases in the productive capacity and purchasing power of the poor. This kind of economic thinking, the liberal dream of fusing "rationality," "decency," and "self-interest," is expected to come true, and provide the world economy with a painless apolitical "fix." The catch, however, is that there is virtually no chance of winning support for such an approach in most rich countries, and even if such support could be found and the plan put into effect there is no reason to expect poor countries or poor sectors of societies to benefit to any large extent.

The analogy drawn between economic conditions in post-World War II Europe and in the contemporary Third World is unconvincing. First of all, Europe in 1947, had a disabled industrial capability damaged by war that could be rebuilt by an efficient, generally disciplined, work force provided only that the capital became available. In contrast, much of the Third World has an industrial sector that is restricted to a small physical area, that involves only a fraction of the labor force, and that lacks a large reservoir of skilled labor to draw upon for purposes of rapid economic expansion. Third World poverty tends to be concentrated in the rural sector and its alleviation would require dramatic shifts in public investment priorities so as to stimulate overall rural development that would benefit the rural population as a whole.[15]

Secondly, the governmental structures of Europe after World War II were genuinely determined to rebuild their economies in an efficient manner, whereas governments in Third World countries are often unable to organize themselves for large-scale undertakings, being disabled as much by corruption as by capital shortages.

Thirdly, the short-term effects of such a stimulus of Third World productive capacity would be to export Trilateral jobs and markets in a period of rising economic nationalism and protectionist sentiment in the North.

Fourthly, there is no assurance that such a growth spurt, even if it occurred, would bring substantial benefit to the really poor segments of Third World societies—especially the rural poor.

The tensions extend even further. If investment, for instance, was heavy in agricultural development of the sort required for food self-sufficiency then it would deprive North American farmers of part of their market for exportable grains and cereals, depress world prices, and cause severe domestic problems in those countries. In fact the situation of the U. S. farmer is already described as worse than it has been at any time since the depression and steps have been taken by the government to cut back wheat production by as much as 20%. These steps have been taken, incidentally, at a time when famine conditions exist in Laos, Mozambique and elsewhere.

Among others, Arthur Lewis has shown that "mutual gain" based on North-South trade, especially in exports of primary goods, does tie the economic hopes of the South to the prosperity of the North. The tie is not mutual, however, because of the extreme dependence of the South on the stability of commodity markets in the North, and because of the absence of any comparable Northern dependence on Southern prosperity. Lewis favors stimulating the growth of South-South trading relationships, as well as diversifying the productive capacities of Southern countries to reduce their import requirements and overall dependency. These policies, Lewis argues, would be beneficial in promoting viable forms of development in the South. Lewis' analysis is powerful, in part, because it proceeds within the confines of liberal economic analysis to clarify why present structures of North-South relations are exploitative even if growth rates appear to move in tandem.[16]

b) Naive "Econometric" Solutions. Another kind of "fix" is to abstract the quantum of resources needed to overcome world poverty. Roger Hansen, for instance, reports "that two estimates resulting from different approaches and methodologies suggest that absolute poverty could be virtually ended within ten to fifteen years at a cost of $125 billion (in 1973 dollars); and that an asset-transfer policy to assure the 'forgotten 40 percent' of a firm floor above that level in the future might cost approximately $250 billion." As Hansen notes, such a program could be financed for $10-13 billion per year for 15-25 years, "depending on the thoroughness of the job." Since the present flow of aid from OECD countries is at the level of $13.6 billion, with much of it going to middle-level countries or for purposes unrelated to basic needs, it would be possible, Hansen contends, to reallocate this amount around the priorities of the basic human needs approach without even necessitating increases in aid totals.[17] This contention seems so simple that it raises the obvious question: why doesn't it happen?

Hansen also points out that according to a World Bank estimate "a 2 percent annual transfer from the upper classes to the bottom 40 percent of the populations of the developing countries could successfully finance both the short-term and the long-term goals of the strategy over a twenty-five year period." [18] Again, we are intrigued by the apparent triviality of the effort as compared to the grand character of the promised effect; and again, as with an international transfer, the political constraints emerge when we ask "why doesn't this happen?" Here, as well, the technical vision seems flawed: resource transfers by themselves will not induce self-sustaining growth.

How does one get the capital to the countryside intact and then invest it in such a way as to meet the human needs of the poor, including infrastructure deficiencies, in a manner that will generate a dynamic of productive growth? Without convincing scenarios, targets and numbers are misleading, diverting us from an appreciation of the structural difficulties of rural development in a polity where the capital allocation process is generally dominated by growth-oriented technocrats and profit-oriented urban industrial capitalists. Such arithmetic targets are useful to the extent that they underscore the availability of economic capabilities to meet human needs and call attention to the structural distortions of priority and control that make these reallocations highly implausible. However, to the extent that such "econometric" solutions are meant to provide a *real* solution via an appeal to good faith rationality of policy-makers, they are naive about the nature of power, as well as insensitive to the exploitative character of human relationships implicit in capitalism. As Fernando Henrique Cardoso puts it, "Because they fail to recognize the banality—social and economic exploitation of man by man, of one class by another, of some nations by other nations—so-called 'counter-élites' often go round in circles, dreaming of technical solutions." [19]

c) The Bariloche Model. On a different level of seriousness, large-scale economic models project ways to help the poor and/or eliminate disparities. Perhaps, the most significant initiative to date is the Bariloche inquiry into the kind of development strategy appropriate for the realization of basic human needs. Unlike "the fix" of resource transfers the Bariloche model examines scenarios that involve indigenous Third World investment reallocations designed to produce a needs-oriented development path. [20] Stress is placed upon the kinds of productive outputs called for to satisfy distributional minima for the poorer sectors of the population, as well as on activating demand from those who are now enduring severe levels of deprivation. The model demonstrates, essentially, that a needs-oriented, demand-pulled "engine of growth" is technically feasible when appropriate resource reallocations are made.

This formal demonstration that needs could be satisfied fulfills an educational function, as well as creates a political instrument of criticism and advocacy. The fact that the Argentinian government has withdrawn support from the Bariloche Foundation, evidently in reaction to the publication and widespread discussion of the model (with its implicit critique of GNP-maximation development strategies that tend to skew investment patterns in directions that perpetuate and even intensify income inequalities), is one indication that rigorous demonstrations of alternate development paths is politically threatening to the extent that makes a needs approach appear feasible.

The technocratic style of reactionary regimes in the South claim that their approach to developmental choices possess 'objectivity' and the toleration of continued poverty is unavoidable for the present. Such approaches dismiss criticism calling for greater equity as sentimental or polemical, or misguided. The Bariloche type of model, with its increasingly rigorous methodology, erodes these official claims to speak objectively, and therefore, helps to expose the ideological and class character of prevailing developmental policy. As such, it is naturally perceived as dangerous by ruling groups, as it weakens the legitimacy of governmental claims to be doing as well as possible on the most explosive of all issues in the South.

Beyond this, such a drastic critique of prevailing policies cannot easily be dismissed as a Marxist effort to overthrow the existing order. Indeed, such model-building is often attacked by those who insist that Marxist categories of perception are the only adequate tools for understanding what is going on at the interface between economics and politics. In these regards, those who favor humane development patterns and yet are disillusioned by hardened ideological claims, can take heart. The Bariloche approach seeks to create a knowledge-base that can give policy-makers a real possibility to shape development patterns in ways that meet the needs of the poor. However, the demonstration of economic feasibility should not be confused with demonstrations of political feasibility. The latter demonstration depends on understanding the basis of the governing coalition in a given country, and the extent of discretion that exists among the leaders to alter the bases of support for that coalition within the bureaucracy and in relation to public opinion.

Coercive Transfers

OPEC, since 1973, has achieved a massive North-South transfer of resources without producing a war, although a rising level of threat occurred during the period of embargo. The bulk of these resources, however, have benefitted only a few countries. Most of the additional oil revenues have been recycled in the North, and have been financing huge arms purchases to build up powerful military establishments in several oil-rich countries, especially Iran and Saudi Arabia. Such a use of the market mechanism to achieve rapid international *redistributive* outcomes is certainly effective, but it does not appear to be generalizable beyond oil, nor does it assure a contribution to international equity, as measured by human effects. Recycling of earnings in safe, productive sectors of the world economy is self-interested behavior by OPEC members. The diversion of resources to poor country economies would almost certainly lead to a global depression, provoking an atmosphere of crisis and danger, as well as depriving the oil producers of their best customers. The OPEC strategy is not, in any event, generalizable because oil has special properties. It is a critical resource for which no available substitute exists in sufficient quantities in the short-run. No other commodity is nearly as vital as oil, although some gains for the South can surely be achieved in other trading contexts by a concerted and intelligent assessment of the market.

It is not realistic to envision the OPEC-strategy as capable of solving the challenge of either disparities or poverty. It is true, however, that the radicalization of Iran and Saudi Arabia could make a sizeable difference in the international climate, possibly sufficiently reinforcing the more militant overall demands for a new international economic order to make some genuine restructuring begin to happen.

Nevertheless, there is no reason to suppose that domestic radicalization will produce solid benefits for people other than those living within state boundaries, although the reality of such benefits might stimulate revolutionary activity elsewhere. In essence, the secondary effects of coercive transfers (via resource cartels) are not likely unless, of course, the main militant governments themselves move toward socialism, which in itself is not a likely prospect for the immediate future, or unless, an even less likely prospect, the overall international economy is restructured along non-capitalist lines.

International Institutional Arrangements

There are some possibilities for wealth sharing that exist at the frontiers of technology. The mineral wealth of the ocean sea bed, for example, was for a time conceived to be a part of "the common heritage of mankind" which could be largely administered by international institutions. Most of the income derived could then be distributed according to equity criteria, giving resource-poor Third World countries a source of capital that came without strings or with an interventionary presence, provided only that the recipient governments were pursuing a development strategy of benefit to the society as a whole.

What is now apparent is that ocean idealism has been super-
ceded by selfish pressures to divide up ocean wealth according to
criteria of geopolitical clout, technological capability, and availability
of venture capital. The expected result is that the richest and most
powerful countries will acquire most of the economic benefits, either
because a treaty arrangement favorable to their interest is negotiated,
or because it isn't, and exploitation then proceeds on the basis of
relatively unregulated competition.

Statist imperatives have been in the foreground of the ocean negotiations, exhibiting the extent to which each government seeks the
best possible deal for its country regardless of effects on other, less
favored, states. This kind of statism implies that there is no real
prospect of getting a progressive distributive arrangement based on
relative societal need, but that each state will bargain for its "fair
share" based on its size, ingenuity, and capability. What becomes
more important is that behind these governmental positions have
been the special economic interests of the multinational corporations, which have pressured their particular government to create
investment incentives that include assuring that the lion's share of
economic reward goes to developers.

Here again the main point is that the existing structures of power
in global society will be generally reflected in the arrangements that
are likely to emerge to govern ocean mineral wealth. Even new
sources of wealth are not significantly subject to redistributive pressures. The idealism associated with such global negotiations is subordinated, in practice, to the persisting selfishness of governmental
outlooks. This generalization includes the behavior of the Soviet
Union (as well as its group of dependent socialist countries) which
has taken a position similar to that of the United States on ocean
minerals, and seeks an arrangement that will reward its superior developmental technology and its supportive polity. Although the
South has so far resisted this solution, it has done so on behalf of
Third World governments as a whole, rather than on behalf of equitable arrangements designed to channel profits from ocean mining
to the governments of poor societies.

What is evident here is the same pattern that can be discerned
everywhere; namely, the predominance of statism. There are small
variations among governments as to the degree to which global interests are incorporated, but official behavior seems generally designed
to maximize state interests and to conceive of international negotiations as interstate bargaining situations, rather than as a cooperative search for a global solution expressive of human or planetary
interests. Given the diffusion of state power associated with the
spread of formal independence and with political and military capa-

bilities, there are some international redistributive effects arising from statist logic, but the intranational impacts are barely discernible.

Multinational Corporate Globalism

In a recent full-page advertisement in the *New York Times*, an investment banking firm epitomized the new globalist perspective of big business by a huge picture of electronic equipment dwarfed by four huge globes in the background. The caption read in bold letters: "THE ROOM IS NOW GLOBAL." Underneath was an explanation: "Why? Because the needs of the corporations, governments, and institutions we serve are now global." [21]

Beneath this public display lies the dynamic of corporate growth reinforced by electronic capabilities now available to manage operations spread around the globe almost as efficiently as if their geographical extent was confined to a single city. The particular pattern of interests vary from industrial sector to industrial sector, even from firm to firm. In some areas where the domestic market is being encroached upon by foreign competition there is a growth of economic nationalism in the form of protectionist sentiment. Occasionally, these positions are advocated by a coalition of labor (fearing an export or loss of jobs) and management (fearing losses of domestic markets and profits).

Overall, the Multinational Corporations (MNCs) seek to deal with the world, or with as much of it as possible, as a single market. One tendency, evident in textiles and electronic assembly, is to locate productive facilities where taxes and labor costs are low and environmental regulation minimal. South Korea and Taiwan have been beneficiaries of such policies. It is alleged that the expansion of MNCs weaves a network of trade and investment interests that erode conflicts at the political level and make for a more peaceful world. IBM's motto is expressive of the wider MNC global ethos: "World Peace Through World Trade."

More relevant, however, are MNC claims that jobs, capital, and technology are being beneficially transferred to poor countries. Indeed, spokespeople for the MNC outlook applaud the noninterventionary contributions being made to economic growth throughout the Third World. Such a positive interpretation of MNC roles remains unconvincing. First of all, the beneficiaries of the MNC are a tiny proportion of the work force, who tend to be concentrated among the most skilled, and already well-off workers. Secondly, in countries with mass poverty, MNC operations depend on the creation of stable political conditions, which often require a deliberate effort to eliminate drastic challenges from below. The search for "discipline" to reduce the economic costs of social uncertainty inevitably leads to the denial of human rights, to repression and to subordination of populist claims for redistribution, full employment, and the like.[22] Indochina, Argentina, Indonesia, the Philippines, and Thailand are among the countries that illustrate political solutions of a highly authoritarian character that can be explained, in part, by the priority their leadership attaches to attracting foreign capital (including loans from international financial institutions). At least for the short-run this insistence upon discipline tends to mean that increased activity by MNCs is not likely to result in greater satisfaction of basic needs of poor peoples. Indeed, the bargaining leverage of the poor may be cut down by government policy to assure an attractive investment climate for MNCs and national capitalists.

Thirdly, economic nationalism in the Third World may be a greater force than the benefits derived from MNC operations. The Brazilian government seems willing, during this present period of its history, to complicate the lives of MNCs so that it can fulfill nationalistic goals, including the reduction of foreign encroachment.

Fourthly, the markets for MNC output have tended to concentrate on the goods that could be purchased by those people with the disposable income, i.e. the middle classes. Necessities associated with nutrition, housing, health, and education are impossible to mass produce for profit when most potential customers lack purchasing power. As a consequence, most MNC production related to the domestic markets of Third World countries is associated with luxury items, thereby widening the consumption gap.

As matters now stand it is difficult to be positive about MNCs as agents of societal change and reform. Their direct impact seems concentrated among favored strata of the population, and their generally unintended, but definite, influence is to encourage repressive tendencies by placing a premium on domestic stability. Such stability in contexts of mass poverty tends to close off avenues of domestic reform for a long time. Often, also, the technological sophistication associated with MNC operations is extended to police administration in these countries, although this "modernization" of law enforcement procedures may occur in the absence of MNCs. In any event, there can be no positive example of a country where high levels of MNC operations have yielded dramatic distribution gains for the poorest sectors or where income disparities have narrowed. Even resource-rich Third World countries have no adopted policies designed to achieve domestic equity.

Domestic Radicalism in the South

a) Economic Achievements of Socialist Regimes. It seems correct to credit socialist governments in the Third World with substantial achievements, at least, with respect to intranational equity. To the extent that resource capabilities exist, the basic needs of the population are met, and internal disparities reduced. External penetration is reduced, as well, either by way of corporate behavior or from foreign governments, and economic structures of self-reliance generated. The trade-offs have involved relinquishing "space" for various kinds of diversity—as the regimen of socialist governance in the Third World has severely inhibited oppositional politics of every variety. A bureaucratic élite has also emerged, threatening to evolve into "a new class," and give rise to domestic disparities. Despite these difficulties, the economic achievements of China, Cuba, and Vietnam suggest that the material needs of Third World populations can be rapidly and substantively satisfied by socialist regimes.

b) Lessons of the Allende Experience. These socialist success stories, however, have all involved triumphant revolutionary movements in a position to reshape the apparatus of state power after a prolonged armed struggle. The contrary experience of the Allende period in Chile (1970-73), and possibly of Portugal since 1974, confirms the observation. A mandate for structural reform—in other words, shifting income to the poor and orienting economic planning around needs—engenders resistance from a state bureaucracy dominated by military officers and civil servants wedded to the old order. Such resistance makes it difficult, if not impossible, to carry out a program of domestic reform in an effective manner.

This resistance poses a serious dilemma for a progressive leadership that does not have its own people in dominant positions throughout the state bureaucracy. If the program can be blocked by hostile forces within the official hierarchy then it can be discredited as "incompetent," while if the program is effective despite resistance, then counterrevolutionary forces are mobilized. Allende's experience involved a mixture of these elements: strong bureaucratic resistance, considerable popular success despite obstacles, and a counterrevolutionary takeover justified both by the alleged incompetence of Allende's governance and necessitated by its persisting popularity, which evidently was understood to mean that it was unlikely that Allende could be unseated by constitutional means.

External factors, of course, reinforced this pattern. The United States Government, via the Central Intelligence Agency (CIA) and other intelligence agencies, mounted a campaign of "destabilization" designed to foster an impression of incompetence on the part of the Chilean government. The powerful MNCs, especially International Telephone & Telegraph (ITT), did their best to keep Allende from power and then harassed the government during his tenure. Furthermore, by means of CIA actions and a variety of intergovernmental military relationships, the United States maintained contact with and gave encouragement to the counterrevolutionary leadership in Chile. It remains difficult as yet to assess the cumulative influence of the US role in this period. Pressure was also successfully used at American initiative to deny Allende the benefit of loans and credits from international financial institutions, including the World Bank. These institutions are dominated by OECD capital and voting power, lack any countervailing socialist participation, and, therefore, tend to resist any kind of radical redistributive policy by a national government despite the degree to which such a policy does what virtually everyone says is desirable.

A final factor involved the failure of the Soviet Union to take protective action on behalf of Allende to offset the effects of American pressure. Soviet motivation is difficult to fathom, but some speculations are possible. One interpretation suggests that the Soviet expense of offsetting American economic pressure on Cuba may have been as much as the Kremlin was willing to accept for the sake of securing "friendly" governments in Latin America. Another view maintains that Allende was "a Marxist" rather than "a Communist" and, consequently, was not sufficiently deferential to Moscow to engender Soviet support. Finally, detente may have been a factor, especially when considered together with the deference the superpowers have been giving to each other's spheres of influence. Soviet leaders may have regarded Chile as within the American sphere and that serious pro-Allende support would have destroyed detente and its related economic relations.

Whatever the causal sequence accounting for Allende's bloody downfall and the harsh militarist aftermath that has befallen Chilean society since 1973, it has tended to reinforce the Leninist insistence that socialism cannot be introduced except as a sequel to a prior armed struggle. This realization is a grave setback for those social forces in the Third World seeking a non-violent path to a socialist political economy.

Cultural Revolution in the North

Together with the notions of helping the South is a new, and quite autonomous, appreciation that the North itself is suffering from a mixture of pressures that have been provocatively labelled "over-development." Such a term suggests that the alienating and dangerous character of post-industrial civilization is to be partly associated with unchecked technological momentum. In effect, the argument goes, after crossing a certain threshold of affluence, "more means worse."

a) Disintegrating Impact of "Over-Development." The idea of "over-development" is vague and needs some elaboration. The real content of the notion derives from the realization that the food we eat, the air we breath, the water we drink, and the lives we lead are contaminating our bodies and spirits in ways we have yet to understand. A recent scholarly paper concludes that malnutrition from affluent diets is taking almost as great a toll in life expectancy as do protein deficient diets.[23] Along similar lines, a report concludes that at least one of four industrial workers in the United States is exposed, without precaution, to hazardous disease-producing conditions as part of work routine.[24] A great deal more than physical health is at stake, however. There are numerous signs of the breakdown of values, institutions, morale. These signs include the weakening of family ties, the corruption and incompetence of government, the rise of crime, incredible rates of hard drug use, the loss of neighborliness and community sentiments, and widespread evidence of despair and alienation. It is an extraordinary commentary on the breakdown of civility to note that the richest cities in the richest countries are among the most dangerous for the unwary.

Over-development, of course, is compatible, especially in the United States, with deep pockets of poverty, as well as with high levels of unemployment, specifically among minority youth in the cities. Serious deficiencies associated with race, region and class persist in most so-called rich countries. These rich polities, as an aggregate, nevertheless waste resources in large quantities on fashions, luxury consumption, planned obsolescence, and weapons. This waste by the rich occurs during a period of rising consciousness about satisfying basic needs and, more keenly, at a time of an emerging concern about "limits to growth" not necessarily mechanical limits, but limits connected to the forms of growth and its environmental effects.

b) Ecological Ethos—A Rising Social Force. The ecological ethos —a measure of deference to nature—is a rising social force, especially in Western Europe, where green, not red, is becoming the color of radical politics. Its potency is revealed by the expansion of a militant anti-nuclear movement throughout the democratic societies of the industrial world. This movement gains support from many sources, but its principal strength arises from the conviction that official institutions are no longer to be trusted with the protection of human interest, especially where fundamental issues of choice and risk are concerned.

In the nuclear context, many people seem prepared to forego, are perhaps eager to do so, additional energy in exchange for a healthier, more humane surrounding. The prospects of economic growth are no longer as tantalizing as they once were to large numbers of people, especially if the cost is reliance on technologies that are a serious health hazard and that result in further centralization of economic and political activities. On a less spectacular scale than the anti-nuclear movement is the rising resistance throughout the West to dams, highways, and bridges that reflects a growing skepticism about the benefits of progress defined in overly materialist terms.

This skepticism has even penetrated official institutions to varying degrees in different countries, although the dominant consensus in these institutions emphasizes the management of environmental concerns in a fashion that is consistent with rapid domestic growth. A bigger pie—and not a more equitably distributed, stable or smaller pie—remains the major premise of economic policy in every society where the quest for profits and higher aggregate production structures are accepted as goals. This growth bias is especially strong in recent years because profits and net output must be sustained in an atmosphere of sharply escalating costs.

In the background of over-development thinking lie varying degrees of guilt or anxiety about annual allocation of world resources. One assessment suggests that 85% of world resources is being used each year for the benefit of less than 20% of the world's population; the people who comprised this 20% are mainly white Northerners.[25] Over-development prescription adopts the inverse view of "the mutual gain" perspective of liberal internationalists. It suggests that the rich should cut back on their use of scarce resources and allow the poorer countries to have a larger share. This outlook would require drastic changes in domestic economic policies and new trading/monetary relations to become operative without inducing severe disruption. It is not an immediately practical alternative. Nevertheless, the over-development outlook is increasingly endorsed by those who seek an economics with a humane and an ecological face.

c) Skepticism Towards Scientific Rationalism. The values challenge directed at the current affluent patterns is also expressed in affirmative ways. There is a remarkable surge of interest in spiritual possibilities of all kinds, bearing witness, I think, to the widespread refusal of people to accept the reign of scientific rationalism. Science and technology are generating the kind of skeptical reaction that had been directed toward religion in earlier generations. The interest in Eastern religions and practices throughout the West expresses, also, a demand for a more drastic religious experience than what is currently available in most of the established religious institutions. This spiritual impulse has been complemented by a variety of questionings directed at the viability of affluent life-styles based upon mainstream careerism. There is an immense growth of various modes of "voluntary simplicity" in these parts of the world, especially in the United States. In these cultural gropings there is much that is faddish, immature, quixotic, but there is also impressive evidence of serious quests for new, more satisfying and suitable cultural forms.[26]

A relevant line of conjecture goes as follows: if voluntary simplicity grows in scope and depth, becomes politically potent via its role in consumerist and anti-nuclear causes, then it may create a new normative climate for political leadership. In this new climate territorial boundaries may come to mean less than what one author has called "earthmanship." [27] Whether such a drastic shift of consciousness can emerge without violent convulsions is, of course, problematic. Recent descriptions of anti-nuclear activity in Europe suggest, for instance, a pattern of intensifying violence. Last summer at a large demonstration one protester was killed and several others maimed in France by highly armed national guard security forces. There appears to be an escalating cycle of militance in the confrontation between the state and its opponents on these issues of technological choice.[28]

d) Shifts in Life-Styles and Religious Outlook Could Make a Difference. In essence, then, shifts in life-style in the North could cut domestic disparities, as well as make a greater proportion of global resources available for the satisfaction of basic needs of other societies provided, of course, that viable ways to sustain the world economy are found. For such a movement to succeed, it would have to draw upon spiritual energies that reformulated the conditions of happiness and development, including the satisfaction of simplicity.[29] The positive character of this conception would have to prevail against the whole mobilization and manipulation of highly individualized tastes based upon accumulation of goods, high style and fashion, and the identification of success with luxurious living. The rise of such alternative life-styles would have to displace the widely held presumption that virtually all sensible people seek to enjoy the energy-intensive middle class life-style associated with the United States. As one influential commentator puts it, "Attainment of middle-class style of life is what constitutes development in countries as widely separated geographically and ideologically as Brazil and USSR." [30] It would require a reversal of the prevailing policymakers' view that Brazilians on the whole are better off than say, the Chinese, or more aptly, to entertain the possibility that the Chinese mode of development, if perfected, might do more to satisfy the total needs of people than can the perfection of the Brazilian mode. The value shift, in effect, would depend upon "less being better" provided "less" is enough to satisfy basic needs, and that the non-material benefits of community solidarity, socialist consciousness, and equality were made available and widely dispersed.[31]

It is difficult to determine the strength and durability of these tendencies toward voluntary simplicity and associated spirituality. To influence the overall economic setting of the world such tendencies would have to evolve much further and begin to influence policy-making perspective on global economic issues. Such an impact cannot be expected for another several decades, although it is worth noting that the late E. F. Schumacher built an immense following for ideas associated with decentralization, simplicity, and appropriate technology. Influential political leaders, at least privately, have been indicating an appreciation for his kind of approach. It is also relevant that Schumacher's position and influence was infused by a deeply held religious outlook that seems organically related to the radical view of development that he espouses.

IV. A PERSPECTIVE ON TRANSFORMATION: SOME TENTATIVE COMMENTS

Perhaps more than social science or even fiction, children's literature has the clearest and most direct insight into the present situation. A familiar theme in recent children's books is the restoration of the earth after it has been plundered by human activity.

The Earth Belongs to Everyone

One such story, called *Dinosaurs and all that rubbish*, tells of a man who caused great ruin on earth so that he might have a rocket built to allow a visit to another planet. After he leaves a totally polluted planet behind, some dinosaurs, sleeping for ages underneath the earth, awake and fix things up so that landscapes become green again. The man in his rocket, in the meantime, discovers that the distant star of his dreams is barren and looks elsewhere. He finds, finally, a planet that is green and beautiful, and is excited. The man is astonished to discover that this beautiful habitat is the same earth that he had abandoned in disgust. He pleads, then, with the dinosaurs to be allowed to have some land to live on:

"Please may I have a small part of it back?" he asked.
"Please, just a hill, or a tree, or a flower?"

And here is the response of the dinosaur:
"No," said the dinosaur.
"Not a part of it,
but all of it.
It is all yours
but it is also mine.

Remember that.
This time the earth belongs to everyone,
not parts of it to certain people
but all of it to everyone,
to be enjoyed
and cared for." [32]

It is worth noticing this non-territorial conception of using the earth, having it all and yet of owning no part of it—a reversal of prevalent attitudes and arrangements.

Tinkering Is Not Enough

No amount of tinkering can fix up the present international system. Too many fundamental pressures exist: continuing demographic pressures (increasing population and even more rapidly increasing urbanization), increasing destructiveness and instability of the weapons environment, waste of economic resources to fuel the arms race and to sustain affluent life-styles, sterility of an economistic vision that identifies progress with material growth, and societal fulfillment with entry into the middle classes, moral backwardness of an overall economic and political system that imposes "order" rather than orients investment and production around the satisfaction of basic needs, and short-sightedness of growth patterns that are not ecologically sustainable. These pressures are cumulative, interrelated, and their eventual impact could inflict irreversible damage, foreclosing future options. The logic that controls the state system is no longer tolerable. It is too dangerous, wasteful, and stultifying. It inhibits the sort of economic, political, and cultural development that fulfills individual and collective potentialities at various stages of industrialization.

In these respects even reorientations of national political consciousness can only be understood as transitional, generating dangerous, provocative confrontations between social forces. The efforts of governments to opt for basic needs generally collides with the interests of those who currently manage the international economic and political system. Neither Castro nor Allende, for instance, have had an easy time in the Western Hemisphere, and similarly, those who challenge entrenched interests in the post-industrial states are being met with violence and coercion. There is, for instance, a peaceful movement in the Seattle area of the United States to prevent construction of a large submarine facility for the Trident Submarine, on the basis of substantial evidence that it has been conceived by its designers as a first-strike weapons system.[33] The response of governing bodies has not been to reexamine or even to justify its com-

mitment to weapons that appear to make nuclear war more likely, but
to put the protesters in jail for increasingly long terms.

In the OECD world the emergent heroes are those who resist the
bland assumptions that we can go on with nuclear power and
weapons as if they are benign and inevitable ingredients of human
destiny. The refusal to accept such a reality constitutes the center of
a movement for transformation in the most affluent countries just as
the movement for economic and social equity and against various
forms of imperialism constitutes the center of movements for transformation in the Third World.

It is also noteworthy that the convergence of these tendencies is
beginning to be evident. Members of the Pacific Life Community,
which have led the drive against the Trident, adhere by choice to a
life style based on voluntary simplicity, so that their lives will not be
in conflict with patterns of living that are, in principle, possible for
everyone else on the planet. They also insist upon the wholeness and
unity of the species, and self-consciously ignore the boundary between Canada and the United States, soliciting Canadians to take
part in activities on American territory as "planetary citizens."
Every person has a stake in preventing nuclear war, although Canadians may have a special stake in preventing a Trident base so close
to their homes. In striking contrast is the highly territorial response
of the governor of the state of Washington, who has publicly warned
Canadians to mind their own business, as if the dangers of nuclear
war could be cordoned off on the basis of national boundaries.

Main Elements of a Transformative Vision

The main elements of a transformative vision of the future are
implicit in what has been written above:

Solidarity — the sense of vital concern about the human species
as a focus of emergent loyalty;

Unity — the shared and unified destiny of the planet;

Space — the non-territorial circumference of human concerns;

Time — the extension of human concerns in time to the ancient
past and to the most distant future;

Nature — the experience of nature as encompassing, inspiring, and
sustaining;

Peace — the renunciation of violence as the collective basis of security and innovation;

Progress — the gradual realization of human potentialities for joy
and creativity in all dimensions of individual and collective existence;

Humility — the awareness of limits applicable to human endeavor
including an understanding that human society should not proceed

with certain lines of scientific investigation and technological innovation; and

Spirituality—the understanding that awe and mystery are as integral to human experience as bread and reason.

In effect, this set of criteria could be espoused on a high enough level of abstraction by virtually anyone, even today. Indeed, even those in positions of significant power in the existing system with its contrary attributes might endorse, quite sincerely, many of these transformative elements. It is the degree of embodiment that makes all the difference! Nominal or ritual embodiment is possible and, possibly, self-deceptive in a damaging way. Power-wielders often seem quiet and serene, even while engaged in destructive activities, because they do not perceive the tension between what they believe and what they do. Part of human adaptability, that has especially high social costs in periods of fundamental challenge, is to disguise contradictions between actions and ideals.

Internalizing a Religious Perspective

The position outlined above is making a radical claim; namely, that the future prospects of the human species depend upon internalizing an essentially religious perspective, sufficient to transform secular outlooks that now dominate the destiny of the planet. Any prudent calculation of probabilities would, of course, heap scorn on this eventuality, and yet, oddly enough it seems more "utopian" to suppose that we can persist on our crowded, depleted, militarized planet inhabited by many who are miserable, some who are desperate, and most who are scared. Any genuine, hard-headed "rationalist," respectful of evidence and trends, would become a "doomsday prophet." Hope, now more than ever, that is not just an unconvincing expectation of a series of technological "miracles," depends on renourishing religious sensibilities.

In the short-term it is difficult to assess whether or not a religious perspective, as integral to the discharge of official functions, allows a power wielder to advance human values more effectively. The resistances seem too formidable. The overriding necessities of wielding power in the current global setting especially in major states, require levels of moral insensitivity that are of a monumental character including a willingness to endorse uses of weapons of mass destruction, to entertain and honor dictators who torture their opponents, to rely on industrial processes that endanger workers and environments, to protect dubious investments and sources of critical raw materials, to orient policy around short-term horizons of expectations. It seems impossible, then, for a religious perspective associated with the values we have set forth to flourish within current realms of secular power.*

In addition to this, religious spokespeople may actually play a regressive role in social issues—for instance on the status of women. A grotesque interaction of secular and religious sensibilities occurred in Somalia two years ago. The government sought to emancipate women from various forms of bondage and was opposed by traditionalist religious leaders citing the Qur'an as their authority. To demonstrate that it meant business, the government rounded up eleven religious leaders actively working against equality for women one morning and executed them later the same day.**

Purely Humanist Positions Cannot Engender Transforming Vision

It is not necessary to be "religious" (in either the formal or existential sense) to have an impulse to do better, to be more ethical, and to be even more empathetic. Such a reformist platform may seem fully consistent with a secular search for stability in the short-run, and hence very practical, or it may be appealing mainly for idealistic reasons. And it is obvious that humanism can be accepted by individuals who have no confidence at all in the wider realities of religious affirmation. But such purely humanist positions cannot, in my view, engender the vision or the hope required to build toward transformation; and secularist thinking will never extend social contracts (for the present) to conventional arrangements (for the future).[34]

---

*A religious perspective can inform almost any political undertaking, often lending it an aura of certitude that vindicates the most extreme, and brutal, behavior. We are using "religious" in a more restricted way associated with shared ideals that are shared by the great religions of the world.

**Bauer and O'Sullivan, note 13, at pp. 55, use this incident to support their central conclusion ". . . that the liberal ideas and phraseology of the West, once transported to the Third World, often assume fantastic and distorted forms." I question such an interpretation, and regard it, instead, as a clash between two indigenous approaches to well-being resolved in a manner that discloses the consequences of the failure to curb state power. These failures should not be associated mainly with Third World countries. See, for instance, the Soviet state vis-á-vis its own people; the US vis-á-vis the Vietnamese.

FOOTNOTES

1. A strong argument along these lines is found in the Club of Rome study of Ervin Laszlo and others, *Goals for Mankind*, New York, E. P. Dutton, 1977, esp. pp. 367-424.

2. See Fouad Ajami, "The Global Populists: Third-World Nations and World-Order Crises," Princeton University, Center of International Studies, Research Monograph No. 41, May 1974.

3. I have tried to depict the organizational consequence of this mixture of centralizing functional requirements and decentralizing human requirements in Chapter IV of *A Study of Future Worlds*, New York, Free Press, 1975, pp. 224-276.

4. On what needs to be done see, among others, especially Marc Nerfin's preface and Rodolfo Stavenhagen's chapter in Nerfin, ed., *Another Development*, Uppsala, Sweden, Dag Hammarskjöld Foundation, 1977; also Dieter Senghaas, "If you can't keep us with the rich, keep away," in *Forum of Committee of Correspondence*, 9:1, Sept. 1977, pp. VI-143—VI-145.

5. For clear explanation of the needs focus and distinction between the positive stress of a basic needs approach from the negative stress of a poverty reduction approach see Graciela Chichilnisky, "Development, Basic Needs, and the Future of the International Order," mimeographed, pp. 1-7.

6. For text see *New York Times*, May 23, 1977.

7. Julius Nyerere, "The Economic Challenge: Dialogue or Confrontation," *International Development Review* 1976/1:2-8, at 3.

8. Amon J. Nsekela, "The World Bank and the New International Economic Order," *Development Dialogue* 1977:1, pp. 75-84, at 75-6.

9. *Idem.* at 78.

10. Issue posed in this way by Samir Amin, "Self-Reliance and the New International Economic Order," *Monthly Review*, July/Aug. 1977, pp. 1-21, esp. at 2-3.

11. For text see *New York Times*, May 9, 1977, p. 12.

12. Such a position is comprehensively depicted by Richard Cooper in "A New International Economic Order for Mutual Gain," *Foreign Policy*, Spring 1977, 26:66-122.

13. Peter Bauer and John O'Sullivan, "Ordering the World About: the NIEO," *Policy Review*, Summer 1977, 1:55-69, at 57-8.

14. Barbara Ward, "Seeking a Planetary Bargain," *International Development Review*, 1977/2:34-5, at 34.

15. For data and argument along these lines see Stavenhagen, in Nerfin, note 5, at pp. 40-65, esp. 40-47.

16. As Professor Lewis argues, emphasis on agricultural development is the key to economic autonomy. See, in general W. Arthur Lewis, "The Evolution of the International Economic Order," Princeton University, Research Program in Development Studies, Discussion Paper No. 74, March 1977, pp. 1-60, esp. 53-60. See also Samir Amin, "Self-Reliance and the New International Economic Order," *Monthly Review*, July/Aug. 1977, 29:1-21.

17. Roger Hansen, "Major U. S. Options on North-South Relations: A Letter to President Carter," in John Sewell and others, *The United States and World Development: Agenda 1977*, Washington, D. C., Overseas Development Council, 1977, pp. 21-142, at 67-9. These figures are specified in greater detail in Mahbub ul Haq, *The Poverty Curtain*, New York, Columbia University Press, 1976, Statistical Annex, Table 5, p. 229.

18. Hansen, p. 68.

19. Fernando Henrique Cardoso, in Nerfin, note 5, pp. 21-39, at 23.

20. For explication of model see Chichilnisky, note 5.

21. *New York Times,* Oct. 3, 1977, p. 48.

22. For lucid argument along these lines Sylvia Ann Hewlett, "Human Rights and Economic Realities: Tradeoffs in Historical Perspective," (mimeographed paper).

23. Erik Ekholm and Frank Record, "The Two Faces of Malnutrition," Washington, D. C., World Watch Paper No. 9, Dec. 1976, pp. 1-63.

24. Report of an official government survey, *New York Times,* Oct. 3, 1977, pp. 1, 22.

25. Chichilnisky, note 5, p. 5.

26. On "voluntary simplicity" see Duane S. Elgin and Arnold Mitchell, "Voluntary Simplicity: Life Style of the Future?" *The Futurist,* Aug. 1977, pp. 200-209, 254-261. In general, see T. Roszak, *The Unfinished Animal,* New York, Harper and Row, 1976.

27. See G. Tyler Miller, Jr., *Living in the Environment: Concepts, Problems, Alternatives,* Belmont, Calif., Wadsworth, 1975, pp. 29-30, 326-330.

28. Anna Gyorgy, "France Kills its First Protester," *The Nation,* Oct. 8, 1977, pp. 330-333; William Sweet, "The Opposition to Nuclear Power in Europe," *Bulletin of Atomic Scientists,* Vol. 33, Dec. 1977, pp. 40-47.

29. Johan Galtung sets forward some suggestive ideas in an essay entitled "Alternative Life Styles in Rich Societies," in Nerfin, note 5, pp. 106-121.

30. Nathan Keyfitz, "World Resources and the World Middle Class," *Scientific American,* July 1976, 235:28-35, at 28. Professor Keyfitz builds his analysis around the presumed superiority of a middle class society, whatever its other features, contending that if resources limit access then "The Chinese rather than the British-Russian pattern of development may be what people will have to settle for." (p. 28).

31. Evidence that value shifts along these lines is taking place is scrupulously and impressively presented in Ronald Inglehart, *The Silent Revolution: Changing Values and Political Styles Among Western Publics,* Princeton, Princeton University Press, 1977.

32. Michael Foreman, *Dinosaurs and all that rubbish,* New York, Thomas Crowell, 1972, pp. 26-7.

33. For an account by a leading participant see Shelley Douglass, "Bangor Summer Reflection," *Year One,* Sept. 1977, III: 12-14.

34. Distinction between "contract" and "convenant" attributed to Richard Neuhaus in Samuel Hux, "The Holocaust and the Survival of Tragedy," in *Worldview,* Oct. 1977, pp. 4-10, at 7.

SUMMARY

For Falk, no technological "fix" can close today's widening gap between rich and poor, North and South. This poverty gap exists, not of necessity, but because of the way states and systems of states are presently organized. To change organizational patterns on this scale is a complex, difficult, perhaps impossible undertaking that depends among other things on shifting patterns of perceived interests and on changing value formations.

Such fundamental changes challenge all our institutions and traditions, but perhaps especially our religious heritages, to provide us with clues as to what is wrong and what to do about it, as well as with inspiration to strengthen our political will to act decisively to close the poverty gap.

Falk is wary of the new stress on human needs as engendering patronizing concern for the poor rather than understanding that poverty is the "structural" consequence of the way power and wealth have been developed.

He first discusses at length the structural and ideological impasse of present methods to reduce world poverty and unmasks the deep differences in perspectives that lurk behind the abstract idealistic rhetoric of leaders of both North and South. He then points out the inadequacies of proposed "painless" econometric solutions that, unlike the Bariloche model, fail to recognize the overwhelming fact of social and economic exploitation at every level of society.

Falk likewise foresees no easy breakthrough in recourse to coercive transfers, proposed new international institutional arrangements, multinational corporate globalism, or domestic radicalism in the South. He finally finds a degree of hope in a growing consensus of disillusionment with "over-development" in the North and consequent shifts in life-style and religious outlook.

Falk concludes by listing the main elements of this emerging transformative vision and insists that to become effective this vision must be internalized in an essentially religious perspective. Purely humanistic positions cannot engender the vision or the hope required to build toward global transformation.

6

Synthesis of Papers and Discussion

Land's paper highlighted the tentative but very hopeful phenomenon of widespread convergence in the approaches to a new world order found among top-level professional groups working in different parts of the world. But Land was puzzled and Abdalla discouraged by the parallel "deaf dialogue" among political leaders who seem to be little influenced in recent years by this convergence in perspective.

While there are many evident similarities in the papers of Abdalla, Grant/Sewell and Falk, the differences in approach are perhaps more striking. Grant and Sewell argue that in practice any realistic future strategy to meet basic human needs must be linked to the NIEO, but their first priority is clearly not fundamental structural change. It is rather to meet the minimum basic needs of the world's people by the year 2000.

For Abdalla, on the other hand, structural changes in world order are his first priority, since, for him, the South's present underdevelopment is a by-product of the rich North's own particular model of development. Basic human needs must be met, but not as marginal concessions from rich to poor while keeping the present world order essentially intact.

Finally, for Falk none of the technological fixes being proposed can close today's widening gap between rich and poor, North and South. Nothing short of a basic conversion in worldview, perceived interests and value priorities can provide the elements necessary for a transformative vision. And for Falk this vision to be effective must transcend purely humanistic motives and be internalized in an essentially religious perspective.

In brief, there is convergence of perspective and goals among these papers, but there is also sharp disagreement on present priorities and how to arrive at the agreed upon goal of a more human and just world order.

The discussion that followed the presentation of these papers was marked by a certain ambiguity among the participants. A clear methodology of how to discuss the challenge of world order to faith and of faith to world order continued to elude the group. Some seemed to think that when the group talked about the NIEO or even about a new world order, the faith dimension was being omitted; others— especially the economists of all faiths—felt the need to define much more precisely and analytically concrete problems before proceeding to focus a faith critique on them. The discussion took the form of raising points, questions and observations rather than of sustained debate. The following interventions are indicative of the general lines of the discussion.

—A group such as this finds little meaning in talk about an 'economic' world order but rather must immediately focus on a 'human' world order. The only way to escape the 'social-engineering trap' is to transcend the concept of 'economic man' found in neo-classical economics and deal with the whole human person.

—The dialectics of struggle and negotiation seem more relevant today than the painless technological fixes proposed by some economic specialists whose escape into mathematical models allows them to avoid social, political and ethical values and so maintain the status quo.

—Do differences in the group stem more from different anthropologies than from different economic theories?

—The NIEO, as proposed in the United Nations, is premised on national sovereignty, but is not national sovereignty itself the heart of the problem? Is this not clearly demonstrated in the present repression-development syndrome found in many states and in the slow progress being made toward necessary regional groupings?

—No amount of positive sum games and clever bargaining can hide the fact than any new economic order will be costly and painful to rich and poor alike in both economic and human terms, even if ultimately a more human and just world order will emerge to the advantage of all.

—The present transfer into poor countries of a whole value system of consumerism by means of transnational corporations and mass media, whose first priority is not the integrity of the human person, presents almost insuperable problems for the traditions and values of these countries.

— Is it so evident that all countries must accept to be interdependent today? Does this not implicitly assume that there is only one universal model, one world order? Is the self-reliant model of China not to be seriously considered? Is its uniqueness due more to its culture and particular values than to its economic status? Is the group's discussion being short-changed by not looking more explicitly at Communist proposals for a new world order?

— Is there not an inconsistency in promoting social justice at the world level without at the same time with equal vigor promoting social justice at the national level of developing nations, where the gap between rich and poor is even greater than at the world level?

— A de-coupling from former colonial and neo-colonial powers is necessary for the development of "collective self-reliance" among poor countries. There is the need especially to accept a plurality of economic models, as well as a variety of cultures and national identities. The imitation willingly or not of the superpowers is not proving a satisfactory solution for the poor countries.

To the suggestion that the best gift the rich countries could give to the poor countries would be to stop the arms race, some participants raised the puzzling and embarrassing question of why, in spite of their clear teachings on peace, do religions and religious parties so often defend wars and large defense budgets?

In the end, there seemed to be consensus that a new re-structured human world order is essential, one which could meet the basic needs of all. It will require a fundamental change in individual and group perceptions of the world and of value priorities, if the majority of people are to participate willingly in the painful process. This process will inevitably involve shifting some degree of power and privilege from the rich to the poor in the ensuing decades. The group could not proceed further into specifics—though several wished to do so—before turning its focus more directly on the faith communities themselves.

(clockwise from empty chair)
Shestack, Ben Shlomo, Hesburgh, Carr, al-Faruqi, Ivern, Avineri, Ahmad, Wedel, Falk, Sewell, Siegman, Yalcintas, Nasr, Blank, Mejia, Rubenstein, Ryan, Bellah, Hull, Gremillion, Abdalla, Hewage. Not visible in this photo are: Arns, Blewett, Faruqi, Ishikawa, Klompe, Rosenhaus, Sakr.

(left to right)
Abdalla, Mejia, Falk, Gremillion, Hull, Hewage, Hesburgh

(left to right)
Ishikawa, Yalcintas

(left to right)
Blank, Klompe

(left to right)
Wedel, Hesburgh

Avineri

(left to right)
Ahmad, Sakr, Falk

(left to right)
Gremillion, Nasr

(left to right)
Abdalla, Sewell

(left to right)
Arns, Faruqi

(left to right)
al-Faruqi, Siegman, Ryan

(left ro right)
Carr, Blewett

146

PART II

The Dimensions of Faith

7

Faith Communities Challenge — and are Challenged by — The Changing World Order

Robert Bellah

Robert Bellah, a US citizen, is presently Ford Professor of Sociology and Comparative Studies and Vice Chairperson of the Center for Japanese and Korean Studies at the University of California, Berkeley. He did his graduate studies in sociology and eastern languages at Harvard University. Among his past positions and honors, Bellah was research associate at the Institute for Islamic Studies at McGill University, Montreal; a Fulbright Research Grantee in Tokyo, and Professor at the Department of Social Relations at Harvard University. He has lectured and published widely in such areas as the Apache kinship systems, the Tokugawa religion, civil religion in America, and the new religious consciousness.

I. INTRODUCTION

The two titles of this paper express my ambivalence as to how to pose the essential issues. The first title represents the straightforward awareness that there are enormous changes going on in the world—technological, economic, demographic, political—that call in question all of the assumptions of the traditional faith communities and challenge them to radical new responses to new conditions. The second title represents my conviction that meaning, belief, spirit, faith are the ultimate determinants of human action and that socio-economic changes will be judged by those determinants, humanized by them, or the outcome will be failure or disaster.

Religion is the deepest apperception of truth that human beings are capable of, for it is an apperception of truth that transcends human beings. Religious truth in its received form, coming as it necessarily does from earlier and simpler times, is always threatened by major socio-economic and scientific change. But where religious truth speaks directly to contemporary reality, which it potentially can in all of the living religious traditions—it is the task of contemporary men and women of faith to make that possible—it calls in question all the assumptions of the world and challenges us to rethink our presuppositions and redirect our energies.

There is, in short, a tension between God and the world, between ultimate reality and human illusion—all the great traditions have recognized that. For that reason the challenge is always double: from the changing world to our faith and from our faith to the changing world.

II. THE DOUBLE CHALLENGE

A Time of "Real" Crises

The "real" crises of the late twentieth century seem so overwhelming when we enumerate them that the only response possible seems to be some sort of urgent action. There is the food crisis brought on in part by the rapid expansion of the world's population. There is the energy crisis brought on by the growing recognition of the finite supply of fossil fuels but more immediately by the rapid increase in the cost of fuel. There are the explosive consequences of the widening gap between the rich and the poor all over the world. There are the political and ultimately military crises that can be seen looming not far off when the tensions created by food and energy shortages, high prices and high inflation, and the consequent unbearable poverty in large parts of the world, result in desperate acts of nations and groups within nations. The contours of these dark possibilities have been sketched in other papers for this meeting—it is not my intention here to do more than refer to them.

It is natural in the face of such terrifying realities, and even more terrifying possibilities, for some to say—as some did at Bellagio—that we cannot afford to spend our time on theology and theory. What we need is action and our concern ought to be how we can galvanize our faith communities into appropriate action as quickly and effectively as possible. I have rather serious doubts as to whether religious communities can be "mobilized" for direct action and I will spell those out later in the paper. But Wilfred Smith suggested at Bellagio that there are deeper difficulties with the idea of "using" religion to solve problems, even if that were possible.

"Faith is man's relation to ultimates, to absolutes," Wilfred Smith said. "To subordinate faith, or to try to subordinate it, to any practical purpose, however worthy, is explosively distorting." He suggested that the "use" of religion not only undermines faith but may well distort and even destroy the worthy purpose. What Smith is telling us is that people of faith must not assume that they know "what the real problems are" and attempt to use their faith in the solution of them. Faith is radical and ultimate. It speaks to what the real problems are and only when our action comes from the heart of our faith will it avoid distortion and destruction.

Crises in Minds and Souls

Smith hinted at another aspect of our late twentieth century crisis to which I would now like to turn. Overwhelmed by the reality of the crises of food, energy and poverty we may be tempted to forget that the late twentieth century is also a time of crisis in the minds and souls of men. Even when the problems are clear it is not the case that we know what to do to solve them. Indeed, many of our assumptions about how to solve our problems have led to actions that have only created new and worse problems.

"Modernization" and "development" once seemed the panaceas that would quickly bring peace and plenty. Over the last 25 years massive skepticism has grown with respect to that way of posing the problem, but genuine alternatives are as yet far from clear. To rush into action without knowing what we are doing or with ideas that produce just the opposite of what we intend is not after all very "realistic." It may be that a pause for reflection, for asking deep theoretical questions, for assessing the insights the great theological traditions of the world might have for us would be far more "realistic" than any precipitate action we could presently think of. Perhaps we are shaken enough in our confidence as modern technical men and women that a time of listening to traditional religious wisdom would be welcome.

But it may be that the overwhelming dominance of modern technical culture even in the minds of those who are critical of it makes it very difficult for us to hear what traditional religious wisdom might have to say about our present condition. Perhaps the only way to understand traditional cultures is to understand modern Western culture, the "monoculture" that invades all our consciousnesses, and that threatens to remake everything in its own image. Or perhaps the two endeavors, to understand traditional culture and the modern West, are really only one after all. Only by seeing modern Western culture in comparative perspective can we understand it or the traditions it everywhere seeks to replace.

III. VIEWING THE MODERN WEST IN COMPARATIVE PERSPECTIVE

Modern Western "Natives"

It is certainly modern Western culture that has unleashed the explosive powers that are changing the world and challenging all traditional religious communities, including Western ones. All individuals with a "modern" education (which includes surely all of the members of this symposium) are in a sense "natives" of this modern Western culture, wherever they may have been born and whatever their religious affiliation. But it is an aspect of the arrogance of modern Western culture that it does not see itself as one culture with its "natives" alongside other cultures with their "natives."

Rather, modern Western culture assumes itself to be neutral, objective, scientific, at least among its highly educated intellectuals, who are the first persons in history to have freed themselves from the distortions of myth, superstition, religion and ideology. I would submit that all of us participating in this symposium, though we have learned deeply about cultural relativity, have tended to exempt ourselves and our colleagues from that relativity when we are operating within the framework of serious intellectual reflection.

We may assume, for example, that the documents prepared for this symposium, because they are highly critical of aspects of the modern West and what Western culture has done to the world, are themselves not products of Western ideology. I would suggest that all of them (including mine) are at least in part products of such ideology and that it is part of the challenge of faith to the changing world as it applies to us that we try so far as possible to become aware of that fact.

In other words we are all, to a certain extent, modern Western "natives" and we must make the effort to stand outside ourselves in order "to see how the natives think." I am convinced that it is the great religious traditions that provide us the best places to stand in making that difficult, and perhaps for many of us even contorted, because so unaccustomed, effort at self-perception.

Limits of Modern Ideology

I will follow Louis Dumont in speaking not of culture but of the slightly narrower notion of ideology. I will, with Dumont, view ideology as "a social set of representations" that largely determine how the world appears to those who subscribe to it. There is no presumption that ideology as such is false. The term is not used pejoratively but descriptively. As Dumont says:

> The fact that one particular representation . . . is judged as true or false, rational or traditional, scientific or not, is irrelevant to the social nature of the idea or value. For example: that the earth revolves around the sun is, I take it, a scientific statement, but it is admitted by most of our contemporaries without their being able to demonstrate it. Moreover, even for those who are able to do so, this statement is part of their world view, together with many other statements they cannot demonstrate. As such, it may legitimately be taken as an integral part of the ideology as a whole, that is, as entertaining certain relations with other components of it.

To define the ideology of the modern West (or more specifically modern Western intellectuals) is a daunting undertaking but with the help of E. F. Schumacher and Louis Dumont I will make the attempt to the extent necessary for purposes of this paper. Schumacher neatly sums up modern ideology with the following terms: *positivism,* the belief that "valid knowledge can be attained only through the methods of the natural sciences"; *relativism,* the belief that there can be no valid objective knowledge about ends or norms; *reductionism,* the belief that "all the higher manifestations of human life, such as religion, philosophy, art, etc." are nothing but disguised expressions of class interests, libidinal energies or other "real" determinants; and *evolution* as based on "competition, natural selection, and the survival of the fittest."

Louis Dumont, with other problems in mind, emphasizes different but related points. For modern ideology *the individual human being* rather than society "bears the basic and ultimate value," and *the relation of man to objects* (things, nature) "is more valued than the relations between men." Because as Dumont recognizes for modern man "everything is knowable" by natural science methods (Schumacher's *positivism*) the individual, considered even as a moral individual, is basically the biological individual with his needs, desires and fears and nature is basically the disenchanted nature of modern physics. Man may have a psychological "self" but he cannot have a "soul" for that would imply that he stands in correlation with an ultimate reality of which modern ideology knows nothing. "Nature" similarly is merely matter and cannot be a "cosmos" which would again imply a context of ultimate meaning of which positivist modern ideology has no knowledge.

Piecemeal Approach Embarrassed by Religion

Dumont is also helpful in spelling out for us the implications of Schumacher's term *relativism* when he says that "modern man knows what he is doing but not what it is 'really about.'" More explicitly he says,

> . . . in the modern world each of our particular viewpoints or specialized pursuits does not know very well — or does not know at all — what it is about and the reasons for its existence or distinctness, which is more often a matter of fact than of consensus or rationality. Just as our rationality is mostly a matter of the relation between means and ends, while the hierarchy of ends is left out, so also our rationality manifests itself within each of our neatly distinct compartments but not in their distribution, definition, and arrangement.

Here Dumont is close to Wilfred Smith when he complained of modern man's tendency to separate all the various parts of life and deal with them "piecemeal," as merely presenting "technical" problems. This standard way of dealing with issues has the result, according to Smith, of leaving out the fundamental questions (which would involve the hierarchy of ends) and ignoring religion:

> These objectificationist trends also meant that the fundamentally human questions as to what sort of person one is or shall become, and what overall vision deserves one's loyalty, were hardly incorporated into the model. In this scheme, the religious tended to be seen as just one more factor in the social complex, although it was tacitly recognized as being different from the others at least by the consensus that it was to be left alone — whether because it did not really matter any more, or because it was too unmanageable.

In general, as Smith implies, when the modern intellectual has to deal with religion there is some embarrassment. There is really no place for religion in the structure of modern ideology, yet religion remains a social force, even in the West. There are also moments when one *does* have to say something about ends and one turns to religion, embarrassment and all, for there is nowhere else to turn.

Doubts in Heartland of Ideology

But for many reasons, which should be obvious to members of this symposium, doubts have arisen in the heartland of modern ideology. As Dumont puts it,

> . . . we are witnessing a crisis of the modern ideological paradigm. It is true that the tendency to see crises everywhere is strong in modern ideology and that, if crisis there be, it was not born yesterday but has been there for quite some time; in a wider sense, the crisis is more or less congenial, to the extent that some of us take pride in it. Yet, we may perhaps say that the twentieth-century crisis of the paradigm has recently gone through an intensification, deepening, or generalization.

Modern ideology and its scientific and social correlates, far from solving all the age-old problems of humankind, seem to have created a whole series of difficulties wholly unforeseen by the traditional cultures except in their darkest chiliastic visions. This being the case it is well to remember that modern ideology did not spring chastely into the world from the head of Zeus nor is it any more neutral than any other way of looking at the world.

It was born at a particular time and place with tremendous polemic intent, with powerful political, economic, and (anti-)religious ends in view, and it has never succeeded even in its heartland in replacing the older traditions that it opposed. If it dominates all of us modern educated individuals beyond our imagining, it is also true that for none of us does it supply all of our picture of the world, for it cannot. All of us, consciously or not, must live in part by ends, symbols, myths, plucked from the great storehouse of the traditional religions, for otherwise we could not live at all.

Necessity to Relativize Modern Ideology

Nonetheless, even those of us who consciously take our stand in one of the great traditions do so in ways saturated with modern ideology. And we are often all too ready to bracket our "peculiar beliefs" and deal with others in purely "secular" (modern ideological) terms. We are all to some extent aware of the schism in the soul, but to deal with it creatively is no easy matter.

What I am suggesting as a first task is to relativize the relativizer, to look at modern ideology as only one among many, as one of the native ways peculiar to us. As Dumont says, "to isolate our ideology is a sine qua non for transcending it, simply because otherwise we remain caught within it as the very medium of our thought." A brilliant observation but an enormously difficult task.

Following all the authorities I have cited so far—Schumacher, Dumont and Smith—I would suggest that the only way to isolate our ideology in order to transcend it is to place ourselves radically in another worldview that will give us comparative perspective. Indeed, each of those I have quoted have done exactly that: Schumacher with traditional Catholicism, Dumont with classical India, Smith with Islam and Hinduism.

But that is a strategy more difficult than first appears, especially when we try to use our own tradition as a point of leverage. For most of us have been brought up in a modernizing religious context where it has often seemed to be more important to show the complete congruence of our religious tradition with the features of modern Western culture and ideology than to maintain a critical distance between the two.

In the case of one tradition, my own, Protestant Christianity, many of the features of modern ideology have been directly derived from it, it has been argued. But we should not forget that Max Weber, the creator of the famous "Protestant Ethic" thesis, believed that the modern world is an "iron cage" in which the spiritual meaning of Protestantism is being destroyed.

If we are to get our proper bearings on modern ideology we must start not from liberal religion, which has already half-compromised itself in its eagerness to prove itself up-to-date, (though we must not forget the exceptional figures who, like Paul Tillich, sometimes under the banner of liberal religion have actually begun the process of the reappropriation of tradition that we need), but from the integrity of the great traditions as they were understood before modernity ever appeared. Perhaps such an endeavor is impossible—surely we cannot as modern individuals leap wholly out of our skins and become what we are not—but the effort, even if only partially successful, to see what it would be like to live in a radically different worldview may yet prove deeply instructive.

No Such Thing as "Traditional Culture"

But here we are faced with another difficulty in our endeavor to attain a comparative understanding of traditional and modern Western cultures. There is no such thing as "traditional culture," as such. The great traditional religions are as different from one another, from many points of view, as they are from the ideology of the modern West. We would be foolish to overlook or deny the diversity and even conflict between the religions. That diversity is a continuing concern of the Interreligious Peace Colloquium and was brilliantly addressed by Wilfred Smith at the Bellagio Symposium.

It may be, I think it is, true that at a high enough level of generality the great religious traditions all do contrast with some of the most fundamental assumptions of modern Western ideology. None of them could adequately be characterized by the terms positivism, relativism, reductionism and competitive evolutionism. None of them are radically individualistic in the modern sense and none of them believe the relation of man to material things is more important than the relation of man to man. But diversity is of the nature of the case in the religious traditions and we must face that issue head on before we can see how the traditional religions might instruct us in our modern plight.

IV. THE DIVERSITY OF THE RELIGIONS AND ITS RELATION TO THE HUMAN CONDITION

If modern Western ideology makes the claim, unjustified we would argue, of being rooted in no particular time and place but of simply being objectively and scientifically true, every traditional religion, however universal its claims, knows that it emerged in history and carries its historical particularity as part of its self-consciousness. Perhaps the difference is related to the fact that modern ideology takes natural science, the relation of man to nature, as its model whereas the religions take human interaction or human consciousness as their models for understanding reality.

Religions Reflect Diversity of Social Existence

In emphasizing the diversity of the religious traditions I do not want to exclude the possibility of their convergence at the highest level of spiritual aspiration. That is an important question for us and must remain open. Nor do I wish to exclude the possibility that in the very midst of the diversity it may be possible for the various faith communities to experience a sense of identity, of "we," with those of other faiths, a possibility for which Wilfred Smith has argued so eloquently that he claims it to be a necessity.

Whatever may be the case with these important possibilities the fact is that at the day-to-day level of religion as it actually operates in the lives of ordinary people there is enormous variety stemming from profound differences in geography, historical experience, social location, political tensions, etc.

Religion is so deeply rooted in the texture of ordinary social existence that it cannot but reflect the diversity of that texture. This involvement in social reality is religion's strength but also in some respects its weakness. Certainly if we imagine that it would be easy to mobilize all the world's great faith communities in an effort to deal with the grave problems of the changing world order, sociological reality will soon disabuse us of that idea.

Religions Are Not Political Monoliths

Diversity and closeness to the texture of varied social reality are features that operate not only between religions but within them. A religious community is not a political structure and certainly bears little resemblance to a modern centralized state. Wilfred Smith has suggested that there is variation between the religious communities as to how centralized they are and how "poised for action." But even the most apparently centralized structures like the Roman Catholic Church are in no sense political monoliths.

The structure of the Catholic Church varies vastly in different parts of the world. Not only are bishops in a sense kings in their own dioceses but priests are often kings in their own parishes, and the religious orders exercise enormous autonomy. To understand why Spanish Dominicans are so different from American Jesuits and a parish church in Erie, Pennsylvania, is so different from a parish church in Lucca, Italy, would involve major studies in historical sociology. It is possible to issue pronouncements in Rome, but it is not possible, not even for the Pope, to launch all the world's millions of Catholics on a campaign of social action to meet the crises of the changing world order. If that is true for the Roman Catholic Church it is all the more true for the other great religious communities.

Religions Operate Through Symbols

Religion operates usually not through the direct manipulation of political power but through the interpretation and application of symbols. It is the nature of the symbolic process, so crucial to the way religion operates, that helps us to understand why religion remains so close to the varied texture of social life. Political power can affect millions of people "externally," so to speak, through force, intimidation or simply "the rule of law." There are limits to the externality of political power. That is one of the reasons political power needs religion to legitimate it.

Politics however, can often operate "externally" where religion cannot. The reason is that religious symbols must be *internalized* in the faithful if they are to be operative. And when they are internalized they are interpreted with all the particularities of time and space that exist in the lives of the faithful. It cannot be otherwise: if religious symbols are to be effective they must touch people close to their deepest feelings.

But their deepest feelings are inevitably bound up with feelings of family, locality, language, ethnic group, race. It is not only religion as such that causes the catastrophes of Northern Ireland, Cyprus or Lebanon, but the tendency of religion to become entwined with and often to symbolize the primordial identities of populations. If the religious leaders in Northern Ireland, for example, controlled their faithful in the sense of political control we may be sure that the difficulties would long since have been over. Instead they have attempted, often working together, to reassert Christian symbols in the midst of the chaos. That process is slower and very different from the manipulation of political power, though its consequences may be major over the long haul.

In order to understand further the diversity of religious life and the reason that religious communities are not easily mobilized for direct action we may turn to a basic typology in the sociology of religion. I would like, adapting from Ernst Troeltsch, to speak of church, sect and religious movement, though I would like to use the terms so broadly that they apply to all the major religious traditions.

Role of "Church" Religion is Ambivalent

It is the essence of the church type, as I am loosely using the term, that it accepts the existing social order while trying to penetrate it with its religious values. Church type religion basically accepts the existing family system, political order and class structure while trying to mold them into closer conformity with ethical norms derived from religious insight. How successful this will be depends largely on the degree of independence that the religious community can maintain relative to non-religious structures, particularly the state.

Church religion, because it is close to the centers of power in its function of legitimating the existing order, may be effective in implementing its vision. But just that closeness to power often proves to be corrupting. Religion, instead of molding society to its own vision, may be itself molded into the image of society, offering little more than a pious sanction for the existing status quo.

Much was said at Bellagio about the role of traditional religion in apologizing for injustice and oppression instead of opposing them. The sacred is powerful and often disruptive of current beliefs and structures. Religiously inspired innovators are often viewed as troublemakers by the satisfied and the privileged. Church religion, which at its best directs the power of the sacred toward the gradual transformation of society, may instead act as a defense against the sacred and a structure of power to suppress religious innovators.

For these reasons the critique that modern ideology has leveled against religion has often been justified and modern ideology has often been liberating. But, as in many rebellions, modern ideology has itself become oppressive and stands in need of new religious critique. But we are getting ahead of ourselves.

Danger of "Sect" Religion is Irrelevance

Sect type religion attempts so far as possible to avoid compromise with society and to exist independently of the state. Normally it does not rebel against the existing order or attempt to change it through direct action. Rather, it seeks to avoid the contamination of the world while pursuing purely religious ends. The sect may nevertheless have an indirect influence on society through its demonstration effect. It offers an alternative model of living to that of the environing society. On occasion the sect may directly confront society, as when sect members refuse military service on the basis of conscientious objection. Monastic communities in various traditions have often, though not always, offered models of more just and harmonious social organization than the larger society.

The danger in the sectarian mode of being religious is that it may involve a withdrawal into harmless irrelevance in which smug concern with one's own purity replaces any genuine concern for others. The modern critique of the contemplative life in general and the monastic life in particular is that they are idle, selfish and non-productive. This criticism, though fundamentally unjust because it lacks any real understanding of the religious life, may yet be apt relative to a corrupted monasticism or a self-satisfied sectarianism.

Religious Movements and Charismatic Leaders

What I am calling the religious movement may arise from church or sect, is usually focused on a religiously charismatic leader, and, though it may eventuate in a new religious group, in its incipient phase it tends to cut across many groups and be more concerned with articulating new symbols or furthering particular ends than with creating new permanent structures. Religious movements are particularly interesting for us for they are usually the way novelty appears in religious life.

But if it is difficult to manipulate either church or sect for any particular end religious movements are even more intransigent. They do not arise on demand. No one can say, "It is time for a Luther in our tradition," or they can say it but not produce one. Luthers come as the spirit moves them, so to speak. Who could have predicted a

Gandhi or a Martin Luther King? The danger in religious movements is that, as religions have long known, there are false prophets as well as true ones and it is not always easy to discern which is which.

Yet for all their intransigence and for all the difficulty in discerning truth and falsehood among them it is probably religious movements and their charismatic leaders that are most likely to provide spiritual insight into our problems and religious inspiration for their solution. Yet, as we have seen, such movements cannot be concocted. Perhaps all that a group of intelligent laymen and clerics at a symposium meeting in a lovely hotel can do is to try to discern those movements and leaders in the world that deserve our support and encouragement and prepare ourselves to be sensitive to the emergence of those that are to come. Some reflection on past movements and leaders of this type may be helpful in both regards.

Embodied Symbols are Most Powerful

Religion, as we have seen, affects people not primarily through political power but through symbols. It is the religiously charismatic leader and his movement that articulate new symbols and ideas, usually not out of whole cloth but as a reworking of tradition. Often, however, the leader of a movement is freer in his reworking of tradition and freer in his borrowing from other traditions than is the spokesman of church or sect. Sometimes such a leader is primarily a thinker and through the sheer power of his writing and speaking achieves an influence over large numbers of people often in many countries. One can think of Rabindrinath Tagore or Mohammed 'Abduh or D. T. Suzuki or Paul Tillich or Martin Buber.

But the most powerful religious symbol is the embodied symbol, the person (or the movement) whose whole life shows forth the meaning of religious truth. Of course all those I have just mentioned embodied to more than a small extent what they preached, as did, for example, E. F. Schumacher. But it is leaders like Gandhi or Vinoba Bhave or Uchimura Kanzō or Martin Luther King who by the radical commitment of their lives remind us most of the saints and founders of the past. Or one thinks of Simone Weil, more a solitary than a leader but whose life challenges every assumption of the twentieth century.

This is not the place to summarize in detail the various teachings of these outstanding thinkers and leaders. Yet I believe there is more than a little convergence among these twentieth century saints and theologians. Some of this is due to actual influence. Everyone knows that Gandhi was nourished by the New Testament and Tolstoy as well as by the Hindu scriptures, just as everyone knows that Martin Luther King was influenced by Gandhi. Yet I believe much of the convergence derives from the similar reaction of religiously sensitive persons to certain trends of life in the twentieth century. Some of these convergences will appear in the final section of this paper.

In presenting the typology of church, sect and movement I do not mean to imply that these are watertight categories. If movements originate out of churches and sects they also permeate and transform them. By offering new symbols or reinterpreting old ones they change the symbolic climate of whole cultures. We are used to thinking of change in economic and political terms but it is symbolic change that goes the deepest and lasts the longest.

If we are to surmount the growing crises of the late twentieth century, symbolic transformation must be part of the process. It is possible that traditional religion freshly embodied in individuals and groups may provide much of that symbolic transformation that may deflect us from the fatal course upon which modern ideology has embarked us.

V. THE RELIGIOUS CRITIQUE OF MODERNITY AND ITS SIGNIFICANCE FOR THE NEW WORLD ORDER

Modern Ideology Mimics Religion

Seen in comparative perspective modern ideology, though it usually despises or ignores religion, is itself religious, in that it unconsciously mimics and performs many of the functions of traditional religion. It demands faith, indeed a rather uncritical form of faith, in its basic assumptions (positivism, etc.) to such an extent that I have on occasion referred to it as "enlightenment fundamentalism." It has a well developed soteriology. It is a form of self-salvation but it often reifies the salvific agent so that it seems that "science," or "technology," or "economic development" will save us. The classical bearer of modern salvation was "Progress," but the deepening crisis of modern ideology to which Dumont referred has made that word a bit less magical and less frequently invoked. It lurks just below the surface, however, of much modern rhetoric.

Modern Ideology, the Religion of Many Intellectuals

Because of the nature of modern ideology — it knows nothing that cannot be known by natural science, it knows of means but not of ends — it tends to concentrate on a this-worldly instrumentalism as the solution to all problems, social, psychological, and cultural. It assumes that if only our tangible instrumentalities are developed enough, in short if our technology is able to produce sufficient wealth and power, all our problems will be solved. Disease, poverty, even war can be overcome.

Since modern ideology has a strongly naturalistic bent it tends to concentrate on rather material considerations, two of which have become almost obsessively central: physical comfort and mastery of the environment. I might reiterate here that no society has ever embraced modern ideology in unadulterated form. Every society, however "advanced," continues to draw sustenance from traditional moral and religious beliefs, often in uneasy tandem with modern ideology. This does not make modern ideology any the less pervasive, particularly among intellectuals.

Religion and Modern Ideology are Profoundly Incompatible

Traditional religions, whatever the differences between them, tend to be skeptical of modern ideology as an adequate response to the human condition. They believe that, however problematic it may be, it is possible to know about more than the purely material. They live in the *metaxy* (Plato: *Symposium* 202-203), the "In-Between," the spiritual realm between the divine and the human. The traditional religions, however variously they may express it, hold forth an ideal of human fulfillment, both personal and inter-personal, that goes far beyond the search for wealth and power, comfort and control, because it promises to bring human life into some kind of harmony with the Holy or the Good that infinitely transcends it.

From the point of view of the traditional religions, modern ideology, in its search for material salvation cultivates just those motives, greed, envy, the desire for domination, that most undercut the possibility of spiritual fulfillment. Among other things the stress on the relation between the individual person and nature in modern ideology tends to make human community a secondary phenomenon derived as an instrumentality for the pursuit of rational self-interest. For the traditional religions self-interest alone provides no adequate basis for community, since real community must be grounded in common spiritual aspiration, mutual love, and compassion.

With respect to all of these issues modern ideology has vigorously counter-attacked religion. Religion, it is claimed, prevents people from improving their lot in this world by leading them into illusory dreams about another world. Religion relies on ineffective moralistic preachments while modern ideology builds on real human motives. Religious communal solidarities undermine effective political mobilization and create bitter hostility toward other religious groups, whereas the rational self-interested individual is the only true citizen of the modern world.

Finally, in its Marxist form, modern ideology attacks religion as a bulwark of privilege and oppression, an instrument of the ruling class. We have detailed these criticisms and counter-criticisms not so much in order to adjudicate between them as to show how profoundly incompatible the basic premises of the two ways of thinking are.

Religion's Long Tradition of Social Criticism

We must remember, however, that social criticism, an insistence on justice and equality, can be found in the religions centuries and even millennia before the birth of modern ideology. This criticism has not always been effective, to be sure, but neither has its impact ever been wholly lost. Let us cite a few examples.

From the *Hebrew Scriptures:*
Hear this, you who trample upon the needy,
    and bring the poor of the land to an end, . . .
Shall not the land tremble on this account,
    and every one mourn who dwells in it, . . .
                                        (Amos 8. 4 & 8)

From the *New Testament:*
    Come now, you rich, weep and howl for the miseries that are coming upon you. Your riches have rotted and your garments are moth-eaten. Your gold and silver have rusted, and their rust will be evidence against you and will eat your flesh like fire. You have laid up treasure for the last days. Behold, the wages of the laborers who mowed your fields, which you kept back by fraud, cry out; and the cries of the harvesters have reached the ears of the Lord of hosts.
                                        (James 5. 1-4)

The *early Christian church* worked out the doctrine of the natural equality of the goods of the earth and attributed inequality to human sin. Victricius about 400 A.D. wrote:

Does the rich man enjoy the blessings of fresh air more than the poor man? Does he feel the sun's heat more keenly or less? When earth received the gift of rain, do larger drops fall upon the rich man's field than upon the poor man's . . . What God himself distributes . . . is shared equally; what we own in unjust inequality is everything whose distribution was entrusted to human control . . . Is there one sacrament, one law for the rich, another for the poor? . . . inequality of wealth is not to be blamed upon the graciousness of God, but upon the iniquity of men.

Saint Thomas Aquinas believed that men are only stewards of the goods of the earth. For a starving man to take food from a rich man is not theft, for the rich man has no just claim to a superabundance of food while the poor are starving.

John Winthrop, first governor of Massachusetts, wrote in his famous shipboard sermon of 1630, "A Modell of Christian Charity":

Now the onely way to avoyde this shipwracke and to provide for our posterity is to followe the Counsell of Micah, to doe justly, to love mercy, to walke humbly with our God. For this end, wee must be knitt together in this worke as one man, wee must entertaine each other in brotherly Affeccion, wee must be willing to abridge our selves of our superfluities, for the supply of others necessities, we must uphold a familiar Commerce together in all meeknes, gentlenes, patience and liberality, wee must delight in each other, make others Condicions our owne, rejoyce together, mourne together, labour and suffer together . . .

Winthrop's words, intended for the Massachusetts Bay Colony might well be applied to the world today.

Islam is rooted in the fundamental belief in the equality of all believers. Injustice toward the poor and oppression of the people by despotic government have sparked revolts led by ulama (religious leaders) in many parts of the Muslim world in pre-modern times.

Nizam al Mulk in his advice to princes wrote: In the eyes of God (be He exalted) there is no sin greater than a king's sin. The right way for a king to acknowledge God's grace is by looking after his subjects, giving them justice, and preserving them from oppressors. When a king is a tyrant all his courtiers begin to practice tyranny; they become forgetful of God and ungrateful for His bounty. Verily God abandons them in his wrath . . .

Again, *Ibn Khaldun,* a great thinker but also a qadi, a judge in the system of Muslim religious law, explicated what Muhammad had in mind when he forbade injustice:

Injustice should not be understood to imply only the confiscation of money or other property from the owners, without compensation and without cause. It is commonly understood in that way, but it is something more general than that. Whoever takes someone's property, or uses him for forced labor, or presses an unjustified claim against him, or imposes upon him a duty not required by the religious law, does an injustice to that particular person. People who collect unjustified taxes commit an injustice.

Those who infringe upon property (rights) commit an injustice. Those who deny people their rights commit an injustice.

It may be more difficult to find such sharp assertions of justice and equality in the *Hindu and Buddhist traditions*. But the life of the ashram or sangha is a living example of justice and equality. Non-dualism, an essential belief in Buddhism and some strands of Hinduism is perhaps the most radical of all rejections of inequality, even though it has not often been used as the basis for the criticism of the existing social order.

Justice and Equality Not Ends in Themselves

I wished to give a series of examples for the sake of concreteness. But taking these quotations and examples out of context runs the risk of misunderstanding. Justice and equality for the religious traditions are not ends in themselves, useful norms for the construction of a social order where individuals can pursue their self-interest with as little constraint as possible, as they have often been for modern ideology.

Rather, they are part of an over-arching set of beliefs that link God or ultimate reality to the cosmos, to human community and to the individual soul. They take on their meaning and value as part of the religious life, the spiritual aspiration of men to do the will of God or enact religious truth. They are a part of a whole set of symbols and images that would limit man's inexorable drive toward wealth and power, comfort and control. They would assert the finitude and limits of the human condition. Thus even when the religious traditions speak the same language as modern ideology the meanings may be different and the tensions between them deep.

Special Meaning of "Needs" and "Rights"

All the faith communities are challenged by the immense changes taking place in the world today to reach back into their traditions and find the teachings that would be applicable to our present condition. Such application cannot be mechanical—it involves the painful labor of interpretation. That labor cannot be avoided simply by repeating the old language without seeing how it relates to present circumstances. But neither can it be avoided by simply translating traditional teachings into terms derived from modern ideology.

Just to take an example of the latter sort, in several papers for this symposium it is suggested that basic human needs and rights may provide criteria for evaluating a "New International Economic Order." Such a suggestion is a valuable one. However, "needs" and "rights" are key terms in modern ideology. Needs in that context are grounded basically in biological appetites and rights derive essentially from the right of self-preservation as the highest of all rights. Placed in a religious context the terms take on entirely different meanings.

"Needs" in this case would include not only the individual appetites but the needs for community, meaning and spiritual aspiration. "Rights" would be grounded not merely in the self-preservation of the individual but in divine justice, law, or dharma.

Above all, the use of "needs" and "rights" in a religious context would involve a critique of how those terms have been used precisely to justify the devotion to the endless accumulation of wealth and power that has done so much to create our problems. If the poor and powerless of the earth simply wish to join the presently privileged in their quest for wealth and power the result will only increase the rate of our escalating crises. Only an assertion of needs and rights in the context of a general critique of modern ideology could contribute to the solution of our long-run problems.

Here I can merely cite the teachings of those thinkers and saints that I have referred to above. In Winthrop's words, only if we can "make others' conditions our own, rejoyce together, mourne together, labour and suffer together," are we likely to survive on this planet.

The religious communities of the world are divided and not very well organized. If one were looking to them with an eye to political mobilization one would be discouraged indeed. In many parts of the world the religious communities are still reeling from the intellectual and ethical critique of modern ideology. Many of the ablest intellectuals and young leaders have abandoned religion and espouse secular causes that derive from the basic premises of modern Western ideology.

Yet the religious traditions remain the guardians of the deepest truths men and women have discovered and the still small voices are to be heard everywhere by those who would listen. Perhaps that is our most important task at this symposium: to listen and to discern as far as we are able what the world is saying to us and what the religiously inspired are saying in return.

VI. A PERSONAL CONCLUSION

As I reflect on what I have written it is clear to me that my paper is implicitly autobiographical. Perhaps some of the fervor in my attack on modern ideology derives from the fact that I was once a believer in it, as a university student in its Marxist form, later in its positivist social scientific form. Even though I was never wholly convinced I did see the world through the categories of positivism, relativism, reductionism and competitive evolutionism. That was an interlude, however, between my having been raised as a Christian and my later return to an appreciation of the meaning and validity of Christianity and also of several other religious traditions.

But in fairness I should say that it was important for my maturation that I went through the phase of modern ideology. It liberated me from all kinds of narrownesses and parochialisms. It left a permanent residuum that I would not want to reject. It has also made my return to religion different from the religion of my childhood. Here I would invoke Paul Ricoeur's notion of a "second naiveté," forever different from primary naiveté. The second naiveté is religious faith not in spite of criticism (using "criticism" to represent modern ideology at its best: a negative but cleansing critique), but religious faith achieved in and through criticism. Another way of speaking is to use the phrase "dialectic of return." Having experienced something radically other, one returns to one's faith in a new way.

What was true for me personally is I think also true historically. Traditional religions have often been terribly narrow, immensely repressive and oppressive, both personally and socially. Modern ideology in its early phase and still today for many of us has its liberating role. Yet where modern ideology is not part of a dialectic of return, where it becomes absolute in itself, it is, I believe, deeply destructive. It is the ideological counterpart of all those structures that threaten us today—uncontrolled technology, bureaucracy, the worship of means and the loss of ends. At another moment I might have been championing it. At this moment I am opposing it, at least in its reified form.

It is well to remember that what I have called modern ideology does not include everything thought by modern intellectuals. There has been a civil war within the modern mind. My own discipline, sociology, particularly in its French roots and in the work of Emile Durkheim, was as much or more a protest against modern ideology as an exemplar of it, a point recently emphasized by Louis Dumont. William Blake, who could hardly be called "traditionally religious," was already in the late 18th century worrying about the "dark satanic mills" and their intellectual progenitors, Bacon and Newton and Locke.

There is certainly in the West and incipiently in other parts of the world a third tradition critical of traditional religion and modern ideology alike. Without coming to terms with and reappropriating the enormous resources of traditional religion this third tradition may be too slender to oppose the massive weight of modernity. But as a catalytic and suggestive tendency it has much to teach us.

We are in these late years of the 20th century, as I have written elsewhere, "at sea and in a rising storm." None of the three traditions to which I have pointed can in their received form save us. Only our own intelligence and will as intellectuals and as citizens, together surely with what Paul Tillich called "the structure of grace in history," can make it possible for us to avoid shipwreck.

REFERENCES

Louis Dumont, *From Mandeville to Marx: The Genesis and Triumph of Economic Ideology,* University of Chicago Press, 1977.

Paul Ricoeur, *The Symbolism of Evil,* Harper and Row, 1967.

E. F. Schumacher, *Small is Beautiful: Economics as if People Mattered,* Harper and Row, 1973.

Wilfred Cantwell Smith, "Divisiveness and Unity," Chapter 5 in *Food/Energy and the Major Faiths: An Interpretive Account of the Interreligious Peace Colloquium,* Joseph Gremillion, ed., Orbis Books, 1978.

SUMMARY

Bellah begins by refusing to consider that a changing world order is a one-way challenge for faith communities, because of his conviction that meaning, belief, spirit, faith are ultimate determinants of human action. For him the challenge is always double: from the changing world to our faith and from our faith to the changing world.

He then proceeds to describe modern Western ideology and its limits, and shows how in its piece-meal approach it is embarrassed by religion. He sees as a first task of religion that of "relativizing the relativizer" that is modern ideology—the practical religion of many intellectuals today—and letting it be seen for what it is, one of the "native" ways of perceiving reality.

This task will be difficult because of the great diversity among religions' traditions. However, in their fundamental assumptions, all religions stand in stark contrast to modern ideology. For example, the stress on the relation between the individual person and nature in modern ideology tends to make human community a secondary phenomenon derived as an instrumentality for the pursuit of rational self-interest. Whereas, for the traditional religions, self-interest alone provides no adequate basis for community, since real community must be grounded in common spiritual aspiration, mutual love, and compassion.

In assessing the influence of religions, we must be aware that religions—even the Roman Catholic religion—are not political monoliths, and that they usually operate most effectively through embodied symbols. That is why religious movements with charismatic leaders usually are more creative than either "sect" or "church" religions, though these categories are not mutually exclusive.

However vulnerable in practice they may be to modern ideology's criticism of indulging in illusory dreams, all religions have a long tradition of social criticism—a historical fact that Bellah exemplifies for the different world religions.

Finally, he cautions religious leaders that in the current dialogue, justice and equality cannot for them be ends in themselves, and that "needs" and "rights" have special meaning in a religious context that cannot be presumed in popular usage.

In a personal concluding note, Bellah reflects that the implicitly autobiographical nature of his paper accounts for his fervor in attacking modern ideology. He admits that there is a third tradition critical of traditional religion and modern ideology alike, but he fears that it has not yet sufficiently come to terms with or reappropriated the enormous resources of traditional religion.

8

A Muslim Response

Khurshid Ahmad

Khurshid Ahmad, formerly a citizen of Pakistan, presently lives in England and is Director General of the Islamic Foundation, Leicester. He is also advisor to King Abdul Aziz University, Jeddah, and Vice Chairperson of the First International Conference on Islamic Economics at the same university; a member of the Executive Committee, Islamic Council of Europe; and Vice President of the Standing Conference on Jews, Christians, and Muslims in Europe. Among his many past positions, Ahmad was editor of THE NEW ERA, a Karachi weekly, as well as of CHIRAGH-E-RAH, a Karachi monthly. He has lectured and published widely on the Pakistan economy, the Third World's dilemma of development, the meaning and message of Islam, the principles of Islamic education, family life in Islam, and Islam and the West.

I. INTRODUCTION

Although an economist by profession and training, I have no hesitation in suggesting that the problems involved in changing the world economic order are too serious and too complicated to be left solely to the economists or the politicians of our time. It augurs well that the religious leaders of four major faith-oriented communities are meeting here to deliberate upon the issues that confront mankind in the context of the contemporary international economic crisis.

My own interest in the subject is rooted in my two major roles, that of an economist and more important that of being a Muslim, a worker in the Islamic movement. Yet, these two roles do not drive my thoughts into conflicting directions; instead my ideas and aspirations, emanating from both these roles converge amicably. Separation between economics and religion has launched economics into chaotic waters on the one hand, and driven religion into isolation from life and its multifarious problems. Fresh efforts are needed to impregnate economic thinking with moral insights. The present symposium can make some contribution towards this challenging end.

I propose to present this paper in two parts. First, I will make a few observations on the subject of the main paper written by Professor Robert Bellah, outlining the relation between faith and the changing world economy. Secondly, I will present my own response, as a Muslim economist, to the overall problem of the new international economic order.

II. RELIGION'S PLACE AND ROLE

Professor Bellah's paper is full of stimulating ideas and insights. His formulation of the problem is clear and incisive. That the changing world order could be a challenge to faith-oriented communities is acknowledged on all hands, but what is not realized generally is that faith can be, and is, a challenge to the changing world order. It is idle to assume that religion is necessarily at the receiving end. This is somewhat typical of the West to always formulate the proposition in a way that would assign a secondary position to religion. It is fashionable to assume that religion must change to give way to the demands of economic and political change. Professor Bellah brings into sharp focus the other dimension, suggesting how faith could be looked upon as a challenge to the changing economic scene and be a positive factor influencing its future dynamics.

Professor Bellah's critique of modern Western ideology has especially interested me. His presentation is as thoughtful as it is sharp
and trenchant. He has candidly shown the limitations and biases of
the Western approach. That helps one to some extent in having a
clearer idea about how and why humankind has been plunged into
its contemporary crisis. This part of his presentation is illuminating.

I have, however, strong reservations about some of his other observations, particularly the ones about the nature of religion and its
role in the solution of human problems. I am afraid his approach remains very much tainted, albeit unconsciously, by the biases of the
Western ideology which he has so forcefully criticized.

The idea of the "mobilization of faith communities" for "direct
action," of the "use" of religion "to solve problems," of "religion going beyond the articulation and internalization of symbols" by creating "new structures" are not necessarily repugnant and self-defeat-
ing, as he seems unfortunately to assume. His typology of religion is
very much attuned to the history of the religious tradition of the West.
He has failed to comprehend all the ramifications of the movement
type model of religion. He gives an exaggerated importance to the
idea of 'religiously charismatic leader' and too little to the social
transformation and societal reconstruction that such an approach
involves.

I feel strongly that the Islamic model does not conform to any of
the three arch-types he has outlined. I will try to elucidate some aspects of the Islamic approach in the second part of my paper, and
would like to submit that religion can be a factor of critical importance
in our search for a new world order.

III. ISLAM AND THE NEW WORLD ORDER

A. Grounds For Hope and Disappointment

A careful perusal of the current debate on the New International
Economic Order leaves one with two rather conflicting feelings: hope
and disappointment. The fact that some of the major incongruities
and injustices that characterize relationships between individuals,
institutions and nations in our times are no longer being accepted
passively as a fait accompli, and the fact that the need for changing
the present state of affairs is being voiced from all quarters and not
merely by the aggrieved parties, give some cause for hope. Smug
complacency over the status quo that has held the ground for so long
has now begun to dissipate.

This in itself is a significant development, as it opens up new opportunities for review and reappraisal, for fresh thinking and for an

examination of alternatives available to humankind, in its search for creative possibilities to rebuild and restructure society and its institutions. This gives rise to new hope, even though it be a tiny flicker. The worry, however, is that this little newborn flicker of light and hope is trembling in the face of confounding winds. The level at which the entire debate is taking place is, to put it frankly and bluntly, quite disappointing.

B. Themes and Issues in the NIEO Debate

It would be fair to suggest that the discussion on the New International Economic Order in almost all international forums, academic as well as political, is being undertaken at three levels—descriptive, analytic and prescriptive.

1) The Level of Description

At the level of description, the plight of the Third World is being brought into focus. There is an increasing acknowledgement of the revolting facts of poverty, misery and deprivation, of disease and illiteracy, of death and starvation, of underdevelopment and retardation of growth, of widening gaps in economic wellbeing and the mounting weight of international debts, of deteriorating terms of trade and depletion or mismanagement of natural resources, of apathy and misdevelopment.

The failure of the developmental effort made over the last three decades in the underdeveloped world, which contains two thirds of the human race, and the deterioration of relations between the developed and the underdeveloped worlds are being highlighted. The leaders of the Third World are becoming more and more vocal and assertive. Those who speak for the industrialized world are increasingly willing to acknowledge some of these realities, even though still haltingly and with reservations.

There is greater consciousness of the transfer of resources from the Third World to the developed world because of a number of built-in mechanisms in international trade which favor the industrialized world and limit the options open to the Third World. The prices of raw materials have been a very unstable factor, with the result that the relative value of the exports of the Third World has been going down, while that of their imports from the industrialized world has been increasing. Many an effort to stabilize the prices of raw materials has been frustrated because it has been regarded as being against the interests of the industrialized world.

The first significant effort on the part of the Third World to gain control over the prices of their products has been the case of oil. This attempt to get an economic price of an essential source of energy has been treated as a declaration of war against the industrialized world. Utterly neglected has been the fact that the North has deliberately kept the price of oil much lower than its real economic price and has built its own economic prosperity by keeping this source of energy cheap.

The technological dependence of the Third World on the industrialized world, and the unsuitability of the technology of the North to the conditions of the Third World, is another major theme in the debate. In spite of some transfer of technology, it is claimed that the new technology is unable to act as an internalized agent of growth. Instead, it is producing new technological destabilization, without really meeting the technological needs of these societies. Moreover, this increases the technological dependence of the Third World on the North and as the prices of capital goods are escalating, this technological dependence is also producing financial dependence.

The hope that foreign aid would act as the chief stimulant to development in the Third World countries has been dashed to pieces. In view of these failures, the Third World countries are asking for a new deal. In the new deal, they are demanding, among others, the following changes.

(a) A restructuring of the international institutions, particularly of the International Monetary Fund, the World Bank and the operative organs of the U.N., particularly at the Security Council. The first major demand of these developing countries is the restructuring of the international institutions so that they may have a greater voice in economic and political decision making at the international level.

(b) Their second major demand is for an acknowledgement of national sovereignty over their own raw materials. This would mean that a country, where a certain raw material or source of energy is found, should have the right to own it, to price it and to benefit from it. Presently, these raw materials are either in the hands of multinational corporations, which are not fully under the control of the national governments, or their extraction, development and trade are so much under the influence of the developed countries that the latter are in a controlling position to manipulate prices and supplies. This puts these resources at the mercy of outside forces.

(c) Their third demand is for revision in the international division of labor. The present situation perpetuates the role of the Third World as producers of raw materials, while the industrialized world specializes in the production of secondary and tertiary goods. It also leads to the type of economic development the Third World is expected to have, with its consequences for the relative shares of economic power allotted to different parts of the world.

(d) Freedom of movement for their goods, particularly for their manufactured products, but also for agricultural and dairy produce, into West European and American markets is another demand of the underdeveloped world. They insist on access to these markets to accelerate their own economic development while seeking some permanent mechanism to stabilize prices.

(e) Finally, because the financing of development is becoming more and more difficult, Third World countries are now suggesting some form of compulsory transfer of resources from rich to poor countries through international institutions, as against bilateral aid. Due to the deterioration of the terms of trade, most of the underdeveloped countries are facing balance of payments crises, and foreign aid has failed to provide any real relief.

First of all, "foreign aid" is a misnomer because it is not a grant or subsidy. Almost 90 per cent of it is made up of tied loans, extended on commercial terms, and subject to a number of restrictions. The result is that the net benefit is often in favor of the giver more than receiver. The volume of aid is also far below the needs of the developing world. Total foreign aid from the developed world is substantially below the targets set by the U.N. for the 1960's and 1970's, with the result that the voluntary transfer of resources from the rich to the poor is not taking place. Then too, the burden of external debt has risen excessively high, and quite a significant part of the export earnings of most of the Third World countries is eaten up in service charges and debt repatriation.

This is why the Third World is now suggesting some form of compulsory transfer of resources. There is a general feeling in the Third World that the time has come when, instead of negotiating about each one of their specific problems, they must try to enter into a new deal with the North to restructure economic relations worldwide. And so a number of possible bargaining packages and strategies have been developed to help bring about a new economic order.

2) The Levels of Analysis and Prescription

At the level of analysis and consequent prescription, there is wide divergence of opinion. Even when some of the facts about international economic disorder are not in dispute, there is great controversy about the factors responsible for them.

Most economists and statesmen from the rich North emphasize the fact of greater interdependence between different parts of the world and the relative obsolescence of the idea of national sovereignty and autarchy. They throw light on the benefits that the Third World has derived from its contacts with the industrialized world and the continuing help and assistance the North is extending to it. They suggest that natural economic factors are not being allowed to play effectively their proper role and thus yield their final benefits.

They also suggest that the internal organization of society and the economy in the Third World countries leaves much to be desired, with the result that it obstructs efforts towards economic development. According to this thesis the prosperity of the two is interdependent. The Third World can prosper only if the industrialized world prospers. Anything that damages the North and its economic prospects is bound to adversely affect the prospects of the Third World.[1]

Third World theorists too have now developed a framework for the analysis of the relationship of their countries with the North. As against the North's concept of a benevolent world economy, in which their growth and prosperity results in spreading wealth to the under-developed world, the general thesis of these writers is that the industrialized countries constitute the powerful central core of the world economy, while the entire Third World is its weak periphery, dependent upon this center which sucks in resources from the periphery. The result is a hierarchical and exploitative world order with built-in arrangements for the transfer of resources from the underdeveloped to the developed world. Development and underdevelopment are not two autonomous realities, but two aspects of the same process. This state of affairs has its roots in the imperialist mode of production, established during the colonial period and it continues unabated today, although some of its forms and instruments of control have changed. The multinational corporation now figures very prominently as the midwife of this neo-imperialism.

These theorists argue that the Third World cannot reasonably hope to achieve self-sustaining development without breaking away from this system of dependence and bondage.[2] Marxian analysts try to develop this thesis in the context of their own thinking on the nature and dynamics of international capitalism and of imperialism and neo-imperialism, while other analysts lay greater emphasis on the elements and structures of dependence without committing themselves definitively to the nature of the system.

The prescription each group offers for the solution of the contemporary international economic crisis emerges largely from their analysis of its causes. Most Northern economists believe that solutions to the problems raised are possible within the overall framework of the present order through more efficient allocation and use of resources, and by transfer payments within the system. The Third World group, on the other hand, insists that structural changes are an essential precondition for any real change in the situation.

C. The Real Challenge of our Times

This lengthy digression recapitulates the mood and the themes of the debate on the new international economic order. The facts of the situation are not very much in dispute. The 'interdependence' thesis and the 'dependentia' theorem both contain elements of truth, but none of them goes far enough to explain the whole truth. They remain partial in their explanation of the present crisis. Each explanation is very much rooted in the overall sympathy-framework to which the analyst happens to belong, psychologically, culturally and economically.

My contention, on the other hand, is that the crisis is not confined to economic relations and institutions. It is rather an all-pervading crisis, and as such, the real causes will have to be traced in the context of the crisis of civilization and not merely of the economic order. It is too partisan and consequently too unrealistic to assume that the disease is specific to the context of capitalism.

The basic problems that confront us today are very similar, whether under capitalism or socialism. In fact, both these systems are products of the same culture system, Western civilization. Capitalism and socialism are both equally exploitative and unjust. The establishment of a just and humane order for the moral wellbeing of people is not their primary concern. They deal with different blueprints of mechanistic structures of society. Their real failure has not been their inability to answer correctly some basic questions but their inability to ask the right questions. They do not treat the universe as a moral order. They regard men and women as self-sufficient, and regard material and economic progress as their real objective. They cannot offer as ultimate goals anything higher than material privileges: economic wealth, political power, military strength, international influence. Conflict of interests is built into this concept of life, and is bound to result in a crisis of values.

Because Joseph A. Camilleri, a perceptive analyst of contemporary history, describes this crisis of our times brilliantly, I quote him here at length:

"The contemporary human crisis is so profound and pervasive that the very attempt to analyze it—let alone resolve it—seems to defy the power of human reason and imagination. The battle for survival is currently being waged by millions of men whose precarious existence is one of poverty, squalor and even hunger. Man's predicament impinges on the future of entire nations that are threated by external attack or internal disintegration. It dominates the vast network of international relations so delicately poised on the dangerous and ultimately unstable 'balance of terror'. . . .

Traditional conceptions of time, space and movement have been overthrown by the technological revolution and the shift to an exploitative, power-centered culture. The ensuing social and psychological discontinuity and moral vacuum have produced a severe crisis of conscience and a large-scale flight from reality. . . .

The crisis which confronts twentieth century man is truly global, not simply by virtue of countless men and women, but in the more far-reaching sense that it permeates and vitiates the whole fabric of human relations and human institutions, and is now distorting man's entire relationship with the natural order. . . . No human community, no individual, no corner of the globe, however remote or isolated, however powerful or well endowed, can now escape from the disorder which affects the entire planet. . . . Perhaps we can best describe the global crisis in terms of a fundamental disequilibrium which severely limits and may ultimately destroy man's capacity for biological and cultural adaptation to his environment.

Among the most common forms of pathological behaviour in modern industrial society, one would include the preoccupation with having and acquiring, rather than with being or becoming; the obsession with the power to dominate rather than liberate; the profound sense of alienation from rather than participation in the wider social reality; the attitude towards work and leisure as means of killing time rather than creatively living in time, the predisposition to an in-group rather than an out-group psychology which discriminates on the basis of sex, race, creed or nationality; the tendency to resolve conflicts through the use or threat of force. . . . What distinguishes the super-industrial system—and the global spread of its empire—is the high degree with which social pathology has been institutionalized through the pyramidal stratification of wealth, power and knowledge, but above all through the growing monopoly of industrial production over the satisfaction of human wants. . . . The institutional integration of pathological behaviour has now reached such proportions that it is not merely the quality but the very survival of human life which is at risk. . . . If this is an accurate diagnosis of the serious and deteriorating condition of our civilization, then no piece-meal, provisional, or parochial remedy is likely to prove efficacious. It would appear that in order to sustain the organic evolution of the human species it will be necessary to develop perspectives and responses that are both radical and global in inspiration." [3]

D. A New World Order—Not Just NIEO

In face of this real challenge to humankind today, all men and women of faith must state with all the force at their command that the real issue is not simply one of a new international economic order but of a new world order, based on a new concept of the human person and a different vision of society and of the destiny of the human community. Any effort at reform under the inspiration of the world faiths in general and of Islam in particular must start by correcting this perspective for understanding the human predicament.

The real need is not to seek concessions here and there to bring about some changes in the superstructures. It is rather to re-examine the foundations on which the entire structure of society and the economy is built and the ideals which the culture aspires to achieve. The crisis in economic and political relations is the natural outcome of those ideals and the structures which have been built to realize them. Islam, therefore, suggests that it is only through inviting humankind towards a new vision of man and society that its house can be set in order. This calls for a basic change in our approach. This change of approach must contain the following elements:

1) More than a new economic arrangement

The real problem is more basic and covers a much wider area than that of mere economic crisis. As such the economic crisis deserves to be examined in the wider context of the overall human crisis—of the crisis of civilization. Our objective should be to strive for the establishment of a just and humane world order and not merely to create a new economic arrangement. This cannot be done in isolation from the totality of the human situation.

2) A value-oriented or moral approach

Economic analysis provides valuable insights but it is idle to assume that even economic problems can be solved merely by resort to the tools of economic analysis and policy. People's efforts to solve economic problems by isolating the economic from the total matrix of the moral are collapsing in futility. Economic science is moving deeper and deeper into the throes of a crisis. For if crisis in a science is symbolized by its continued inability to meet the challenges that confront it, then few would disagree that economics is in serious trouble.

The phoenix-like rise of macro-economics from the charred debris of the crash of the 1930's generated a new confidence and valor among economists. A solution to almost every problem seemed within sight. All looked green in the valley of economics. This confidence has proved false and short-lived. Not only the old problems have remained unsolved; new ones have emerged with threatening overtones. Mass poverty; frustrated take-offs in development; increasing disparities at regional, national and international levels; coexistence of hunger and affluence; irrational use of non-renewable resources; incongruity between technology and developmental needs; unsuitability of production and consumption processes to environmental needs; exploitation of the poor and the afflicted by the rich and powerful; inflation and stagflation; structural deformities in relations between developed and developing countries; all of these and many more problems fail to be tackled within the framework developed by post-Keynsian economics. This is being realized even by those economists who had earlier thought that their sophisticated economic models could now deliver the goods.

Nobel Laureate, Paul Samuelson, for example, of the Massachusetts Institute of Technology (MIT) laments the disarray into which economic theory has fallen. He warns "there are no signs that we're converging towards a philosopher's stone that will cause all the pieces to fall neatly into place." Professor Otto Eckstein of Harvard says, "We are always one inflation too late in specifying the exact form of the price-forecasting equation." And Robert Heilbroner goes a step further when he says, "Economists are beginning to realize that they have built a rather elaborate edifice on rather unsubstantial narrow foundations."

The predicament of economics has been searchingly examined by Kurt Dopfer in his *Economics in the Future: Towards a New Paradigm*.[4] The near consensus that emerges is that what is needed to salvage "the duck of economics" from the "tangled weed" in which it is stuck at the bottom of a rubbish-ridden pool—to use Veblen's analogy—is not just some new interpretation of this or that economic theory or some changes within the current paradigm of economics. There is, rather, need to change the paradigm itself and to move towards a new paradigm under which economic problems can be approached not as economic problems in isolation but in the context of an entire social system and as part of the overall moral problem.[5] What is needed is a widening of our approach from merely an isolated economic approach to a moral approach within which the technical aspects of the economic approach are fully assimilated.

Our approach should be value-oriented. In economics, as in any branch of human activity, there is an area which deals with technological relationships. But such technological relationships *per se* are not the be-all and end-all of a social discipline. Technological relationships are important and they should be decided according to their own rules. But technological decisions are made in the context of value relations. Our job is to weld these two areas together, to make our values explicit and to assign to them the role of an effective guide. It is only through a thorough understanding of the social ideals and values of religion and of a realistic assessment of one's socio-economic situation—resources, problems and constraints—that faith-oriented communities can develop a creative and innovative approach to change.

This approach would be ideological as well as empirical and somewhat pragmatic. Pragmatic not in the sense that ideals and values can be trimmed to suit the exigencies of the situation, but rather pragmatic in the sense that ideals and values are to be translated into reality in a practical and realistic way.

3) A unique approach to social change

The real objective which inspires faith-oriented communities is not a package of economic and political concessions or even some changes in the economic superstructure but the construction of a new world order, with its own framework of ideals, values and foundations. The approach of faith communities to social change has to be unique.

The Western approach has always assumed that radical change can be brought about by changing environment. That is why emphasis has always been placed on change in structures. This approach has failed to produce proper results. It has ignored the need to bring about change within men and women themselves and has concentrated on change in the outside world. What is needed, however, is a total change—within people themselves as well as in their social environment. The problem is not merely structural, although structural arrangements would also have to be remodelled. But the starting point must be the hearts and souls of men and women, their perception of reality and of their own place and mission in life.

4) The Islamic approach

The Islamic approach to social change takes full cognizance of these three elements. For Islam,

(a) Social change is not a result of totally predetermined historical forces. The existence of a number of obstacles and constraints is a fact of life and history, but there is no historical determinism. Change has to be planned and engineered. And this change should be purposeful, that is, a movement toward the ideal.

(b) Man is the active agent of change. All other forces have been subordinated to him in his capacity as God's vicegerent and deputy (*Khalifa*) on the earth. Within the framework of the divine arrangement for this universe and its laws, it is man himself who is responsible for making or marring his destiny.

(c) Change consists in environmental change, and change within the hearts and souls of men and women — their attitudes, motivation, commitment, their resolve to mobilize all that is within them and around them for the fulfillment of their objectives.

(d) Life is a network of inter-relationships. Change means some disruption in some relationships somewhere. So there is a danger of change becoming an instrument of disequilibrium within men and women and in society. Islamically-oriented social change would involve the least friction and disequilibria, with planned and co-ordinated movement from one state of equilibrium to a higher one, or from a state of disequilibrium towards equilibrium. Hence, change has to be balanced, gradual and evolutionary. Innovation is to be coupled with integration. It is this unique Islamic approach which leads to revolutionary changes through an evolutionary trajectory.

These basic changes, if implemented, will revolutionize our approach to the problems of a new world order.

E. Islam: Its Meaning and Message

I would now like to briefly explain what Islam is and how it proposes to establish a new order.

No departmentalization of life

Islam is an Arabic word. It is derived from two roots; one *salm*, meaning peace and the other *SLM*, meaning submission. Islam stands for "a commitment to surrender one's will to the Will of God" and as such be at peace with the Creator and with all that has been created by Him. It is through submission to the Will of God that peace is produced. Harmonization of our will with the Will of God brings about harmonization of different spheres of life under an all-embracing ideal. Departmentalization of life into different water-tight compartments, religious and secular, sacred and profane, spiritual and material, is ruled out. There is unity of life and unity of the source of guidance. As God is One and Indivisible, so is life and our human personality. Each aspect of life is inseparable from the other. Religious and secular are not two autonomous categories; they represent two sides of the same coin. Each and every act becomes related to God and His guidance. Every human activity is given a transcendent dimension; it becomes sacred and meaningful and goal-centered.

A worldview

Islam is a worldview and an outlook on life. It is based on the recognition of the unity of the Creator and of our submission to His

will. Everything originates from the One God, and everyone is ultimately responsible to Him. Thus the unity of the Creator has as its
corollary, the Oneness of His creation. Distinctions of race, color,
caste, wealth and power disappear; our relation with other persons
assumes total equality by virtue of the common Creator. Henceforth,
our mission becomes a dedication to our Creator; worship and obedience of the Creator becomes our purpose in life.

Divine guidance

The Creator has not left us without guidance for the conduct of
our life. Ever since the beginning of Creation, He has sent down
Prophets who conveyed His message to humankind. They are the
source for finding God's Will. Thus we have the chain of Prophets
beginning with Adam (peace be upon him) and ending with Muhammad (peace be upon him). Abraham, Moses, Noah, John, Zecha-
riah and Jesus (peace be upon them) all belong to this golden chain
of Prophets. Prophets David, Moses, Jesus and Muhammad (may
peace be upon them all), brought revealed books of guidance with
them. The Qur'an, the Book revealed to the Prophet Muhammad, is
the last and final of these books of guidance.

The Qur'an contains the word of God. In it is preserved the divine
revelation, unalloyed by human interpolation of any kind, unaffected
by any change or loss to the original. In it is distilled the essence of
all the messages sent down in the past. In it is embodied a framework
for the conduct of the whole of human life. There are explicit criteria
for judging between right and wrong; there are principles of individual and collective conduct. In it are depicted the human follies of
the past. In it are warnings for humankind, and in it are assurances
of continued guidance for those who seek God's help.

The Qur'an has depicted a path, the Straight Path *(Sirat ul-Musta-
qim)* which when followed revolutionizes the whole of life. It brings
about a transformation in character and galvanizes us into action.
This action takes the form of purification of the self, and then un-
ceasing effort to establish the laws of God on earth, resulting in a
new order based on truth, justice, virtue and goodness.

God's vicegerents

Men play a crucial role in the making of this world. They act as
God's vicegerents *(Khalifa)*—His deputies and representatives on the
earth. They are morally prepared to play this role. Success lies in
playing it properly, by enjoining what is right and forbidding what
is wrong, by freeing people from the bondage of others, by demonstrating that a sound and serene society can only result if one har-
monizes one's will with the Will of God. This makes seeking the

Creator's pleasure one's purpose in life, treating the whole of Creation as one's partner, raising the concept of human welfare from the level of mere animal needs to seeking what is best in this world and what is best in the Hereafter.

This is the Islamic worldview, and its concept of men and women and their destiny. Islam is not a religion in the Western understanding of the word. It is at once a faith and a way of life, a religion and a social order, a doctrine and a code of conduct, a set of values and principles and a social movement to realize them in history.

No priesthood

There is no priesthood in Islam, not even an organized 'church'. All men and women, who are committed to this ideal, are expected to live in accordance with its principles and to strive to establish them in society and history. Those who commit themselves to Truth try to see that Truth prevails. They strive to make a new world in the image of the Truth.

A system of life

Islam, as a system of life, prepares us to play this role and provides us with guidelines for the development of a new personality and a new society. For the purification of self there are prayers *(Salat)* performed five times a day in the confines of the home and in congregation in our mosques, strengthening our commitment to God, refreshing our loyalty to truth, reinvigorating us to work for the realization of our ideals. Prayer is supplemented by fasting *(sawm)* for the achievement of these objectives.

If prayer and fasting integrate us with God and provide us with the spiritual discipline we need to become godly in the midst of the rough and tumble of life, *Zakat* commits our wealth—our worldly resources—to the achievement of divine purposes in the socio-economic realm.

Zakat is a monetary obligation. Every Muslim who possesses more than a certain minimum amount of wealth has to contribute at least a certain percentage of his/her total wealth for welfare functions within society. It is not a charity; it is a religious right which the rich owe to the needy and the poor, and to society at large. But the spirit of this compulsory contribution is that it is paid by the rich as an act of worship and not merely as a tax.

This is how all that Muslims have, soul, body or their belongings, are harnessed for the service of virtue, justice and truth. It is also obligatory on Muslims to visit the *Ka'ba* at least once in their lifetime for *Hajj* (pilgrimage). This, among others, is an index of the unity of the Muslim community *(Ummah)*, a community of faith and a symbol of the unity of humankind. A universal order can come into existence only on the basis of a universal faith and not on the basis of commitment to the 'gods' of race, color, region or riches. The ideal of human brotherhood seeks actualization in Islam.

Unique in values and principles

A new model of human personality and a new vision of human culture are here presented. Science and technology are developed but they are not directed towards destroying either nature or our abode therein; they add to our efficiency as much as to life's sublimity. Islam aims at a new harmony between man and nature and between man and society.

The uniqueness of Islamic culture lies in its values and principles. When Muslims, after an illustrious historical career, became oblivious of this fact and became obsessed with the manifestations of their culture, as against its sources, they could not even fully protect the house they had built. The strength of Islam lies in its ideals, values and principles, and their relevance to us is as great today as it has been in history. The message is timeless and the principles Islam embodies are of universal application.

F. Islamic Role in the Establishment of a New World Order

In our search for a new world order today, Islam emphasizes that we must aspire to a new system of life which could approach human problems from a different perspective, not merely from the perspective of limited national or regional interest, but from the perspective of what is right and wrong, and how best we can strive to evolve a just and a humane world order at different levels of our existence, individual, national and international.

That the present order is characterized by injustice and exploitation is proved beyond any shadow of doubt. But Islam suggests that the present order fails because it is based upon a wrong concept of man and of his relationship with other human beings, with society, with nature, and with the world. The search for a new order brings us to the need for a new concept of man and his role. From the viewpoint of world religions in general, and of Islam in particular, the focus of the discussion must be shifted to a new vision of man and society, to an effort to bring about change at the level of human consciousness, of values, leading to new cultural transformation.

A movement-oriented approach to religion

Islam is a movement for social change. It not only gives a clear concept of society and the *modus vivendi* of bringing about the coveted change in history, but it also gives clear guidelines for socio-economic policy, for some of the key institutions that guarantee the implementation of that policy, and an organized social effort under disciplined leadership to see that these objectives are achieved in space and time.

Muslims have this movement-oriented approach to religion. This model operates at three levels, that of the individual, of society and of the world. First, unless the individual has a new faith, a new consciousness and a new perception of his/her own role, required changes cannot be brought about. Second is the level of society. Initially it may be at the national level but later at the level of the whole world. The Islamic strategy is that it starts with creating a new consciousness in the individual, who imbibes its values and strives to work for the establishment of a just life, not on the basis of expediency or to seek personal or group interests, but to do what is right and just. The Qur'an shows us how an individual problem has to be approached at the universal level when it says that if one person is unjustly killed, this is tantamount to killing the entire human race, and that whoever saves one single life saves the whole race.[6] This is how an individual incident is transformed into a world problem, how an event moves into the realm of values.

Clear guidelines for action

Islam is not a defense of the *status quo*. Instead, it is a critique of human life, including the lives of Muslims and the organization of Muslim society. The present day Muslim society falls far short of Islamic standards. Thus we believe that Muslim society has to be changed in order to establish those social, economic and political institutions which would establish justice in human relations. Islam wants to bring political power under the control of its moral ideals. Such a society and state would be established as a result of a social movement directed towards Islamic revival. Then the Muslim world would be in a position to play its ideological role in the world, by making its own resources available to build a model society where it has political power, and then by sharing it with others in the interests of justice, acting on the same principle as the Prophet used when he helped the famine-stricken people of Makka who were politically at war against him.

The Islamic State was not at war with human beings as such, but only with the institutions which represented belligerent political power. This may help lead humankind towards the model of a new world order where justice will be done to all, friends and foes alike, and where wealth will be shared with the needy not because it is expedient but because this is just.

Zakat is a right of the poor. According to the Qur'an, those who do not help the needy or who scorn the orphan are committing the crime of denying *din,* the Islamic way itself. This idea of the sharing of wealth as a right is a revolutionary idea. It is with these insights that Islam enters this debate and gives to it a new direction, a new perspective and also clear guidelines for action. In the light of these guidelines a strategy for change can be formulated. A new just order is not merely the need of Muslims, it is a need of people everywhere, in the West as well as the East.

Islam — more than a religion

Islam is a faith and a way of life. It provides a definite outlook on life and a program for action, a comprehensive milieu for social reconstruction. It reshapes the entire personality of men and women and produces a new culture and civilization. It is deeply concerned with their moral and material existence, their psychological attitudes as well as their socio-economic behavior patterns. All aspects of individual and collective life are developed in a harmonious fashion, within the framework of overall human development known as *Tazkiyyah* [7] (purification).

Islam influences people at different levels of their existence: belief, motivation, personal character, individual behavior, social institutions, collective action. That is why it is more correct to say that Islam is a faith, a way of life, a process of change, and a social movement for the reconstruction of society and the establishment of a just world order, not just a religion.

Basic values for world order

The basic values on which this world order is established are as follows:

1) *Tawhid.* (God's Unity and Sovereignty).

This is the foundation on which Islam's worldview and its scheme of life is based. It lays the rules of God-man and man-man relationship. *Tawhid* is not merely a metaphysical doctrine. The human approach to social reality is an inextricable part of this belief. The establishment of justice in human relations is a demand of this faith. Belief in God's Unity and His Sovereignty means that all human beings are equal, and that their rights *(Huqùq al 'Ibàd)* are a natural extension of God's rights *(Huqùq Allah).* The Qur'an says:

"Have you observed him who denies the *din?*
(the faith and religion, the divine law)
He is the one who spurns the orphan,
Does not urge the feeding of the needy.
Bitter grief to worshippers

Who are neglectful of their prayers;
Who would be seen in prostration
Yet refuse kindnesses and charity." [8]

2) *Khilafah* (vicegerency).

Islam defines our status in the world as that of God's vicegerents
—His deputies and representatives. Everything that exists is at our
disposal for the fulfillment of this role and is like a trust in our hands.
This means that we are not the masters, we are God's agents and our
primary concern should be the fulfillment of the Will of the Lord. We
are in the position of trustees in respect to all that is in the universe,
our own personal faculties and all our possessions and belongings.
All authority is to be exercised within the framework of this trust and
we are accountable for whatever we do. This principle stipulates our
active participation in life and invites us to treat the entire creation,
not as foe, but as partner and friend, made to fulfill the same objectives. The Islamic concept of man's equality and brotherhood and the
creation of the ideological fraternity of the *Ummah* (the community
of faith) are essential elements of this principle of *Khilafah,* our trus-
teeship and stewardship.

3) Establishment of justice among human beings.

Establishment of justice among human beings is one of the basic
objectives for which God raised His prophets and sent down His
guidance.[9] All human beings have rights upon all that God has provided and thus God's bounties are to be shared equitably.[10] The poor
and the needy have a right upon the wealth of the rich and of society.[11]
They must be helped and enabled to participate in the struggle for
living with skill and honor.

4) Political and economic power are not evil.

It is a part of our religious mission to harness them for the fulfillment of moral objectives. Instead of remaining instruments of oppression and exploitation, they must be made to serve the ends of justice
and to promote good and virtue and to forbid evil and vice.[12]

5) There are no intermediaries between God and man.

God's guidance is available in the form of His Book, the Qur'an
and the life-example of His Prophet, the *Sunnah*. They clearly state
the ideals, values and principles that we need to build our individual
and collective lives on truth and justice and there exists in this guidance a built-in mechanism to meet the demands of changing times.
Evolution is possible within this framework. Only the divine law is
eternal, all human expedients are temporary and time-bound. Pursuit

of the divine law is the greatest guarantee against human arbitrariness and relapse into injustice.

Islam's all-embracing approach to rebuilding world order

These are the basic principles on which Islam wants to rebuild the world order. The first contribution that Islam wants to make is at the level of one's approach to this problem. Islam adopts an all-embracing approach, based on a spiritual appreciation of reality. It approaches men and women in the context of their total existence, in relation to their Creator and His entire creation. It admits of no dichotomy between matter and spirit, nor between physical and moral. It welds the religious with the secular and treats life as one integrated and harmonious whole.

Islam stands for total change, as against all contemporary ideologies and some religious systems which are content with partial change. It purifies the individual and reconstructs society, making both the individual and society achieve a still higher ideal: fulfillment of the Divine Will.

Its approach is based on values and not on the demands of expediency, personal or national. Its outlook is positive and constructive, and not just negative or destructive. It seeks the person's total welfare—moral, social and economic. It stands for the realization of justice in all aspects of human living. It upholds the principle of universal good and justice and invites the entire human community to work for its establishment. It affirms the integrity of the individual and sanctity of his/her human rights, as rights guaranteed by the Creator and tries to establish a social order wherein peace, dignity and justice prevail.

Islam's strategy for changing world order

Islam's strategy for the establishment of such a world order consists in inviting all human beings to take this path, irrespective of their color, race, language, nationality, ethnic or historical origin. It does not speak the language of the interests of the east or the west, of the north or the south, of the developed or underdeveloped. It wants the new order to be established for all human beings in all parts of the world. Through this universal approach Islam wants to bring about a new consciousness of the ideals and principles on which the house of humanity should be rebuilt and invites them to spell out its implications for the reconstruction of human thought and policy.

Islam also launches a social movement, an international movement involving all those who accept these ideals and values to establish the new order. Islam is eager to establish the new model in any part of the world. If it reconstructs its social order on these principles, the Muslim world could be the living example of this new order. But the present reality of the Muslims is far removed from the ideal. Once this model is established in some part of the world, this experiment can be shared with all the rest, as sunshine is shared by all. The prospects of this depend very much upon the Islamic movement that is trying to spearhead this social effort for the establishment of a new world order.

FOOTNOTES

1. See Richard N. Cooper, *The Economics of Interdependence: Economic Policy in the Atlantic Community*, New York: McGraw Hill, 1968; "Economic Interdependence and Foreign Policy in the Seventies," *World Politics*, 24th January, 1972, pp. 159-81; and "Macroeconomic Policy Adjustment in Interdependent Economics," *Journal of Political Economics*, 83, February 1969, pp. 1-24; Fred C. Bergston, *The Future of the International Economic Order: An Agenda for Research*, Lexington, Mass.: D. C. Heath & Co., 1973; Harry G. Johnson, *International Economic Questions Facing Britain, the United States and Canada*, British North America Research Association, June 1970; Raymond Vernon, *Sovereignty at Bay*, New York: Basic Books, 1971.

2. See Raul Prebisch, "Commercial Policy in the Underdeveloped Countries," *American Economic Review*, 49, May 1959, pp. 251-73; Andrew Grunder-Frank, "The Development of Underdevelopment," *Monthly Review*, 18, September 1966, pp. 17-31; Gunnar Myrdal, *Development and Underdevelopment*, Cairo: National Bank of Egypt Fiftieth Anniversary Commemoration Lectures, 1956; Benjamin J. Cohen, *The Question of Imperialism — The Political Economy of Dominance and Dependence*, New York: Basic Books, 1973; Osvaldo Sunkel, "Big Business and 'Dependentia': A Latin American View," *Foreign Affairs*, 50, April 1972, pp. 51-131; Stephen Hymer, "The Multinational Corporation and the Law of Uneven Development," in *Economics and World Order — From the 1970's to the 1990's*, edited by Jagdish Bhagwali, New York: Macmillan, 1972.

3. Joseph A. Camilleri, *Civilization in Crisis: Human Prospects in a Changing World*, Cambridge: Cambridge University Press, 1976, pp. 1-2; 5; 9; 11; and pp. 179-180.

4. Kurt Dopfer, *Economics in the Future: Towards a New Paradigm*, London: Macmillan, 1976.

5. See also, E. F. Schumacher, *A Guide for the Perplexed*, London: Jonathan Cape, 1977, pp. 135-154.

6. *The Qur'an*, 5: 32.

7. *The Qur'an*, 2: 129, 151; 19: 9-10; 87: 14.

8. *The Qur'an*, 107: 1-7.

9. *The Qur'an*, 57: 25.

10. *The Qur'an*, 14: 33-34.

11. *The Qur'an*, 51: 19.

12. *The Qur'an*, 2: 143; 3: 110; 17: 80-81.

SUMMARY

For Ahmad, a Muslim and professional economist, changing
the world economic order is too serious a matter to be left solely
to economists and politicians. The initial mistake has been to
separate economics from religion.

He finds Bellah's critique of modern Western ideology
illuminating but tainted by the biases of the very ideology he is
criticizing so forcefully. Bellah exaggerates the role of the religious
charismatic leader, Ahmad contends, and fails to understand all
the ramifications of religion as a "movement" for social change.

Ahmad then reviews the central themes and issues on the NIEO
debate. He finds the facts not much in dispute, and the two chief
contending analyses rooted alike in the overall sympathy-framework
of their authors. Both analyses give merely partial explanations of
the crisis which now pervades capitalism and socialism alike. For
him the real failure has been in not asking the right questions,
in not treating the universe as a moral order.

Faith communities must not be satisfied with such partial
analyses nor with their proposed bargaining packages. Rather,
they must call for a basic reorientation in the approach to social
change. This approach must provide not merely for a new economic
arrangement but also for having it take place within a value-oriented
framework of accepted basic ideals, values and principles.

Ahmad concludes with a lengthy description of the meaning
and message of Islam and how it proposes to establish a new
world order. He explains how Islam is not only an integrated
system of life which sees people as God's vicegerents here on
earth working out their own destinies in harmony with His
will. Islam is besides, in marked contrast with all contemporary
ideologies and some religious systems, a movement for total social
change with clear guidelines for socio-economic policy. It even
provides some of the key institutions and organized social efforts
that guarantee the implementation of its proposed policies under
disciplined leadership.

Ahmad admits that present day Muslim society falls far short of
these Islamic standards. Nevertheless, such a model if implemented
anywhere in the world would serve as a living example to all people
of a new world order. Therefore, he believes that the future prospects for a new world order depend greatly on the social effort that
the Islamic movement is presently trying to spearhead. Finally,

Ahmad assures us that Islam's strategy for establishing such a world order is not sectarian or exclusive—it consists in inviting all people to take this path irrespective of their color, race, language, nationality, ethnic or historic origin.

9

A Jewish Response

Irwin Blank

Irwin M. Blank, a US citizen, is presently Senior Rabbi of Temple Ohabei Shalom, Brookline, Massachusetts. He did his graduate studies at Hebrew Union College and Columbia University Teachers College. Among his positions and honors, he has been a member of the faculty of Hebrew Union College School of Education and the Department of Theology of Fordham University, and served as a chaplain in the US Navy during the Korean war. Blank is past president of the Synagogue Council of America, and presently a member of the Board of Ministry of Harvard University and Chairperson of the Committee for Justice and Peace of the Central Conference of American Rabbis. He has lectured and published on such topics as Judaism and ethics, Rabbinic counseling, secularism and Judaism, and intra-religious experience in America.

Unfortunately, it does not lie within the scope of my assignment to discuss with you the economic institutions which have developed within the Jewish community over these many centuries designed to establish an equitable distribution of goods and property, humane working conditions and an appropriate balance between the spiritual and material needs of human beings. Had we the time, I would like to have discussed with you the institutions of the Sabbatical year, tithing, the forgiveness of debts, free will offerings and Tzedakah which is generally mistranslated as charity but which, in fact, is the doing of simple justice by sharing material goods.

It is my belief that God, by virtue of having created the material world is, in effect, the first materialist. It is the view of God which, for me, makes it possible to relate pure spirit to the material needs of human beings. In my view the Sabbath is, in part, a celebration of materialism intended to reorient us spiritually to our material needs, a necessary reorientation in the light of the disorientation which is the by-product of the work-week.

I am grateful to Mr. Bellah for presenting a richly textured, many faceted paper which places high priority values and conflicting perspectives in juxtaposition. This challenges our ability to make decisions and take action in the realm of political action which can be said to flow from our faith and be an appropriate expression of our faith.

It is this very juxtaposition of values and perspectives which pushes us in the direction of quietism, on the one hand, and on the other, waiting for the emergence of a charismatic leader as one of very few options open to us.

The two titles of Mr. Bellah's paper express his ambivalence. Since I do not believe in waiting for the coming of the Messiah or in hoping for the arrival of a charismatic leader, I would suggest a third title: Changing Faith: Challenging the World Order.

Quietism is fostered by the concept of "not knowing what it's about." Waiting for the charismatic leader is encouraged by the thought that church religion, sect type religion and religious movement do not provide a group process by which the faithful can be effectively mobilized since these manifestations of faith are distortions of the pursuit of "the deepest apperception of truth that human beings are capable of," which is offered by Mr. Bellah as one definition of religion.

Discussions focusing on the nature of reality, truth, faith and the ordering of values, demonstrate that such modalities as positivism, relativism, reductionism and competitive evolution cannot be discrete modalities. In their most absolute formulations they are merely reference points. They may be useful analytic tools. But, in the living situation they are not mutually exclusive, discrete entities or at all absolute. Sometimes one perspective is the valuable tool, sometimes another. More frequently more than one perspective is brought into play before we decide what to do. It is only when these opposing perspectives are thrown into a state of tension that human beings can hope to approach something which approximates the truth.

The fact that the rabbis understood that there were several sets of hermeneutic rules did not paralyze them. Neither quietism nor following the lead of a charismatic leader makes for a democratic community. Quietism makes for withdrawal from community, charismatic leadership tends towards fascism. Insofar as they do not make for a democratic community, Mr. Bellah's contention that the most important goal is to achieve profound person-to-person relationships cannot be realized, other than in an inferior-superior relationship or in a collection of very private individuals who may present the appearance of community but who are certainly a long way from a true I-Thou relationship. Thus we have a pseudo-community, the lonely crowd of Riesman.

The I-Thou relationship is realized only after risk taking. Risk taking is the opposite of quietism. There are no guarantees that one is not following a false prophet, or committing one's self to a false value, or pursuing a physically or spiritually self-destructive process. Is that not the basic definition of faith. Abraham does not have any real guarantee when he leaves his birthplace. He certainly does not have one when he is prepared to sacrifice Isaac. Kierkegaard makes that dramatically clear. Esther has no assurance that she will not be beheaded by Ahasuerus.

Risk taking is a necessary element of faith. Wilfred Smith may have implied this in saying that "when the modern intellectual has to deal with religion there is some embarrassment." (cf. Bellah, p 153). No more or less so than is true for men and women of faith through the ages. Faith is frequently a source of embarrassment. Abraham and Sarah were embarrassed. Jeremiah was embarrassed. Jonah was embarrassed. Maimonides was embarrassed. But that did not prevent them from being people of history, doing something in time and space.

Just as we have expressed the thought that categories, relativism, reductionism, etc. are not discrete, unrelated or non-interacting categories, so too the concept of the charismatic leader has to be modified.

Moses was a charismatic leader. He was able to take a mixed multitude, an *erev rav*, and lead it through forty years of hardship in the wilderness and there to mold this rag-tag group into an identifiable people. But, what is most significant for us is that every step along the way he was challenged by the people. His brother and sister challenged his marriage. The people challenged the wisdom of his decisions. His father-in-law challenged his ability to judge the people properly without assistance. God challenges his stability of character and finds him wanting. Everybody reserves the right to test this charismatic leader, and he must respond to the challenge not as an authoritarian leader but as one who is responsible to the people and to God.

This concept of responsible interaction is more fully realized when the local priests in the period of the deuteronomic reformation become teachers to the people rather than the sole performers of sacerdotal functions, or the elite manipulators of symbols. Learning becomes democratized. Holiness becomes democratized. The people come closer to becoming a kingdom of priests and the people of the book.

The process is continued in the rabbinic period with the establishment of the academies. Rabbis are authorities. They are not authoritarian. They are not guardians of the mystery. They must withstand challenge. They must teach. They must decide. They must do. Some questions are left for the Messiah to solve. But, they are few.

Men and women must take the risk of being historical entities. They must decide what it is they have to do in time and space. Facts, feelings, fantasies, phenomena are synthesized in the service of the pursuit of truth. Values are ordered, but the order is not immutable. Absolutes are few in Jewish tradition, three in number. Just as the "I" is defined, in part, against the ground of the "Thou" so too men and women are defined by their deeds which stand against the ground of time and space. It is the *commandment* to which they ultimately must respond since the mystery is unfathomable.

Chapter 38 of the *Book of Job* is overwhelming in its delineation of the cosmic. But, Chapter Nineteen of *Leviticus* is more useful. That is not my judgment alone. That is the judgment of my faith community in response to God's first words to Abraham which are also addressed to us, לֶךְ לְךָ , "Get going."

Let us cite two Midrashim. The first Midrash demonstrates the concern of the rabbis for determining the nature of the commandments which ought to be acted upon. From this concern there evolves their consideration of the specific patterns of behavior which define men and women in history. The second Midrash has to do with the fact that once the data of revelation are accepted the time for decision is at hand. It is human beings in confrontation with one another who must decide what is to be done. They cannot rely on further revelations, the coming of the Messiah or the emergence of a charismatic leader.

THE ONE COMMANDMENT

Rabbi Simlai expounded:
Six hundred and thirteen commandments were given to Moses,
three hundred and sixty-five "Thou shalt nots," the number
    of the days of the solar year,
and two hundred and forty-eight "Thou shalts,"
corresponding to the parts of the body.

David came and brought them down to eleven;
as it is written:
"Lord, who shall sojourn in Thy tabernacle? . . .
He that walketh uprightly, and worketh righteousness, and speaketh
    truth in his heart; that hath no slander upon his tongue, nor doeth
    evil to his fellow, nor taketh up a reproach against his neighbour;
    in whose eyes a vile person is despised, but he honoureth them
    that fear the Lord; he that sweareth to his own hurt, and changeth
    not; he that putteth not out his money on interest, nor taketh a
    bribe against the innocent" (Ps.15:1-5).

Isaiah came and brought them down to six;
as it is written:
"He that walketh righteously and speaketh uprightly; he that despiseth
    the gain of oppressions, that shaketh his hands from holding of
    bribes, that stoppeth his ears from hearing of blood, and shutteth his
    eyes from looking upon evil" (Isa.33:15).

Micah came and brought them down to three;
as it is written:
"It hath been told thee, O man, what is good . . . : Only to do justly, and
    to love mercy, and to walk humbly with thy God" (Mic.6:8).

Isaiah came again and brought them down to two;
as it is said: "Thus saith the Lord,
Keep ye justice, and do righteousness" (Isa.56:1).

Amos came and brought them down to one;
as it is said:
"For thus saith the Lord unto the house of Israel:
Seek ye Me, and Live" (Amos 5:4).

Rav Nahman bar Isaac objected:
"Seek ye Me"—may it not mean: in all the Torah?
Rather Habakkuk came and brought them down to one;
as it is said:
"But the righteous shall live by his faith" (Hab.2:4).

TORAH ON EARTH

. . . On that day Eliezer brought all the proofs in the world, and the
masters would not accept them.
He said to them: If the law is according to me, let this locust tree
prove it.
The locust tree moved a hundred cubits. (And some say: four hundred
cubits.)
They said to him: The locust tree cannot prove anything.
Then he said to them: If the law is according to me, let this stream of
water prove it.
The stream of water turned and flowed backward.
They said to him: The stream cannot prove anything.
Then he said to them: If the law is according to me, let the walls of the
House of Study prove it.
The walls of the House of Study began to topple.
Rabbi Joshua reprimanded them:
If scholars are disputing with one another about the law, what business
is it of yours?
They did not fall down out of respect for Rabbi Joshua, and did not
straighten up out of respect for Rabbi Eliezer, and they are still
inclined.
Then he said to them: If the law is according to me, let the heaven
prove it.
A voice came forth from heaven and said:
Why do you dispute with Rabbi Eliezer?
The law is according to him in every case.
Rabbi Joshua rose to his feet and said:
"It is not in heaven" (Deut.30:12).
What is the meaning of: "It is not in heaven?"
Rabbi Jeremiah said:
The Torah has already been given once and for all from Mount Sinai;
we do not listen to voices from heaven.
For You have already written in the Torah on Mount Sinai:
"After the majority must one incline" (Exod.23:2).

Rabbi Nathan came upon Elijah.
He said to him: What was the Holy One, blessed be he, doing at that
moment?
Elijah said to him:
He was smiling and saying: My children have defeated me, my children
have defeated me!

   It is possible that we may not be able to establish a community
because of our varying perspectives and the different ways in which
we order our values and structure reality. It is also possible that we
may be able to establish a limited community, but a real community,
nevertheless, which will enable us to be effective in confronting a

limited number of issues. It is also possible that we will not be successful in establishing any kind of community. But, we will not know unless we confront one another here and now. Perhaps we can agree on two rules of the road: that we will not kill one another and that we will be prepared to settle for something less than our whole vision of truth.

SUMMARY

Blank believes that God is "the first materialist" by virtue of having created the material world. For him, it is this view of God that makes it possible to relate pure spirit to the material needs of human beings. Thus, it is easy to understand the Jewish community's endless preoccupation with creating institutions, such as the Sabbatical year, tithing, forgiveness of debts, free will offerings, Tzedakah, etc., that assure a more equitable distribution of goods and property. Indeed, even the Sabbath is, in part, "a celebration of materialism" intended to reorient God's people spiritually towards their material needs.

Blank rejects Bellah's apparent ambivalence between religious quietism or "waiting for the coming of the Messiah" and hoping for the emergence of a charismatic leader, and suggests rather that changing faith should challenge present world order. Quietism makes for withdrawal from community, while charismatic leadership tends to fascism. Believers must be risk-takers. They must challenge all leaders in responsible interaction. They must risk being historical actors without any certainty of the outcome of their actions. Few questions can be left to the Messiah to solve.

Now is the time for the faith community to "get going" according to God's first words to Abraham. Blank finds confirming evidence of this faith attitude in the two Midrashim he cites in conclusion.

10

An African Christian Response

Burgess Carr

Burgess Carr, a citizen of Liberia, is an Episcopal priest and presently the General Secretary of the All Africa Conference of Churches. He did his graduate studies at the Harvard Divinity School. Among his many past positions and experiences, he has been Executive Secretary of the Commission of the Churches on International Affairs, as well as African Secretary, Commission on Inter-Church Aid, Refugees and World Service of the World Council of Churches, Geneva. Carr was moderator of the negotiations that produced the "Addis Ababa Agreement on Southern Sudan" and thus ended the civil war in the Sudan. He has lectured and published extensively on theological and social issues facing the churches in Africa.

INTRODUCTION

Let me begin by stating that my response to the theme of this Symposium is that of an African theologian. African theology is influenced by the radical politics of "Liberation" and the Christian doctrine of "Incarnation." It is by no means the normative theological point of view current within the church, not even in the African church. But for those of us who are struggling against the forces of "modernism," in spite of our education (cf. Bellah), in order to situate our obedience to faith in God revealed in Jesus Christ within the religious traditions of our own cultural and historical experience, "Liberation" and "Incarnation" represent the heart of the Gospel.

In other words, I am one of those striving to liberate even the Christian faith in Africa from the "monoculture" of that minority of humankind located in the North or in the West, i.e., the white imperialist world. It is from within the crucible of this struggle that I theologize about the New International Economic Order.

Secondly, by way of further introduction, I should say that I am an ecumenical theologian. That means that the interpretation of my response to Faith is naturally set within the larger context of the whole church and indeed of the whole human family (oikoumene). For this reason I can perceive the need for a new international economic order only in terms of the larger need for a new world order.

The economic order is sustained and sustainable through the political, social and cultural order in the world today. Therefore the change must be total if it is to be a new order. Our efforts cannot succeed as long as we persist along the path of isolating the economic order and dealing with it as though it were autonomous.

This said, I will turn to the heart of the matter and make two propositions.

1) The Need to Demythologize the Present Order.

Professor Bellah in his paper has said that "religion operates . . . through the interpretation of symbols," and that "religious symbols must be *internalized* in the faithful if they are to be operative." (p. ⌐157) I agree, but would go on to say that it is primarily Christian symbols taught by the church which have shaped the structures of the world over the last five hundred years.

I suspect many of you are aware of the deep division within the church over matters such as the Christian's relationship to the state, or the Christian's response to repressive and unjust governments. A considerable part of the Christian Faith community takes what Paul wrote in *Romans 13* — "There is no authority except from God, and those that exist have been instituted by God" — to be a universal prescription governing their attitude to the political and social order in the world. Those of us who have experienced colonization know that perhaps no single verse in Scripture has been preached to us more incessantly and vigorously. And what is more, Paul goes on to say, "therefore he who resists the authorities, resists what God has appointed, and those who resist will incur judgement."

The Christian Faith community has consistently bestowed sacred sanctions upon the prevailing social, economic and political order in this world, in spite of its glaring injustices. Furthermore, it has used the social teachings of Paul concerning slavery and the status of women in the church in the first century, for example, as normative for all time. So the first task of Christians in the present crisis we are dealing with here is to demythologize the present world order.

A few months ago I had occasion to tell a Canadian audience that Jesus' words, "Man shall not live by bread alone" were addressed to Satan and not to hungry people who had no bread. On the contrary, when Jesus observed that a bridegroom was on the verge of becoming embarrassed because his wedding party had run out of wine, he performed his first miracle. Similarly, he multiplied the loaves and fishes in order to feed a multitude of some five to seven thousand people who were hungry and had nothing to eat.

I am suggesting that the process of demythologizing the religious symbols that Christians have internalized and which sustain the present structures of injustice and oppression in the world, must involve identifying — both in time and in situation — the relevance of those symbols to the Faith response we are called upon to make.

This is as much a political action as it is religious. Take for instance the most efficient system of repression ever devised by human beings. I refer to apartheid. Everyone knows that the ideological foundations of apartheid are grounded in the kinds of religious interpretation I have already alluded to. The bulwark of Afrikaaner nationalism is the Dutch Reformed church in South Africa. Some would say that radical changes would occur within South Africa immediately if the Dutch Reformed church could be converted and withdraw its theological support from apartheid.

So I would differ with Professor Bellah when he says "there is really no place for religion in the structure of modern ideology" (p. 153). I maintain that every ideology relies upon certain Faith symbols and that demythologizing those Faith symbols is as much a political act as it is religious. The French Justice and Peace Commission stated the position accurately when it said,

> "If, they (world structures) . . . industrialized societies, have since freed themselves of the Church's tutelage, they neverthe-

less found in evangelization the moral justification they needed, as Christian regimes, for the colonization of the rest of the world."[1]

And as an African I maintain that colonization is the one phenomenon in the modern world that continues to offer the most stubborn resistance to the New International Economic Order.

This assertion implies not only culpability, but more importantly, a reading of history which demonstrates that the process of domination, dependence and dislocation, now recognized as the principal factors responsible for under-development and poverty, are linked to Western Christianity. Che Guevera was therefore right when he said, "Only when the religious masses struggle for liberation will liberation be total."

2) Christian Symbols That Are Liberating

In the second part of this paper, I will sketch briefly some of the religious symbols in Christianity that support the struggle for liberation toward a new world order.

a) Men and Women are the Incarnation of God in the World

Incarnation is a unique Christian doctrine. It derives from the "image of God" concept found in almost all religions. But it goes further in stating that the sacredness of human beings is related to the fact that, in Jesus of Nazareth, God took human flesh and form and lived on this earth.

The incarnation of God in Jesus was the maturation of God's initial work in creation, when He made man and woman "a little lower than the gods." Now through the life, death and resurrection of Jesus Christ, humanity is elevated and given its primal place as part of the life and being of God himself.

Thus the holistic view of *man-and-woman-in creation* passes beyond into a view of *man-woman-above creation*. Their humanity and all that relates to it are infused and energized by the divinity of God. Their material development can therefore be seen as part of their coming to the mature person revealed in Jesus Christ. This is not the same as materialism, because although men and women are integral to the material universe of nature which God animates with His word and with His breath, they are also destined to receive the "glory and worship" of nature. Their constant struggle must be to resist becoming the central object of faith, since they too must join their voice to the chorus of creation in ascribing the ultimate glory and worship to the Lord in whom all things have their origin and in whom all things are ultimately summed up.

In the penultimate, humanity's calling is to push forward those positive and progressive forces which enlarge the humanity of men and women, for in so doing we bring nearer the reign of God's sovereignty.

The cry for bread therefore is not merely a cry for justice. It is a cry for *God's justice* through which His glory is revealed in all its fullness "as the waters cover the sea."

b) Men and Women are Stewards of Creation

A consistent theme common to Judaism, Christianity and Islam is that of man's and woman's stewardship to dominate the earth. But this word "dominate" does not imply exploitation. It rather means enjoyment. The earth is delivered to man and woman as a "good thing" to develop and enjoy.

In this way they can fulfill their own humanity in a multi-directional way. They can give praise to God for the gift of creation and they can bring nature to fruition through the fulfillment of their own joy. They are an integral part of nature and only as nature is released from bondage can they experience salvation. They are not set over against nature as though to acquire and possess it in whole or in part. This is the "non-dualism" common to all traditional religions (Bellah p.165). And the implications Professor Bellah draws about the "rejection of inequality" are apt and accurate. No part of God's creation is not good; therefore no part is unequal. This theological principle gives profound meaning to man's and woman's responsibility as stewards of God's creation.

c) Justice, Freedom and Dignity are Spiritual Needs

The religious insistence on justice, freedom and dignity means more than a critique of the prevailing social order. The issue is not merely greater access to material prosperity, however broadly defined, political participation or human rights. To speak of justice, freedom and dignity, as spiritual needs is to imply a theology of human wholeness which is praxis-oriented and at the same time inspired by symbols of solidarity, hope and transcendence. When Jesus stood up in the synagogue at Nazareth and read the text from Isaiah 61 (see Luke 4:16 ff), he demonstrated to his hearers that God's justice (righteousness) is revealed in His partisanship with the poor.

In his address to the Fifth Assembly of the World Council of Churches (WCC) in Nairobi, M. M. Thomas of India spoke of the Church's need for a "spirituality for combat." And he quoted another WCC colleague, Canon David Jenkins, as saying,

> "Perhaps what Christians are particularly called to work out
> . . . is what might be called a *spirituality for combat*. Can our strug-

gles become part of our celebration of man as we understand him, in the image of God and died for by the Son of God? How might we help one another to so conduct our struggles that they become part of our worship?" [2]

M. M., as he is affectionately known, goes on to reflect upon these searching questions from the perspective of his own Asian and Orthodox Christian background:

"In this context, the Orthodox concept of a humanity in community with transfigured nature, society and cosmos, needs to be redefined and reaffirmed in relation to the spirituality of contemporary struggles for the defense of the *humanum* and the unity of mankind." [3]

d) The Symbol of the "Kingdom of God"

Finally, Christian engagement in the struggle for a New International Economic Order falls under the sign of the "Kingdom of God" leitmotif in Biblical eschatology. Here we are not dealing only with the fascination of the "new." More than that the "Kingdom of God" symbol addresses itself to the fatalism which derives from the notion that history is in bondage. The Christian doctrine of the resurrection negates all fatalism. Even our last enemy, death, is "swallowed up in victory." (Corinthians 15:54-56).

Today, Third World theologians insist that "the realization of the values of the Kingdom of God requires not only the good will of individuals, but also the good organization of the structures of society." [4] If the churches are to avoid "withdrawal into harmless irrelevance in which smug concern with one's own purity replaces any genuine concern for others" (Bellah, p. 159) they will have to work out concrete strategies to overcome their systemic relationship to structures of domination and dependence in society.

Paul's exhortation to the Romans to be subject to the higher powers, quoted earlier, was given with the assumption that rulers are to be "not a terror to good works, but to evil." When "powers" are detrimental to society, then Christians have a God-given duty to transform their behavior, says a Report of a WCC Consultation on Transnational Corporations held in Geneva last June.[5] And the French Justice and Peace Commission adds that this struggle is a precondition for the conversion which gives birth to faith and which has to be constantly repeated until death is conquered by the fullness of the resurrection.

The symbol of the "Kingdom of God" means that Christians are called to transform despair into hope and uncertainty into positive certainty. "Faith is confident assurance concerning what we hope for, and conviction about things we do not see." (Hebrews 11:1). Today, it is the struggle to establish a new order that challenges the creative calling of Christians to work hand in hand with other men and women of Faith.

The World Council of Churches Assembly in Nairobi two years ago said,

"The role of Christians and the Churches will be to assist in the definition, validation and articulation of just political, economic and social objectives and in translating them into action. Specifically it will involve:

1. joining hands with all who are engaged in the task of organizing the poor in their fight against poverty and injustice;

2. educating the more privileged to cooperate in the establishment of new socio-economic orders . . . favoring the needy; and

3. searching for new structures for human beings to live together in justice, freedom and peace." [6]

To sum up, I will quote from a recent Consultation organized by the Social and International Committee of the World Methodist Council, with the cooperation of SODEPAX, on the theme, *In Search of a New Society and the Social Dimensions of Evangelism:*

"Christians know what elements of the old disordered society must be changed, such as the loss of hope by many, glaring social and economic injustices, the violation of human rights, the armaments race, pollution, the waste of the earth's limited resources, widespread violence, all of which lead to a frequently held view, especially among youth, that there is no meaning to life and that society is incapable of change. In light of this situation, the need for repentance becomes emphatically clear." [7]

This is the conviction that inspired the Roman Catholic Synod of Bishops in 1971 to proclaim: "the struggle for justice is a constitutive dimension in the preaching of the gospel."

"The Kingdom of God is at hand. Repent and believe the Gospel!" (Mark 1:15).

FOOTNOTES

1. Quoted in CHURCH ALERT (No. 16, September-October 1977) a SODEPAX Publication, 150 Rue de Ferney, Geneva.

2. Cited in *Breaking Barriers* (Nairobi, 1975, WCC Geneva, P. 240)

3. *Ibid.*

4. *CHURCH ALERT, op. cit,* p. 9

5. *Loc. cit.*

6. *Breaking Barriers, op. cit.* p. 123

7. *CHURCH ALERT, Ibid. op. cit.,* p. 19

SUMMARY

Carr insists that his response is that of an African Christian theologian for whom "liberation" and "incarnation" represent the heart of the Gospel in his present struggle to liberate even the Christian Faith itself from the imperialist "monoculture" of the West.

As an ecumenical theologian his interpretation is set in the context of the whole church and of the whole human family and, therefore, cannot limit itself to the "economic" order, but rather must be extended to a "new world order." He sets out two propositions: 1) that the present order needs to be demythologized, because the Christian Faith community has consistently bestowed sacred sanctions upon the prevailing social, economic and political order of this world, in spite of its glaring injustices; and 2) that Christian symbols are in themselves liberating.

He then goes on to elaborate on these symbols: a) man and woman as the "incarnation" of God in the world; b) man and woman as stewards of creation; c) justice, freedom and dignity as spiritual needs; and d) the "Kingdom of God." All of these symbols support the present struggle for liberation toward a new world order.

11

A Buddhist Response

Lankaputra Hewage

Lankaputra Gonadeniya Hewage, a citizen of Sri Lanka, is presently Professor and Chairperson of the Department of Humanities Education at the University of Sri Lanka at Colombo. Among his many past positions and honors, Hewage was Founder Chairperson of the National Educational Council of the All Ceylon Buddhist Congress; Founder Chairperson of the Sarvodaya Educational Institute; Chairperson of the UNESCO Committee of the World Fellowship of Buddhists; and Founder Director of the Middle Path International. He has lectured and published widely on such topics as educational psychology, community education, and the relevance of Buddhist culture for development and peace in adult education.

WHAT THE BUDDHA DISCOVERED

Prince Siddhartha, who later became the Buddha, enjoyed all the material comforts that the son of a king (chieftain) of India (now Nepal) during the sixth century B.C. could afford to get. As an infant, as a child, as an adolescent and as a married youth, he had all the educational experiences and the luxuries needed at each stage of his personality development. At the age of twenty-nine after his wife Yasodara gave birth to a child, he renounced worldly life and became an ascetic. During the six years that followed his renunciation, he went through a life of extreme asceticism, often denying even basic physical and psychological needs. Thereby he experienced the two extremes of excessive indulgence in sensual pleasures and self mortification respectively.

During this period of six years, he had acquired many psychomotor skills necessary to control his senses and to adjust his behavior to any difficult situation. Simplicity, non-violence, mindfulness, pleasant speech, diligence and a search for truth, were some of the outstanding characteristics he had acquired by this time. When he was thirty-five years of age, he had studied and tried out all the systems of *"mind culture"* that were then known to all religious leaders of India. His was a life-long *(Yava-Jiva)* education process. Even more, it was a process that would not end till the ultimate goal *(Yava-Nirbana)* was realized. Still, he was not satisfied with the outcome of his experiences gained by following these systems, although they did help him in acquiring certain worldly psychic powers not attainable by ordinary people in other ways.

Thereafter, avoiding both extremes and following a middle path for a time, he started a search within himself by focussing his full attention on the nature and functions of his own psycho-physical organism, his mind and body. In his unique experiment, carried out one day at Gaya within his fathom-long body, he could gradually isolate one by one all the physical and mental conditioning factors that came together in different relationships at successive moments of his waking life. In addition, he could experience the results of such changing conditions of modified greed, hatred and illusion.

He reached a stage when he could maintain perfect equanimity without allowing his attention to be drawn by any stimulus whether pleasant or unpleasant, whether internal or external, physical or mental. At this stage using the psycho-motor skills which he had already acquired by constant practice from his earliest days and subsequently developed to a very high degree under different teachers, he focussed his attention on his own body and found that it was a continuous process of an arising and a ceasing of millions of conglomerations of physical forces.

In the same manner he could see that his mind too was a similar series of ever-changing thought processes consisting of or made up of thought moments. And when he focussed his attention and clear comprehension on what took place outside his body, he saw the same changing and conditioned nature as was found within his psycho-physical organism. At this stage he could see that this conditioning process also remained true in relation to the past irrespective of space-time differences. Now he knew everything about himself. He could guide his own behavior in any direction he wished. He was fully liberated and had totally conquered greed, hatred and illusion.

According to this discovery, any material object, biological organism, mental concept, or any social, economic, political, or psychological phenomenon or structure is the result of conditioning factors called *Sankaras*, coming together to form conditioned units *(Sankatas)*, while each of these conditioning or contributing factors is also a similar unit arising out of other such factors coming together. These *Sankatas* are formed when *Sankaras* come together in certain relationships. Thus no *Sankata* or *Sankara* remain unchanged. All the relationships that cause material, psychological, social, economic, political and spiritual phenomena were seen by the Buddha and were called *Paccayas* or conditioning causes. According to this system of *Paccaya Sankaras and Sankatas*, there is no phenomenon, whether material, mental, economic, social, spiritual or cultural that cannot be ultimately analyzed and explained in terms of this system called the *Paticca-Samuppada Dhamma* (Law of dependent origination).

Any phenomenon, event, concept or structure, within us, around us and related to us can be understood in its true nature only to the extent these *Sankaras, Sankatas*, and *Paccayas* are known and seen. Our future depends on how we understand these relationships, deal with and manipulate them for the welfare or the annihilation of all. Whatever good or ill that comes to this world must result from our handling or mishandling these complex structures within ourselves, within society and within the whole world or the universe.

If we react to this situation diligently with Right Understanding we can change these relationships for our survival, welfare and liberation. Otherwise, we may end up in their opposite conditions. The Middle Path way of life contained in the teachings of the Buddha helps us to understand these relationships and change them to meet our needs while our needs themselves are reduced to the minimum in that process of Right Understanding.

BUDDHISM AND BUDDHIST CULTURE

After he made this unique discovery he attained the highest perfection, equanimity and wisdom any human being or divine being
could ever attain. At Benares he presented the report of his unique
experiment to his colleagues who once worked with him on the same
problem following other methods. It is here that he proclaimed the
Middle Path and the Four Noble Truths. Thereafter when he had col-
lected sixty disciples who successfully followed his Middle Path, he
proclaimed his Middle Path philosophy of Buddhist Education for
the welfare of all.[1] He devoted forty-five years of his life thereafter
until the very moment of his death to an education service for the
welfare of all humankind, regardless of sex, color, creed, caste, race,
age and even intellectual and socio-economic status.

His way of life called the Middle Path (*Majjima Patipada*) is not
limited only to ascetics who renounce worldly life in search of the
ultimate emancipation.[2] He showed ordinary laymen and laywomen
how they could follow the Middle Path in their day-to-day life while
successfully engaged in worldly pursuits. Kings, queens, ministers,
chieftains, bankers, soldiers, statesmen, businessmen, traders, industrialists, physicians, artists, musicians, farmers, barbers, courte-
sans, prostitutes, scavengers, highway robbers, criminals, men and
women, young and old were among those who benefitted from his
teachings and guidance, according to their own understanding, ability and interest.

The present writer has shown how the Middle Path is the general
principle of avoiding extremes and following a positive and peaceful
way of life with a dynamically neutral attitude to all controversial
issues. When one tries to follow the Noble Eightfold Path, one is led
steadily and inevitably to this Middle Path.

Everyone who followed the Buddha's teachings successfully to
any degree became more peaceful, more mindful and more skillful in
life as they modified their greed, hatred and illusion. Every society
that accepted the *Triple Gem* and tried to follow the Middle Path at
least to some extent, became non-violent and non-aggressive to that
extent, except when defense of one's country was at stake. Values
like respect for one's parents, elders, religious leaders of all religions
and righteous rulers were social mores no one dared to challenge.
Simplicity, contentment, diligence, sharing and cooperation along
with a readiness to share one's material and spiritual wealth were
given high social prestige.

Intellectual freedom without accepting anything on blind faith
became the rule rather than the exception when the method of wise

consideration called *Yonisomanasikara* was adopted in comprehending problems by analysis and synthesis, with mindfulness at all times *(Sati-Sampajanna)*. Self discipline with mental peace resulted from the Middle Path system of training which consists of *Sila, Samadhi* and *Panna* (virtue, concentration and wisdom).

For the purpose of applying this Middle Path at different stages and levels according to each one's ability and interest, Buddha recognized the four divisions of the community namely, monks, nuns, lay male disciples and lay female disciples *(Bhikkhu, Bhikkhuni, Upasaka, Upasika)*. His teachings provided guidance and the insight necessary for all these communities to conduct their business for their welfare as a whole, as well as for the welfare of each individual member of the community. All his teachings together are called *Dhamma*, while all those who follow his teachings successfully are called *Sangha*.

Buddhist culture is the result of the impact of these three—the *Buddha, Dhamma* and the *Sangha*, popularly known as the Triple Gem—on individuals and social groups, large and small, in different parts of the world as well as on the whole human race.

Asoka's reign, as recorded on his rock edicts, shows how the Middle Path was applied to politics at that time, because Asoka himself refers to the Middle Path by name, when he indicates his policy and plans for a just and righteous society. *(Dharma Samaja)*.[3] In Japan, Prince Shotoku was sometimes called a second Asoka because he too tried to apply the Middle Path to establish a righteous and just society according to Buddhism.[4]

The history of Sri Lanka provides an example of a social group which has had the impact of the Middle Path ever since the introduction of Buddhism, and continuously for several centuries with only brief periods of interruption due to historical reasons.[5] What is left to us as our cultural heritage resulting from that impact clearly indicates that religious people, religious institutions and religious education according to Buddhism can still play a very significant role in promoting an appropriate way of life which will lead to a new world order where not only economic poverty but also spiritual poverty will be considered as conditions suicidal to the whole human race.

Even today the people of Sri Lanka, with the exception of perhaps the extremely sophisticated urban minority, are making a heroic effort against innumerable obstacles to evolve a national socio-economic, religio-cultural and educational policy based on the Middle Path, without blindly following materialistic philosophies but rather adapting whatever is appropriate for our national culture.[6]

A BUDDHIST RESPONSE TO SOME ISSUES RAISED IN THE BACKGROUND PAPERS

From the foregoing brief introductory statement about Buddhism and Buddhist culture, we have only a bird's eye view of Buddhist teachings about the nature of person, his or her immediate environment and the wider world with which they interact. Nevertheless, we can draw from this brief statement some relevant observations for our discussion on the theme of the seminar and the issues raised in the background papers.

(1) The theme of the seminar and the issues raised appear to focus attention mainly, if not exclusively, on the socio-economic and political structures of society which, for the sake of convenience, we may call the Sociosphere. The Buddhist perspective clearly emphasizes the need for changing the psychological structures of the inner life of the individual (Mind) which may be called the Psychosphere. The latter is the main mission of religious leaders.[7]

(2) The New International Economic Order, which is the main theme of the seminar, cannot be considered in isolation because it is only one dimension of the complex global problem confronting humankind. Even if the problem of the NIEO is solved satisfactorily, the total problem of the New World Order will not be solved unless appropriate changes are brought about in the attitudes, values and interests of the people concerned and involved. This conclusion is based on the Buddhist perspective of both global problems and individual ones.

(3) Regarding the question raised in the background paper whether men and women are educable or not, the Buddhist point of view is in the affirmative, subject of course to the recognition of individual differences due to various factors. The Middle Path philosophy of education provides for these differences.[8] The history of education also clearly indicates that education may be used for the welfare as well as for the destruction of people because of this modifiability and educability of each person. The present world order is a result of an educational system based on false assumptions and values which has to be radically changed. For this, Buddhist educational resources may be relevant and useful.

(4) The problem of world poverty and how to solve it appears to be a main focus of the seminar. Poverty has been understood in our context in terms of material wealth or economic means, and what is sought is international cooperation to meet this problem of world poverty only in an economic sense. A Buddhist perspective is quite different from this. People can be wealthy or affluent economically

but still may be poor spiritually. The same is true of a society or a nation, even of the whole world. It is the inner growth and development of an individual (Psychosphere) that indicates the true wealth which alone leads to true happiness and contentment for the individual as well as for society.

Quantifiable indicators could be evolved to evaluate this aspect of poverty as well. Therefore, unless and until we accept this spiritual poverty and take necessary steps to solve that problem together with the problem of economic poverty, neither a new world order nor a new economic order will be realities.

How this can be done, articulated and measured and what tangible steps have to be taken to fight against the spiritual poverty of the world in general and among the economically affluent in particular, are vital issues for consideration when global problems are viewed from a Buddhist perspective. This is particularly so if we hope to move towards a human world order as suggested by Gerald and Patricia Mische or by Falk and others. [9]

(5) The educational role of religious leaders in Buddhist societies has had an unbroken tradition for which the Buddha himself set the best example by his own life-time educational service. His educational policy statement proclaimed to his first sixty disciples *(Arahants)*, has been very loyally followed by the Buddhist monks whenever they had the facilities and opportunities to do so. The results of this educational role can be seen from the cultural heritage of Buddhist countries like Sri Lanka,[10] where the impact of the *Triple Gem* had been predominant in all spheres of individual, social and national life. For example, this influence is quite conspicuous in education, politics, economic development, irrigation systems, music and dance, art and sculpture, architecture and all aspects of the general behavior pattern of the people and the leaders.

Therefore, Buddhist religious communities, if given the opportunity and orientation, can play a very significant role in the education process of re-educating the educated to build a new world order which will be more human than that which presently exists. A proposal made by this writer to establish an Institute of Buddhist Education for the purpose of initiating studies and implementing model projects oriented to development and peace has been held up for several years due to lack of funds.[11]

The combined and collective educational role that all religious communities can play in promoting development and peace has been emphasized by this writer elsewhere, and a proposal to establish an Asian Centre for Religious Education (ACRE) is now under consideration. Its implementation has also been delayed due to lack of funds.[12] By such a centre the untapped Asian religious educational resources may be explored, studied, re-interpreted, revised and re-vitalized to meet the educational needs of contemporary society.

Regarding the significant role that Buddhist religious education may play, we now have little doubt, particularly because most of the philosophical assumptions and principles relating to the theory and practice of life-long education in Buddhist countries like ancient Sri Lanka appear to be relevant even now, after the world crisis in education has been recognized as real and some consequent studies made about it.[13] This is an area perhaps where economically affluent societies can play a very useful role in the interest of humankind, if they are prepared to sacrifice some of their luxuries to save funds for educational projects of this nature.

(6) The emphasis and even over-emphasis on the Psychosphere does not at all mean that the Sociosphere is not important. Especially, basic human needs for food, clothing, shelter and medical care are accepted in the Buddhist traditions as essential even for spiritual growth. Freedom of inquiry, expression and association are also considered necessary according to Buddhism. What is emphasized here is the main function of religious persons who can attract, develop and harness spiritual forces for the common welfare, if they concentrate more on the development of the Psychosphere rather than the Sociosphere, which they should leave to others to be handled with their guidance.

A gradual process of spiritual development indicated in Buddhism creates conditions favorable to internal growth in the individual concerned. The presence of such individuals, their wishes, guidance and inspiration can have an impact on other conditions of the society in which they live. This is in addition to the observable and empirically verifiable results of such persons as behavior models for others in that society. It is through such spiritually developed religious people that the intuitive potentialities of the human race can be tapped to the maximum and harnessed for the welfare of all. It is also by providing facilities and opportunities for such spiritual development that world poverty in the spiritual sphere can be reduced, particularly in the economically affluent countries and among the economically affluent minorities of the other countries.

CONCLUDING REMARKS

Erich Fromm in his recent book entitled *To Have or To Be* shows how two modes of existence are struggling for the spirit of humankind.[14] In a chapter on conditions for human change and features of the new person, Fromm suggests that human character can change for the better if the following conditions exist:

1. We are suffering and aware that we are.
2. We recognize the origin of our ill-being.
3. We recognize that there is a way of overcoming our ill-being.
4. We accept that in order to overcome our ill-being, we must follow certain norms for living and change our present practice of life.

These four points, according to Fromm himself, correspond to the Four Noble Truths that form the basis of the Buddha's teaching dealing with the general conditions of human existence. He also tries to show how this formula appears similar to the method followed by Marx as well as Freud, in presenting their own solutions to human problems. Let us use this as the basis for our concluding remarks of this short paper.

(1) We are suffering but are we aware that we are? Who are these *we* when we think in terms of a New World Order? Are they not the peoples of the world? Do they know the true situation today and what is in store for them and their children in the near future? People do not know. They are ignorant of the true situation. Therefore, the first step to be taken in the right direction is a world-wide adult education program to create awareness in all people in all countries about the global problems confronting humankind. In addition, do they know how to adjust to any of the fast-changing conditions being predicted? That too they do not know because education for them does not include such useful knowledge on the assumption that they are not scientific. Hence the equally important need to popularize such knowledge. Only then will they be able to know and see the global problems as they really are.

(2) Whether we like it or not, we must now admit that the present human predicament is mainly due to our ignorance of the true nature of human nature despite all the scientific knowledge that has been acquired by humankind within the last few centuries. Instead of helping us and guiding us to adjust ourselves to the fast-changing conditions, this knowledge expansion appears to keep us lulled but groaning under its weight, awaiting the inevitable doom in a total annihilation of all, due to our own inability to control its proliferation and abuse for destructive purposes. But it is true that to most of those directly involved in this knowledge industry, it does serve the purpose of maintaining the establishment at any cost.

The situation goes from bad to worse because the Buddhist technique of understanding the true nature of human nature (Psychosphere) is discarded and discredited by scientists as an unscientific method of knowing although every one has a right to know this technique because it is an integral part of the common human culture. As long as we ignore all the traditional religious resources relating to human behavior and depend only on scientific knowledge, we will not be able to know the origin and nature of our suffering. Therefore, the second step to be taken in the right direction to solve global human problems confronting humankind today is to explore all the religious education resources which can help us understand ourselves and the problems affecting us.

Under normal circumstances, it is a UN agency like UNESCO which was founded to build defenses of peace in the minds of people through education, science and culture that should take the initiative in world-wide ventures of this nature with a global significance. But attempts to get UNESCO interested in such studies and projects have not met with success,[15] perhaps due to its holy alliance with "Science God" and the consequent unholy suspicion about all religious resources. Or it may be because UNESCO has not yet been able to escape its policy of propagating the culture of its home country even at the risk of losing all other cultures, as pointed out by some scholars recently,[16] and also as seen from the way funds have been allocated to Non Governmental Organizations (NGO's) in the last thirty years.[17]

(3) Educability and modifiability of human nature along with the availability of adequate unexplored religio-cultural educational resources that have proved their effectiveness in evolving the style of life and type of society appropriate for a new world order provide the hope and the assurance that the present human predicament can be overcome. Studies have to be made about traditional cultures and experiments have to be tried to evolve an appropriate style of life and a social model that can ensure human survival at least, if not human welfare and spiritual liberation.

(4) As Fromm suggests, if we accept that we must follow certain norms for living we must first dethrone the present consumer-oriented, need-proliferating, extremely materialistic style of life which Fromm calls the "having mode." This is according to Buddhism the extreme of excessive indulgence in sensual pleasures. We must also popularize and develop the Middle Path style of life which promotes harmony with nature, moderation, simplicity, non-violence and contentment. The name given to this way of life does not matter.

In order to understand the concept of Middle Path which in general has to be followed as a solution to global problems today by not emphasizing the Sociosphere at the expense of the Psychosphere, I may conclude this with two statements indicative of the two perspectives of the same human predicament—one with emphasis on the Sociosphere and the other on the Psychosphere.

The one uses the scientific method and analyzes only the structures of the Sociosphere. The other uses the insight (Vipassana) meditation method and sees things as they really are (Yatha-Bhuta-Nana-Dassana). The one by the founders of the Club of Rome opened the "growth debate" and the first window to the hitherto hidden global human predicament by publishing *Limits to Growth*.[18] The other was the question posed to the Buddha by a deity and the Buddha's reply to that question.

The one is the opening paragraph of the introductory chapter of a book entitled *On Growth* [19] which assembled the responses to the Club of Rome report from seventy scholars, thinkers and scientists mostly of Western countries and representative of Western culture.

"With man at the pinnacle of his knowledge and power, a profound malaise is spreading through human society. Faced with an increasingly more complex and ever-changing tangle of intertwined problems—some of them overarching all political, cultural, and geographical boundaries—mankind is threatened by an unprecedented crisis."

The other was the theme of a dissertation called the Visiddhi Magga [20] submitted to the Mahavihara Buddhist University of Anuradhapura during the first century by the great commentator BUDDHAGHOSHA to qualify himself as a competent scholar to write Pali commentaries to Buddhist texts based on the Sinhalese commentaries accepted by that university.

QUESTION
Tangles inside and tangles outside, the whole community is entangled in a tangle. And so I ask of Gotama this question, Who succeeds in disentangling this tangle.

ANSWER
When a wise man, established well in virtue, develops his mind and insight, then such a person if ardent and sagacious, he succeeds in disentangling this tangle.

Anto Jata Bahijata—Jataya Jatita Paja
Tan Tam Gotama Pucchama—Ko Imam Vijatye Jatam

Sile Patitthaya Narosapanno—Cittam Pannaca Bhavaym
Atapi Nipako Bhikkhu—So Imam Vijataye Jatam.

The impact of this Middle Path approach to both individual and social life can be seen even today from the cultural heritage of Sri Lanka, and in the way that heritage is shaping the socio-economic and political policies of that nation in the contemporary global society. *Ehipassiko*—come and see!

FOOTNOTES

1. Hewage, L. G., "A Theory of Education based on Buddhist Philosophy," unpublished Thesis for MA (Ed) University of Ceylon, Peradeniya, 1959.

2. Hewage, L. G., "Towards A World Community," (A Middle Path Approach) Paper presented to Multi-lateral Dialogue of W.C.C. Colombo Papers, W.C.C. Geneva, 1975.

3. Rev. G. Saranankara Thero, *Asoka and his Inscriptions,* (Sinhala ed.) Mangala Press, Maradana, Colombo, 1963.

4. Kode Matsunami, *Introducing Buddhism,* The Hode Mission of Hawaii, 1973.

5. Hewage, L. G., "Role of Religion in Asian Development." Paper presented to an Inter-religious Seminar on Religion and Development in Asian Society, Colombo, Marga Publications, 1974.

6. Hewage, L. G., *Metta* (Loving Kindness), Sarvodaya Press. Moratuwa, Sri Lanka, 1975.

7. Hewage, L. G., "Peace Through Religion," Background Paper for Asian Conference Religion and Peace (ACRP), Singapore, 1976 (Full report not yet published).

8. Hewage, L. G., "A Theory of Education based on Buddhist Philosophy," unpublished Thesis for MA (Ed) University of Ceylon, Peradeniya, 1959.

9. Mische, Gerald and Patricia, *Towards a Human World Order,* Paulist Press, 1977; Falk, Richard, *A Study of Future Worlds,* New York, The Free Press, 1975.

10. Hewage, L. G., "Relevance of Cultural Heritage in Development Education" (A Middle Path Approach based on the Experience of Sri Lanka). Paper presented to the Special International Session of Sri Lanka Association for Advancement of Science (SLAAS), Colombo, 1976.

11. "Report of the Inaugural Meeting of the UNESCO Committee of the World Fellowship of Buddhists," Bangkok, 1973.

12. "Peace Through Religion," ACRP Brief Report, Fumon Hall, 2-6 Wada Suginami-ku, Tokyo 166, Japan (pp. 35 to 39).

13. Faure, Edgar and others, *Learning to Be, The World of Education Today and Tomorrow,* Paris, UNESCO, 1972 and also *Education on the Move; A Companion Volume to Learning to Be,* OISE-UNESCO, Paris, 1975.

14. Fromm, Erich, *To Have or to Be,* World Perspective Series, No. 50, Harper & Row, New York, 1976.

15. Hewage, L. G., "BINESCO, A Buddhist Approach to UNESCO Objectives," National Education Council of All Ceylon Buddhist Congress, Colombo, 1971.

16. Pendergast, William R., "UNESCO and French cultural relations 1945-1970" in *International Organization,* Vol. 30 No. 3, Summer 1976, University of Wisconsin Press.

17. UNESCO "Director General's Report to the 19th General Conference of UNESCO, Nairobi, on Activities of NGO's for Thirty Years."

18. Meadows and Others, *Limits to Growth,* Club of Rome Report on the Predicament of Mankind, London, Pan Books Ltd., 1972.

19. Oltmans, William L. (ed), *On Growth,* Capricorn Book Edition, 1974 (USA).

20. Bhikkhu Nyanamoli, *English Translation of the Visuddi Magga by Buddhaghosha,* Revised Edition published by Buddhist Publications Society, Kandy, Sri Lanka, 1976.

SUMMARY

Hewage first describes how Prince Siddhartha, who later became the Buddha, discovered the "Middle-Path" way of life by which he himself was fully liberated and had totally conquered greed, hatred and illusion. He then goes on to show how the Buddah trained disciples and later ordinary lay people to follow the Middle-Path in their day-to-day life, thus following a positive and peaceful way avoiding extremes and retaining a dynamically neutral attitude on all controversial issues.

Hewage believes that the Middle-Path way of Buddhism has had significant influence on shaping the socio-economic, religio-cultural and educational policies of many countries and regions of the world. His own country, Sri Lanka, is, he believes, an excellent example of this influence at the present time.

Finally, he suggests that a Buddhist perspective would empha-size the "psychosphere"—"the main mission of religious leaders"— much more than the present background papers do. Buddhists believe men and women are educable and that Buddhist educational resources are relevant for the radical change required in education today. He deplores the seeming lack of interest in agencies like UNESCO with his suggestion, for he is convinced that if the Middle-Path style of life—or whatever it is called—is developed and popularized in its individual and social dimensions, it will promote harmony with nature, moderation, simplicity, non-violence and contentment among all peoples. He ends by inviting his readers to come to Sri Lanka and see for themselves.

12

Synthesis of Papers and Discussion

Bellah reminds his readers that the challenge which a changing world offers to faith today is not a one-way challenge. In fact, his paper is more concerned with the challenge that faith presents to the changing world, because of his personal conviction that meaning, belief, spirit, faith are the ultimate determinants of human action. For him religion's primary task today is to unmask modern Western ideology and to reveal it for what it is—one very important but particular historical way of perceiving reality.

For slightly different reasons, Hewage, Ahmad, Carr and Blank are all in agreement with Bellah on this central point. Hewage, because he sees modern Western ideology at odds with the Buddhist "Middle-Path" way, which requires a holistic, non-violent, harmonious approach to life focussed on restructuring the human personality. Ahmad, because he sees Western ideology as alien to Islam in its piecemeal, value-free approach to reality. For him, this ideology fails in not being centered on the human-person-in-community under God, and in its Western view of men and women as self-sufficient rather than as God's *Khalifahs* (vicegerents) here on earth. Carr, because as an African he sees the urgent need to demythologize not only the present world economic order but also the African Christian church itself of their smug racial and self-centered biases they continue to call "objective" and even "scientific."

All except Blank stress the need for a holistic view to replace economic and other partial views of the human person and society. Blank is more concerned that believers risk becoming responsible actors in history, getting on with the task of setting up effective institutions rather than being paralyzed, like Job, by an overambitious search for cosmic and holistic visions, or being tempted to wait unduly for the coming of the Messiah who brings perfect solutions for today's problems of injustice.

As before, the participants' discussion took the form of raising points, questions and observations rather than of sustained debate, but it was evident that there was a much wider consensus on the role of faith communities in the world than there had been on the process of structuring a new world order. The group could now build on or nuance each other's remarks and address specific topics.

Several Muslims took exception to sections of Bellah's paper. They insisted that his criticism of Islam as a religion was not scientific but rather autobiographically biased by his own Western experience and perceptual framework. For them, Islam must be judged on its own merits—not as seen through the prism of Western ideology nor in the actions of individuals or groups of Muslims in history.

There were different views about the present status of modern Western ideology—some participants confident that it is dead or about to die, others uneasy that it has become all too much a part of civilization, perhaps irrevocably.

The concept of original sin, of human nature being flawed—alien to Buddhism and Islam—tended to make these believers more confident than the Jews, and in varying degrees the Christians, about potential abuses and contradictions in the best intentioned human enterprises and even in religion itself. And yet most in the group seemed to agree that fear of demonstrating religious triumphalism should not be an excuse for failing to endorse political power put at the service of the universal good. Nor can an option for tolerance and religious pluralism deny the universal claims of truth.

There was strong reaction against the suggestion that religions—or at least religious leaders—should be content to identify issues only and not become openly and actively involved in the socio-economic and political field. But this was not to deny the fact that even religious institutions by the very fact of being human often betray the faith community itself, and are used by the class struggle and by political movements, as well as by the power establishment, for their own purposes. Yet it was agreed that believers cannot stand apart from today's world struggles. Again and again they are called to reread their holy books and reexamine their traditions and listen to their prophets in the light of daily events and try to discern an honest creative response.

The disturbing fact of the multinational corporations not focussing on the basic needs of poor people raised the more fundamental question of private property itself. Arns circulated notes presenting a critique in which he noted that from the time of Moses it has been clear to religious leaders that private property and the power associated with it is a source of egoism and easily leads to a society in which justice is impossible. People of faith have to criticize all ideologies that degrade the human person but particularly those which lie behind the glorification of private property. It is not what persons own but what they are that determines their humanity. All religions have long traditions of social criticism and have also tried to foster institutions that ground human community on mutual love and compassion, not on greed, competition or self-aggrandizement.

Gradually, a growing consensus emerged that religion's role should be to critique present narrow *economic* approaches to a new world order by bringing a broader, more human and comprehensive approach to today's problems. Religion should also define and enhance the creative role for men and women in the building up of the world, supplying them with motivation, a set of values and priorities, and even key institutions to foster their mission of responsible stewardship over the whole of creation. This includes a new cross-fertilization of anthropology and cosmology with theology and eschatology.

It seemed, at least to some, that religion could even provide a process for influencing social change as well as for renewing religion itself, along the lines suggested by Bellah. Religion, in fact, as a "movement" under charismatic leaders has usually proved more creative than either "sect" or "church" religion, though these categories are seldom mutually exclusive and often reinforce each other.

In the overall discussion that centered largely on the role of religion in relativizing the idol of ideology, particularly of modern Western ideology, the participants became more aware of how all speech, thinking, and perception is biographically structured. The miracle of Lisbon was that persons of such different experiences and beliefs could talk together at all. Shared faith in an absolute and transcendent God enabled the participants to see the relativity of all that exists, including all human structures and power. This gave them sufficient common vision to begin, acquire mutual trust, carry on and see the promising possibilities of continuing dialogue and future cooperation toward a more just and human world order.

13

Summary of Recommendations

Jane Blewett

On the final morning of the conference, the participants were divided into three work groups to come up with suggestions of future directions and tasks for IRPC to pursue after Lisbon. The results of their brainstorming can be grouped under five general headings: 1) immediate follow-up by IRPC officers, 2) social teachings and publications, 3) concerns of the world's poorest, 4) development of regional groups and 5) future meetings.

1) Immediate follow-up by IRPC officers:

— develop a declaration or statement to inform the respective faith communities and the world at large of IRPC's existence, what it stands for, the fact of the Lisbon meeting, the issues discussed and the principles agreed upon emerging from the several traditions represented; disseminate this information as widely as possible;

— publish at the earliest possible date, the papers and proceedings of the Lisbon conference;

2) Social teachings and publications:

— encourage leaders in the faith communities to develop social doctrine and sensitize their own people with respect to the prophetic teachings reflecting on the outstanding social problems of our times, problems of mass poverty, human rights, misuse of technology, disarmament, the role of private property and multinational corporations, quality of life, etc.; share this information across faiths;

— encourage faith communities to reflect on how the real costs and burdens of bringing about a new world order will be distributed among rich and poor, both within and among countries. Here, as in other efforts to educate to justice, they should profit from the growth and experience of small or base communities in both poor and rich countries;

— formulate specific positions on various concrete policy proposals drawn from the reflections of the various faith groups, as a guide to those in public policy-making positions;

— sponsor a publications program that would raise the level of understanding of one faith community in respect to the other communities, stressing in particular areas of commonality and affinity rather than separation and differences;

— produce new literature presenting viewpoints of the major religions on specific questions theoretical and theological, as well as practical, such as, the concept of God and person, worldview and natural environment, diet, family, economic justice, race, materialism, secularism, etc.;

— explore the possibility of sponsoring worldwide studies of the role religions have played in the past, play now and might well play in the future to promote a socio-economic system more appropriate for a global society;

— integrate IRPC's thrust into existing faith groups and religious networks;

3) Concerns of the world's poorest:

— to work toward the alleviation of extreme poverty among the 450 million or more who are at bare subsistence living, the so-called 'fourth world', IRPC should prepare and disseminate information on the subject;

— encourage governments and private foundations to assist voluntary organizations already actively addressing this concern;

— serve as a clearing house for existing religious and voluntary aid organizations to focus their efforts on the poorest of the poor;

— identify the resources needed and mobilize expert technologies, particularly in agriculture, appropriate to 'fourth world' situations;

— encourage media attention to this problem;

— sensitize young people to existing inequities through formal school curricula;

— exercise influence wherever possible to encourage governments to cancel debts owed by fourth world countries;

4) Regional growth:

— IRPC should assist in the generation of regional groups and assist them in developing programs appropriate to their areas;

— these groups should work at the level of individual faith communities and at inter-faith levels in order to disseminate the message of IRPC, undertake study programs, and eventually take up whatever action proposals evolve; for instance, an African cultural forum on development similar to the existing Asian forum;

— move toward regional conferences that would cover a variety of topics adapted to certain geographical areas of the world, for example, the question of human rights in Latin America;

— regional conferences on structural changes needed within the developing world itself and within nations in order to make a new international order possible;

— work to insure that regional groups and events link closely to the main body of IRPC and its international network, not only in terms of the practical assistance that might be derived from such linkage, but also to provide a certain degree of security to those participants who live in precarious situations;

5) Future meetings:

— conferences should be held in countries where the issue under discussion is actually being experienced and more local participation included;

— participants should be expanded to include more equal participation of women;

— future meetings should include participants skilled in the area of communications and mass media in order to assist in the process of dissemination of news;

— topics that might be considered in future meetings include: the experience of faith groups when they are in either majority or minority positions in relation to the rest of society; religion as a uniting or divisive force in an interdependent world; religion and human rights; faith and ideologies, etc.

PART III

Followup and Future

14

A Statement on the Lisbon Meeting by Officers of the Interreligious Peace Colloquium

Matthew Rosenhaus, Isma'il al-Faruqi
Henry Siegman, Joseph Gremillion
William Ryan, Cynthia Wedel
Theodore Hesburgh, Irwin Blank

THE LISBON MEETING

We met during the week before President Sadat's visit to Jerusalem. We numbered but thirty. Eight Jews—three from Israel, five from the United States. Seven Muslims—from Cairo and Istanbul, Jordan, Iran, Turkey and Pakistan, two among them exiles from Gaza and Jaffa, Palestine. Thirteen Christians—one each from the Vatican and the World Council of Churches, nine from West Europe and North America, and two courageous leaders of the awakening churches of Africa and Brazil. Two came from South and East Asia, Buddhists of Sri Lanka and Japan.

Most participants were from secular fields: seven with direct political experience, six in business and economic affairs, two from the media, seven in academic life. Only eight were pastors or leaders of faith communities. All acknowledged, however, that their faith traditions and religio-ethical values directly influence their daily work and professions. The large majority actively participate within their respective communities.

JEWS-MUSLIMS-CHRISTIANS

The "mix" of the Lisbon meeting was singular in another significant way. Purposely we brought together believers in the One Personal Creator of all the human family, the God of Abraham and Moses, Jesus and Muhammad.

We did this for three reasons: First, because we Jews, Muslims and Christians share so much in faith from divine revelation; also in our devotional practice and moral imperatives, world vision and hope for the future, in time and eternity. And how that sense of sharing grew and deepened during our week-long live-in together!

Second, because there have been too many periods when we were at enmity with each other, despite our kinship in blood, our spiritual and family roots from Abraham through his sons Isaac and Isma'il, from these brothers on to Mary and Jesus and Muhammad. Together we seek now reconciliation, friendship and cooperation.

The third reason for our unique mixture appears from our theme: The challenge presented to our three communities of faith by the search for a new world order of justice and peace among our globe's one hundred forty-nine nations. What should faith respond to this mounting call for transforming structures, within and among nations, so as to provide basic human needs and to assure human rights and full development of all our planet's peoples?

Can our three monotheist communities present a uniting witness to our four thousand million sisters and brothers under God? All begin to realize their increasing interdependence as nations, regions and blocs, due to a technology at once wonderful and horrendous. All acquire fresh awareness of their human solidarity, of their universal yearning for justice and peace, of their common danger and hope and destiny.

HUMAN DIGNITY FROM GOD

A new world order, it was agreed at Lisbon, must be fashioned, negotiated and constructed. And Jews, Christians and Muslims of the West and Middle East have, we felt, unique responsibilities in this arduous endeavor.

These responsibilities flow from our long historical relationship and from economic, political and military reasons as current and stark as the morning headlines and evening TV reports. Also, our believing Peoples—through temple and mosque, church and synagogue—continue to play major roles, for conflict and/or cooperation, in the nations and civilizations they have helped generate in our regions.

Too, we "People of the Book" share the same conviction in *the* root source of human dignity. We Jews-Muslims-Christians worship the same God Who, in the words of Genesis, creates each human to His Own Image; we adore the same God Who, in the words of the Qur'an, "fashioned him (man) in due proportion, and breathed into him something of His spirit." (Surah 32:9)

Therefore, today when human dignity, human needs and human rights take first place on the world's agenda, we see this as a providential sign. We feel called then to address these issues of "the humanum" precisely as Muslims, Christians and Jews seeking solutions and working together.

By no means do we wish to ignore other faith communities. Two Buddhists were with us at Lisbon; we regret that two Hindu friends had to cancel out at the last moment. Through other sessions and groups we monotheists hope to carry forward our initial exchanges with the other transcendental religions.

THE NEW SKEPTICS

We recognize too the pervasive and often beneficent influence exercised in our era by the social sciences and humanist ideologies. We remain open to the precious natural insights they bring to us about society and the human condition, nation and world community, history and the future. We rejoice at the creativity and discipline which engender modern technology and we would cooperate in many of its projects for human betterment.

But as believers ours basically is a critical stance.

We reject the facile credulity accorded exclusivist rationalism and the scientific method during the past century throughout the West, and infecting now most of the globe. Toward this narrow horizontal approach to total reality, we who believe in God declare ourselves "the new skeptics."

Together we hope to bring fresh dimnsions of love and justice and life's meaning into current debates and struggles among our interdependent peoples. Provided our sustaining Creator awakens us anew to His transforming Message and to our prophetic role in today's world.

For this at Lisbon we began to pray and search together, to strengthen and animate each other. For we, would-be witnesses to the Light, the Good, the Power, are so often myopic, sinful, weak. As individuals, groups, communities; as Jews, Muslims, Christians.

A HUMAN WORLD ORDER

Addressing ourselves initially to the call for a New International Economic Order now debated in the United Nations, we quickly stripped away the modifier "economic." The changes must also be political, social and cultural, we all affirmed.

Our goal then must be a *human* world order, which provides basic human needs and assures the rights of freedom and participation for all.

This goal requires fundamental changes in world structures, we all agreed, through transfers of economic and political power.

Third World participants insisted that the injustice in today's world order derives directly from the colonial and imperialist control of the West over most of the planet's peoples, from 1800 to World War II. During that period the industrialized West organized the globe for their own benefit. The economic, military, political and cultural structures of that global system, the first in history, remain largely intact in our time, despite the formal independence of a hundred nations since 1945. Some Southerners went on to contend that even the United Nations was constituted by the five great powers to shore up that framework.

Underdevelopment, therefore, is not simply national or cultural backwardness of people, according to this Third World view. It comes rather from an exploitative global system and development models imposed by the North. So Southern underdevelopment is the ugly by-product of Northern industrialization for selfish nationalist goals.

The interlacing cobweb of power structures which entangle the South includes the North's technological and financial power, exercised principally through transnational enterprises, together with the North's military might. To this must be added the cultural dominance of Western civilization exerted through education, information and communications systems. This view holds that self-reliant development among nations must be maximized in order to break this inherited stranglehold.

Northern participants raised no direct or absolute challenge to this Third World explanation for the genesis of today's unjust global system. They asked rather, what can be done about it, within and among nations, blocs and regions. Some Northerners tended toward adjustments within the inherited system. They also asked how Southern nations could justify demands for democratic equality and participation in global institutions, when so many denied these rights to their own citizens in their own national institutions. Southerners contended that often these regimes persist because of Northern support.

NORTH-SOUTH CONSENSUS

We reached, however, a solid consensus despite these questions, that significant transfers of economic and political power from North to South are required. The sudden start and growing volume of this power shift through the Organization of Petroleum Exporting Countries received the attention due this historic turnaround. Of unique interest because of Lisbon's interfaith perspective, it became clear that many in the Muslim community have begun grappling with the moral implications for justice and development, human rights and peace, of their sudden responsibility for enormous wealth and power — within their own region and for our interdependent world.

We also agreed that transfers of economic capability must give priority to basic needs for the poorest of the poor, the billion humans who have nothing to be "economic" about, nothing to sell, nothing to buy, the five hundred million who are constantly malnourished, often suffering famine. We reacted favorably to the recent tentative formula for measuring human development, namely, the Physical Quality of Life Index, based on rates of infant mortality, literacy and longevity. This represents a substantial improvement over the Gross National Product.

All accepted that basic transformations would hurt, but still must be carried through. Northerners insisted that the cost of changes resulting from more labor-intensive production, medium level technology, adjusted tariff and trade patterns, etc., must not fall upon the poorest and weakest within their own nations. Even those who could reduce high consumption without really hurting are loathe to forsake their superabundance by simpler lifestyles. The young people in these countries are generally more flexible. We saw the need of personal interior conversion and unselfish motivation for generating the fresh political will to effect changes required among the Northern rich.

Southerners recalled the dramatic suffering inflicted on Third World peoples by the Western world system for many generations. They asserted that the new world order will benefit the North as well as the South, that it is more than a "zero sum game," taking from one exactly what will be given to another. Some, from both North and South, regard it as a "positive sum game," everyone will gain from a more human world order.

This is due to the present interdependence of all nations, unprecedented in history, and the problems shared in consequence. We did admit that North and South must face together problems such as the arms race and nuclear threat, depletion of scarce resources, especially oil, and chronic food shortages, rampant inflation, unemployment and damage to the environment. Continuing arms sales to the

Third World by industrailized nations was decried as particularly tragic and immoral.

We perceived at Lisbon that absolute sovereignty of the nation state and unbridled nationalism fly in the face of this new global reality. We saw that political realism today demands openness beyond traditional national interests and territorial security, beyond our inherited brand of narrow internationalism merely for "reasons of state."

A COMMUNITY EXPERIENCE

As our week drew to a close, we marvelled that our disparate group had drawn so close together.

Our sense of community was nurtured by the informal setting of our small seaside hotel, ideal for confidential talk and sharing. Also, by the scheduled "quiet periods," of some forty to sixty minutes, "each day for prayer, meditation and services, alone or in groups."

The week's highlight, all agreed, was the outpouring of personal experience, doubt and hope, which occurred during the opening session. Each in turn looked inside self to answer: Who am I? Why am I here?

Gradually the probing went far beyond banal embroidery upon curriculum vitae. Self-revelation took over each in turn. "Why am I doing this?" several asked. "I've never exposed my deepest motives and religious quest to anyone. Why now, to total strangers?" The two hours allotted for introductions stretched into six, and remained still the shortest session of all.

OUR JOINT MISSION

And what do we do next? How continue what has begun?

We have reached an initial consensus on the role of religion for promoting a more just and human world order. We see our role as constant appraisal of this arduous secular effort in terms of the value of human beings, their origin and transcendental character and ultimate destiny. We who believe must bring a more comprehensive vision into this long-term endeavor—dimensions which are anthropological and cosmological, theological and eschatological.

While not rejecting the strategy of "positive sum games" and bargaining packages, we are convinced that personal transformation and deep inner motivation are imperative. Our unique message as Jews, Muslims, Christians, is the love and justice of God for all His human creatures, and that we bear true witness to Him through our own love and justice toward all. Our joint mission, we now see, is to move this love and justice into the Monday morning world of economic and political power, into the regular processes of policy-and decision-making.

For that reason we have come to regard ourselves as a faith-inspired movement, a community of friends who offer solidarity and courage to those among us who are exposed to danger on "the front-lines" as defenders of the weakest and poorest and most oppressed.

AN INTERFAITH INTERNATIONAL

The Interreligious Peace Colloquium (IRPC) sponsored the Lisbon conference to carry forward an embryonic peace and justice movement born out of a similar experience two years ago in Bellagio, Italy. The subject of that first session was "The Food-Energy Crisis: Challenge to the World Faiths." The undersigned are officers and directors of IRPC, which was legally constituted a year ago to provide the minimum of structure needed to keep our movement afloat.

Our present group is basically North American in its composition and concerns. At Lisbon all participants agreed that they will begin forming groups in other regions, e.g., in West Europe, the Middle East, South Asia, Latin America, and Black Africa. As these advance we hope to federate as equal partners. Interfaith groups will also be formed in metropolitan centers; these will provide local networks for the regional groups.

We perceived that our movement has a major role to play within our three faith communities. We will communicate the content, motive and meaning of our Lisbon experience to our religious leaders and official bodies, at local, national and world levels. Their understanding and the cooperation of temple and mosque, church and synagogue are necessary for realizing our Lisbon aims. We shared information about the networks of our faith communities, some of which are recently organized, especially among Islamic bodies.

Where appropriate we shall assist interfaith coalitions, and if lacking stimulate their formation, within our respective nations. These interfaith coalitions must bring our Lisbon consensus on a human world order to government officials, scholars and members of the foreign policy community, to business, labor and farm leaders, into educational systems and the media.

At Lisbon we discovered marked convergence on religious principles and practices which can undergird our joint efforts, at local, national and global levels. We agreed that "social ministry" of this sort is needed in the normal teaching mission and prayer life of our faith communities. We shared examples of such ministry and of the religious literature now being prepared to nourish it.

To assist this process, we will encourage research and studies on the relation of faith and justice in our interdependent world, and will publish books, pamphlets and articles which present and enrich the "social teaching" of each community. The papers of our Lisbon conference and a more detailed report of its findings will be published in book form in spring 1978. At that time an interpretative account of the Interreligious Peace Colloquium, 1975-77, and of the Bellagio session which launched it, will also be published; this book's title will be *Food-Energy and the Major Faiths* (Orbis Books, New York).

We now feel called into a sort of "Interfaith International," growing out of this Lisbon experience of our rooted dependence upon our one personal God.

We rejoice at the deep sense of brother-sisterhood we His followers have discovered in each other, and toward all the human family, awakened anew by the interdependence of our one hundred forty-nine nations on this "Only One Earth" provided us by Him.

By this Statement we the undersigned officers and directors of the Interreligious Peace Colloquium, who participated in the Lisbon conference, make known to all who would hear our findings and commitments.

Officers:

Matthew Rosenhaus, President
Isma'il al-Faruqi, Vice-President
Henry Siegman, Treasurer
Joseph Gremillion, Secretary and Coordinator
William Ryan, Executive Secretary

Members, Board of Directors:

Cynthia Wedel
Theodore Hesburgh
Irwin Blank

(Other members of the Board, not present at Lisbon, are Maurice Strong, Henry Schultz, Muhammad Abdul Rauf, Sol M. Linowitz, Philip Klutznick, and Simeon Adebo.)

15

Reflections and the Future

Joseph Gremillion and William Ryan

Four months after the Lisbon meeting, we who have edited this book reflect upon its larger meaning and possible upshot.

As executive staff for the Interreligious Peace Colloquium we two have had prime responsibility for conceiving the Lisbon program in consultation with scores of officers and experts, and for spelling out the thrust of its ten papers with each of their authors. After directing the whole process for over two years, through the actual conference and the Statement given above, we have now studied anew and summarized the papers, sought clarification from their authors, reviewed the discussion, and, we trust, presented the several parts of this Lisbon experience as an interconnected whole.

To conclude, we now reflect upon the deeper significance of this singular experience as an intelligible unit within the much larger whole of the human community now a-borning, formed by trans-national actors of diverse character, endowed with varying kinds and degrees of power and weakness. These we find merely begin to awaken to their self-identity as *transnational* actors, and of their roles in the overarching community of communities—a newly conscious "we" embracing all humankind—which they increasingly beget, often through absent-minded groping.

I. RATIONALE OF THE LISBON PROCESS

A. Purpose

Our basic purpose was to address the changing world order from the dimension of transcendent faith, in order to generate larger vision and stronger commitment for human betterment, social justice, human rights and peace. The present socio-economic and political order must, we felt, be judged in the light of religious convictions and values. Likewise, a critique of religion's worldly role should be made under the challenge of the changing global order.

Through this process we aimed at bringing major Faith Communities into vital relation with each other within the *arena of this-world issues*. We chose to focus particularly upon the three Faiths of the one monotheist family which have been at enmity through much of their history—Jews, Muslims, Christians. And we hoped that common convictions held by the three would be strengthened to provide ground for future cooperation, in lieu of historic and current conflict.

After Lisbon we are convinced that this purpose, however grandiose its scope and rhetoric, can and should be pursued, even by such modest means as there taken. And that such simple steps can and will be multiplied, as the significance of the purpose is grasped.

B. Premise

A basic premise of our Lisbon process was that while the national unit retains considerable power, transnational groups or actors take on increased roles in our interdependent world, and these must consciously interrelate in new modes.

These transnational groups or actors we have, for our purposes, identified under four categories: economic-political blocs, religio-cultural ethnic regions, faith communities, and ideologies.

1) Economic and political blocs, composed of nation-states.

In the context of the New International Economic Order, the two overarching blocs were represented at Lisbon: the North (some 35 nations) and the South, or the Third World (some 110 nations).

More precisely, only the Western bloc within the industrialized North (including Japan) was present, and not the Eastern or Soviet bloc, although it forms part of the North. Nor were there participants from China which creates its own bloc within the Third World. (These absences were deliberate, in view of our purpose and method.) Among Southern participants there were spokespersons from the new economic and political bloc formed by the Organization of Petroleum Exporting Countries, OPEC.

2) *Religio-cultural ethnic regions of geopolitical significance.*

The West and Mideast were the two regions best represented at Lisbon. Only seven out of thirty participants came from the much more populous regions of Black Africa, Latin America and Asia.

3) *Faith communities*

These become transnational actors insofar as their belief and ethical systems affect the socio-economic and political views of citizens from several nation states. This can erode narrow nationalism and generate loyalty to a larger collective "we" among believers of several countries. Usually this influence is exercised through or in concert with cultural ethnic regions and ideologies.

This transnational effectiveness of faith communities is increased if their national units are organized for transnational communication and cooperation as or with universal or regional councils, fellowships, churches, brotherhoods, sisterhoods, and similar associations. Among such transnational actors represented at Lisbon were the Islamic Council of Europe, Synagogue Council, World Council of Churches, Roman Catholic Church, Buddhist Federation, All Africa Conference of Churches, and the Jesuit Society.

4) *Ideologies*

Ideologies, in the double and positive sense of "a systematic body of concepts especially about human life or culture; the integrated assertions, theories, and aims that constitute a sociopolitical program." (Webster's Collegiate Dictionary, 1973 edition)

Capitalism and socialism, nationalism, colonialism and imperialism were ideologies repeatedly in contention at Lisbon, as exercising transnational influence, together with conservatism, liberalism, humanism and individualism, modernism and technological "progress," racism and sexism. Their presence at Lisbon had been foreseen; they thread through the papers and discussion as our report indicates. These ideologies become transnational actors exercising influence through scientific and cultural centers and associations, political parties and blocs, the media, multinational business, foundations, governmental, voluntary and religious networks, etc.

C. Method

Our method through the Lisbon process was to facilitate interchange among these four types of transnational groups or actors, by focusing on the changing world order.

We attempted this by bringing together thirty leaders who are in some measure representative of key economic-political *blocs*, religio-cultural ethnic *regions, faith communities,* and *ideologies.* We spent a week together in formal study and discussion, and in much friendly conversation, within a setting of quiet, prayerful community. Personal examination and expression of motives and ideals were encouraged.

Given the restriction of numbers required for personal sharing, all transnational actors were not represented. As already indicated, complete universality was neither expected nor attempted. Still, on the whole, the "mix" and result were excellent.

The method is, then, workable. Our most telling discovery was the extent to which our deepest perception of reality is biographically rooted. And one's quest for this self-fulfillment is willingly shared in an appropriate setting, and affects the experience by evoking trust.

Secular leaders brought concreteness to the religious exchange, because of the human focus on needs and rights. But economic and political issues as such were not confronted substantially. Faith, value and cultural dimensions were dominant.

II. THE FAITH DIMENSION

Despite the volume and quality of the economic and political input, by four major papers and the personalities present, this served mainly as the basis and focus for religious and value-oriented discourse. Jews, Muslims and Christians showed faith dimensions which can be characterized as follows:

1. Their interchange was substantial and fruitful, despite well-known suspicions and tensions. Spokespersons for each community showed marked preoccupations, respectively:

Jews: the future of Israel, and the past of ghettos and Holocaust; their uniqueness and durability as a people, biblical and historical.

Muslims: awakening again to a world role, confronting modernization, purging out Western cultural intrusions, certainty in their belief and destiny.

Christians: self-criticism in view of past triumphalism and centuries-long abuse of the two other communities through intolerance and imperialism; new openness and concern for justice.

2. These three monotheist Faiths share common sources and history, content and vision, which set them apart from the other great religions. It is fitting that they consciously seek a certain "community" under their One God. Simultaneously however, they should open to

dialogue and cooperation with the other transcendental Faiths, especially with Buddhists and Hindus.

3. Jews-Muslims-Christians share fundamental convictions in areas which affect the changing world order. The extent and depth of this convergence came as a surprise. Agreement is found on human dignity, needs and rights; joint stewardship among all humans over all the earth's resources; critique of private property and unjust power structures; unity of the whole human family, inadequacy of the nation state for solving global issues, and necessity of transnational economic and political bodies in our interdependent world.

Each Faith Community should elaborate its "social teaching" along comparable themes. The three should seek rapprochement of their social ethics and should address world and regional issues conjointly.

4. To an unexpected degree, spokespersons for the faith and social scientists, *as* social scientists, combined to make a strong critique of "exclusivist rationalism and the scientific method . . . and humanist ideologies." Toward these worldviews and ideologies, rampant "during the past century throughout the West, and infecting now most of the globe," participants declared themselves "the new skeptics." (See the Statement for quotes)

Among social scientists, motives for this critique arise because of failures in today's Western society, largely the product of science and modern ideology. Further, rationalism's "narrow horizontal approach to total reality" has been tried and found wanting. They now see that the non-measurable, intuitive and holistic values of human experience must become freshly appreciated and revived. And that these historically derive in large measure from a transcendental, religious view of humankind and the universe.

Among professed believers, their traditional critique of narrow rationalism was re-enforced at Lisbon. Previously they have dealt with ideologies as separate communities. Sometimes, as with socialism, faith communities react with knee-jerk rejection; in other cases, as with nationalism, they fall into naive acquiescence.

The faiths begin now to cooperate in their consideration and judgement of ideologies, and, among Jews-Muslims-Christians, to seek for signs of God's will and presence through the natural, social and cultural creativity which ideologies might reflect. Cooperation or conflict between ideologies and faith communities, as transnational actors, could then become more deliberate and consequential.

III. FUTURE INITIATIVES

Lisbon was a limited experiment by a very small group. Its sponsor, the Interreligious Peace Colloquium, cannot—and never conceived that it could—provide adequate followup. Our modest goal is to point out from our experience a few directions which might be followed, and to join with those organizations, movements and persons who are already proceeding that way.

Our hope is that the many bodies, religious and secular, concerned with human needs and rights, social justice, the changing world order, food and energy, violence and peace, will incorporate our "Lisbon lesson" in fitting form into their own programs and networks. These include:

• world affairs and foreign policy communities, private and governmental, at national, regional and global levels, including the United Nations family of agencies

• educational and research institutions, publishing houses, the media, and information systems

• industry, agriculture and labor, commercial, financial and economic power groups

• cultural, community and voluntary organizations

• faith communities, in their seminaries, colleges and schools; by instruction, preaching and witness; in prayer life and worship; through social ministry and advocacy for the poor and powerless; by interfaith dialogue and collaboration.

We need, in short, to "conscientize" our human communities, until now exclusivist and separate, to their need to communicate among themselves, to beget a new universal awareness of the one whole humanwide "we" which we form, under God.

Appendices

Participants

Participants at Lisbon

ABDALLA, Dr. Isma'il Sabri, Chairperson
Third World Forum, Former Minister of
National Planning, Egypt

AHMAD, Professor Khurshid, Director
The Islamic Foundation, England

ARNS, Cardinal Evaristo
Archbishop of Sao Paulo, Brazil

AVINERI, Dr. Shlomo, Former Director General
Foreign Ministry, Israel

BELLAH, Professor Robert, Director
Center for Japanese and Korean Studies,
Berkeley, United States

BEN SHLOMO, Professor Josef Asher
University of Tel Aviv, Israel·

BLANK, Rabbi Irwin M.
Temple Ohabei Shalom, Brookline, United States

BLEWETT, Ms. Jane, Administrative Assistant
Interreligious Peace Colloquium, United States

CARR, Canon Burgess, General Secretary
All Africa Conference of Churches, Kenya

FALK, Professor Richard
Princeton University, United States

al-FARUQI, Professor Isma'il, President
Association of Muslim Social Scientists
Temple University, United States

FARUQI, Muhammad Hashir
Editor of Impact International, England

GREMILLION, Rev. Joseph, Coordinator
Interreligious Peace Colloquium, United States

HESBURGH, Rev. Theodore, CSC, President
University of Notre Dame, United States

HEWAGE, Professor Lankaputra G.
Middle Path International, Sri Lanka

HULL, Rev. William E., Pastor
First Baptist Church, Shreveport, United States

ISHIKAWA, Rev. Tsunehiko
International Section, Japan Buddhist
Federation, Japan

IVERN, Rev. Frank, SJ
Assistant General for Social Issues,
Jesuit Society, Rome

KLOMPE, Dr. Marga
Minister of State, Netherlands

MEJIA, Rev. Jorge, Secretary
Commission for Religious Relations with the Jews,
Vatican City

NASR, Dr. Seyyed Hossein, Director
Imperial Iranian Academy of Philosophy, Iran

ROSENHAUS, Matthew, Chairperson
J. B. Williams Company, United States

RYAN, Rev. William, SJ, Director
Center of Concern, United States

RUBENSTEIN, Amnon
Member of Knesset, Israel

SAKR, Dr. Mohamed A., Chairperson
Department of Economics,
University of Jordan, Jordan

SEWELL, John W., Executive Vice-President
Overseas Development Council, United States

SHESTACK, Jerome J., President
International League for Human Rights,
United States

SIEGMAN, Rabbi Henry, Executive Vice-President
Synagogue Council of America, United States

WEDEL, Mrs. Cynthia, President
World Council of Churches, United States

YALCINTAS, Professor Nevzad
University of Istanbul, Turkey

The Interreligious Peace Colloquium

The Interreligious Peace Colloquium (IRPC) brings together adherents of the major faiths who determine policy and make decisions at transnational levels, in the fields of politics and economics, communications, education and religion. It addresses current and future issues which concern large portions, and sometimes all, of God's human family—in the light of faith convictions and social ethics, religio-cultural values and history.

IRPC was born out of a conference held in 1975 at Bellagio, Italy, on "The Food-Energy Crisis: Challenge to the World Faiths," attended by thirty Muslium, Jewish, Hindu, Buddhist and Christian leaders. In 1976 four sponsors of the Bellagio meeting, Matthew Rosenhaus, Cyrus Vance, Henry Siegman and Joseph Gremillion, formally incorporated IRPC as an educational and religious organization, with these interlocking programs:

1. The Changing World Order: Challenge to the Five World Faiths

2. The Future of the Middle East: Can Its Three Faiths Work for Healing after Centuries of Conflict?

3. Religion's Role in Current Struggles for Human Rights

4. Religion as a Divisive and/or Cohesive Force in Today's Interdependent World

The organization's character and method of operation is described briefly in Chapter 14 of our present volume, A Statement on the Lisbon Meeting, under the heading "An Interfaith International." A more thorough treatment of its history and purpose is found in IRPC's first book, *Food/Energy and the Major Faiths,* published in April 1978 by Orbis Books. Written by Gremillion, the volume is principally a report and interpretation of the Bellagio conference.

Vance and Siegman explain in the Foreword of the Bellagio book that: "Our purpose was to help believers of these five Faiths, so often in conflict, to work together on issues affecting the fate of the whole human family; above all, to work for peace." They go on to stress the special experience of Muslim, Jewish and Christian participants: "At Bellagio we became especially aware of the conflicts past and present among those of us who share most: we who are believers in the one personal God of Abraham and Moses, of Jesus and Muhammad. Reflecting on this paradox, we asked whether the new fact of economic and political interdependence among all our people provides—perhaps by Providence—a sign calling for greater interdependence among our Faiths."

Because of this, IRPC now focuses primarily on Jewish-Muslim-Christian relations and concerns, as is obvious from our report on the Lisbon meeting.

IRPC officers are Matthew Rosenhaus, president; Isma'il al-Faruqi, vice-president; Henry Siegman, treasurer; Joseph Gremillion, secretary and coordinator; William Ryan, executive secretary. The last two have served only part-time as professional staff, with Jane Blewett as administrative assistant. The Center of Concern, the socio-religious research and educational institute of which Ryan is founding director, provides secretariat services and support staff.

Cyrus Vance was vice-president of IRPC until 1977 when he became Secretary of State in the cabinet of President Carter. Members of the IRPC board are: Simeon Adebo, Irwin Blank, Theodore Hesburgh, Philip Klutznick, Sol Linowitz, Muhammad Abdul Rauf, Henry Schultz, Maurice Strong and Cynthia Wedel.

The budget of IRPC for an initial period of 1977-79 is $365,000. The Rockefeller and Ford Foundations have each made grants of $75,000 for this three year period. The additional $215,000 is being sought from individual donors, family trusts and members of faith communities. The Internal Revenue Service has assigned tax exempt status to IRPC. Its executive office is located at 3700 13th Street, N.E., Washington, D. C., 20017.